Learning to Pass

New CLAiT

2006

Jackie Sherman

Using Office 2007

www.heinemann.co.uk

✓ Free online support
✓ Useful weblinks
✓ 24 hour online ordering

0845 630 44 44

Heinemann

Part of Pearson

Heinemann is an imprint of Pearson Education Limited, a company incorporated in England and Wales, having its registered office at Edinburgh Gate, Harlow, Essex, CM20 2JE. Registered company number: 872828

www.heinemann.co.uk

Heinemann is a registered trademark of Pearson Education Limited

Text © Pearson Education Limited 2009

First published 2009

12 11 10 09
10 9 8 7 6 5 4 3 2 1

British Library Cataloguing in Publication Data
A catalogue record for this book is available from the British Library

ISBN 978 0 435 57949 4

Typeset by Tek-Art, Crawley Down, West Sussex
Cover design by Wooden Ark Studios
Cover photo/illustration © Photolibrary.com / Blend Images
Printed in the UK by Scotprint

Acknowledgements
The author and publisher would like to thank the following organisations for permission to reproduce screenshots in this book:

Microsoft product screenshots reprinted with permission from Microsoft Corporation.

Virus Checker Screenshot from AVG; Information Networks screenshot from uSwitch, used by permission; Connect to the Internet screenshot from thinkbroadband.com; Sign up, GMX 1 screenshot from GMX, used by permission; Sign up, GMX 2 screenshot from GMX, used by permission; Sign up, GMX 3 screenshot from GMX, used by permission; Compose Screenshot from GMX; Receiving messages screenshot from GMX; Reply screenshot from GMX; Forward screenshot from GMX; Attach screenshot from GMX; Message with attachment screenshot from GMX; Receiving an attachment screenshot from GMX; Saving an attachment screenshot from GMX; Downloading browser screenshot from Google; Browser page screenshot from Pearson, used with permission; Hyperlink pointer screenshot from Pearson, used with permission; Engine list screenshot from Yahoo; Techniques screenshot from Google; Search for jobs screenshot from Google; Using Directories screenshot from UK Directory, used by permission; Add favourite screenshot from Pearson, used by permission; Open bookmark screenshot from Google; History screenshot from Google; Ex. 10 using bookmarks screenshot from Yamaha; Save web page screenshot from Pearson, used by permission; Save web image screenshot from Pearson, used by permission; Print preview screenshot from Pearson, used by permission; Print page screenshot from Pearson, used by permission; Police auction screenshot from Bumblebee Auctions; Auction list screenshot from Google; Selling on auction screenshot from Bidsnbuys; Computer for sale screenshot from Cash Converters; Bike for sale screenshot; Wiki and copyright screenshot from Wikipedia; Sent message with attachment screenshot from GMX; Insert hyperlink screenshot from Runner's World

Every effort has been made to contact copyright holders of the material reproduced in this book. Any omissions will be rectified in subsequent printings if notice is given to the publishers.

Websites
The websites used in this book were correct and up-to-date at the time of publication. It is essential for tutors to preview each website before using it in class so as to ensure that the URL is still accurate, relevant and appropriate. We suggest that tutors bookmark useful websites and consider enabling students to access them through the school/college intranet.

Contents

Introduction

The qualification

CLAiT 2006 is a suite of qualifications offered by OCR aimed at improving skills and confidence in general areas of Information Technology (IT) such as word processing, email, the Internet and databases. The qualification can be taken at one of three levels depending on your abilities and experience. These are:

Level 1 – **New CLAiT** (the subject of this book): aimed at boosting the confidence of beginners

Level 2 – **CLAiT Plus**: for those with some experience

Level 3 – **CLAiT Advanced**: for confident and productive IT users

To achieve the full Level 1 certificate, you must complete assessments in the mandatory or core unit together with two others chosen from a range of options. For a Level 1 diploma, you must complete assessments in the core unit plus four others. Study normally takes place at a training centre or college, and depending on the units chosen assessment may be online or centre-assessed.

Full details of the qualifications and accredited study centres can be found at www.ocr.org.uk.

Appropriate software

In 2007 Microsoft released a completely new version of their Office suite of programs that includes Word, Excel and PowerPoint. Until then, new versions of the programs did not differ fundamentally from the previous ones. However, with Office 2007 there has been such a complete overhaul of the look and workings of the software that it is hard for people accustomed to Office 2000, XP or 2003 to use it without difficulty. For this reason, although you can gain CLAiT qualifications using any appropriate software, we have taken the opportunity to introduce readers to Office 2007 programs, as well as the latest version of Internet Explorer 7.

This publication therefore covers the following New CLAiT units:

Core Unit:

001 File management and e-document production

Optional Units:

002 Creating spreadsheets and graphs

003 Database manipulation

005 Create an e-presentation

008 Online communication

Using this book

For each unit, you will find full coverage of the underpinning theoretical knowledge and step-by-step guidance on the practical skills needed to carry out the everyday tasks required for the certificate.

After each section, you will be offered the chance to complete a short exercise to check your understanding, show that you have gained proficiency in the required skills and help identify any gaps in your knowledge. There is also a final assignment for each unit designed to reflect the style and coverage of questions you will face when taking the assessments.

In many of the units, you will also find extra material. Although not required for the qualification, this will introduce you to related topics and can be used to expand your basic skills and competencies.

Throughout the book, instructions involving clicking on-screen, pressing keys on the keyboard or selecting menu options will be shown in **bold**. For example, when asked to open the File menu and select the Save option, this will be shown as: Go to **File – Save**.

Some of the exercises in this book refer to documents on the accompanying CD-ROM.

File management and e-document production

This mandatory unit concentrates on developing your skills in carrying out some of the basic operations, including logging into a computer, managing files and producing word-processed documents.

In particular, you will be able to:

⊕ identify and use a computer and appropriate system software

⊕ use a computer's system software to create and manage files and folders

⊕ identify and use word-processing software to enter text, numbers and symbols accurately

⊕ format basic pararaph and document properties.

1 Hardware

In computing, the term hardware refers to any parts of a computer system that can be seen and touched such as the monitor, disks and cables. The programs that run on a computer, which you cannot see, are therefore known as software.

Although there are different sizes and types of computer in use today, they all work in a similar way. A stand-alone PC (personal computer), for example, has the following hardware components.

- The base unit is the box that everything else plugs into and contains all the major computer components.

- The monitor – also referred to as the VDU (Visual Display Unit) or screen – is needed to view what is going on inside the computer.

- The keyboard is normally used to type in data and instructions, and a mouse gives instructions by clicking a button.

Hard drive

The hard disk or hard drive (referred to as the C: drive) housed in the base unit is a sealed unit built inside the machine that is the main storage facility. Data is recorded onto the magnetic coating on rotating metal discs and there are also heads for reading and writing data.

The hard disk contains all the digital information and programs necessary for the computer to operate effectively. Any files you produce as you work can also be stored here, and the information is permanent (non-volatile), as it is retained even when the computer is switched off.

2 The operating environment

At its simplest, a computer system works as follows:

1   Data input – e.g. accessing a photo from a digital camera
2   Processing – e.g. editing the photo to change its colour
3   Output – e.g. printing the photo onto photographic paper
4   Data storage – e.g. storing the photo on a CD-R.

An operating environment is that combination of hardware and software that enables a computer system to carry out these functions effectively. The three most common environments today are MS-DOS, UNIX and Windows. This book concentrates on computers running Windows programs.

The operating system

The most important program on a computer is its **operating system**. This is the software that provides the platform on which everyday programs (applications) such as word processing and desktop publishing can operate. It is responsible for managing and coordinating activities such as sharing resources, handling input and output and keeping track of files.

Users of Windows machines interact with the operating system through a **GUI** (graphical user interface). This means that items are represented by easy-to-understand windows, small pictures, menus, drop-down lists and checkboxes so that you don't need to know or remember actual code when giving instructions.

To identify the computer's basic system information, such as the operating system, main memory and processor type and speed, simply right-click the **My Computer** icon on the desktop and select **Properties**. For example, Figure 1.1 illustrates that this book is based on a computer running the Microsoft Windows XP operating system that has an Intel Pentium processor with a speed of 1.60 GHz and 0.98 GB of RAM.

Starting up

To turn on your computer, press the **power on** switch. When a Windows machine starts up, the opening screen showing a coloured background is known as the **desktop**. It displays small pictures, or **icons**, representing parts of the computer such as the storage system (My Documents), deleted items (Recycle Bin) or the computer itself (My Computer). In the bottom left-hand corner is the green **Start** button that provides access to all the programs on the computer. Running across the bottom of the desktop is the **taskbar** that houses the Start button and any open programs.

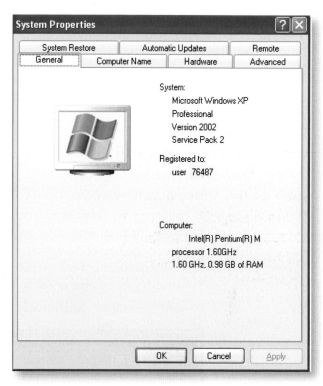

Fig. 1.1 Processor and RAM

Desktop background   Icon   Menu displayed after right-clicking

Fig. 1.2 Desktop icons

Icons

To work with icons, you need to move the mouse so that the pointer is positioned over the target and then press (**click**) one of the mouse buttons:

- left button once – this will select an item
- left button twice (double-clicking) – this will open the item
- right button once – this offers a short menu.

reposition an icon

1 Click on the **icon** once to select it.
2 Position the **pointer** over the selected icon and press and hold down the **mouse button** *without* clicking.
3 Move the **mouse** to drag the pointer across the screen, taking the icon with it.

Changing settings

You can customise a Windows machine in a number of ways. To do this, you have to change the settings, which are accessed via the **Control Panel**. Some of the possible changes include:

- correcting the date or time
- setting the resolution of the monitor
- altering the background images displayed on the desktop
- choosing a different printer as the default
- increasing the volume or turning off the speakers.

The original settings of your machine are referred to as the **default**.

Fig. 1.3 Opening the Control Panel

change settings

1 Click on the **Start** menu button.

2 Click on **Control Panel**.

3 When the Control Panel window opens, select the item you want to change and press the **Enter** key on your keyboard or double-click to open it in its own window.

4 (If you want to change Display properties, you can also do this by right-clicking on an empty part of the desktop and selecting **Properties**.)

5 Make changes by typing in new figures, dragging pointers or selecting from drop-down lists. For example (Figure 1.4):

- open **Display**
- click on the **Settings** tab
- increase or decrease screen resolution
- set alternative colour quality.

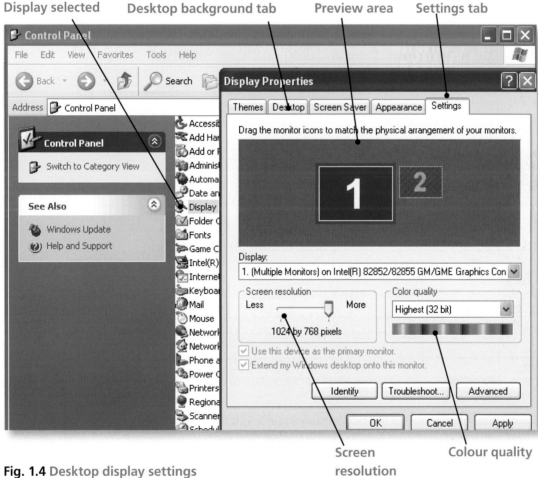

Display selected   Desktop background tab   Preview area   Settings tab

Screen resolution   Colour quality

Fig. 1.4 Desktop display settings

6 Preview the changes if they are displayed in the central area and then click on OK to confirm the new settings, and close the window.

Check your understanding 1

1 Check that both **date and time** are correct. If not, make any necessary changes.

2 Check which **printer** has been set as the **default** (it will show a tick next to its name).

3 Change the **image** set as the **background** via the **Desktop** tab of the **Display Properties** window.

4 Explore the other tabs within Display Properties.

5 Move the **Recycle Bin** to a new position on the desktop.

Working with windows

Windows machines run all their programs within small windows. You can have any number of windows open at the same time, but only one will be *active*. This will be the uppermost window and will display a stronger coloured bar (the **Title bar**) across the top. To change to a different window, click on the Title bar of the window you want and it will become the active window. (As a shortcut to switch between open windows, hold down the **Alt** key as you press the **Tab** key (showing two arrows next to Q on the keyboard). When you locate the target window, let go of both keys and it will open as the active window.)

With several windows open at any time, you can view them all rather than leave all but the active window minimised on the task bar if you use the **tile windows** facility.

tile windows

1 Right-click on the **Task bar**.
2 Select one of the three tiling options:
    a **Cascade** to arrange windows diagonally across the screen.
    b **Tile Vertically** to place them side by side.
    c **Tile Horizontally** to place them one above the other.
3 You can move between them by clicking a particular window, or change the borders if you want to enlarge the one you are working with.

Minimise   Maximise

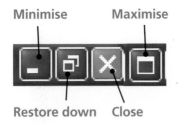

Restore down   Close

Fig. 1.5 Control buttons for closing or amending the window size

All Windows XP icon windows have a similar structure:

● The Title bar that runs across the top houses the control buttons that enable you to close or amend the size of the window.

  o **Close** – click on the button showing a cross to close the window.

  o **Maximise** – click on the button with a square to open the window to its maximum dimensions.

  o **Minimise** – click on the button showing a single bar to minimise the window so that it appears as a labelled button on the taskbar. The window will be reopened when you click on its name.

  o **Restore Down** (alternates with Maximise, so you won't see them both at the same time) – click on the button showing two overlapping windows to restore the window back to its original size after maximising.

● A **Menu bar** offering a range of menu options such as getting help or editing the contents.

● A **Toolbar** that has shortcuts relevant to the item and the program you are running.

● **Scroll bars** to move vertically or horizontally within the window.

● A **Tasks pane** running vertically down the left side of the window that offers shortcuts to various actions.

Note that within the Office 2007 suite windows look very different. They are described in full later.

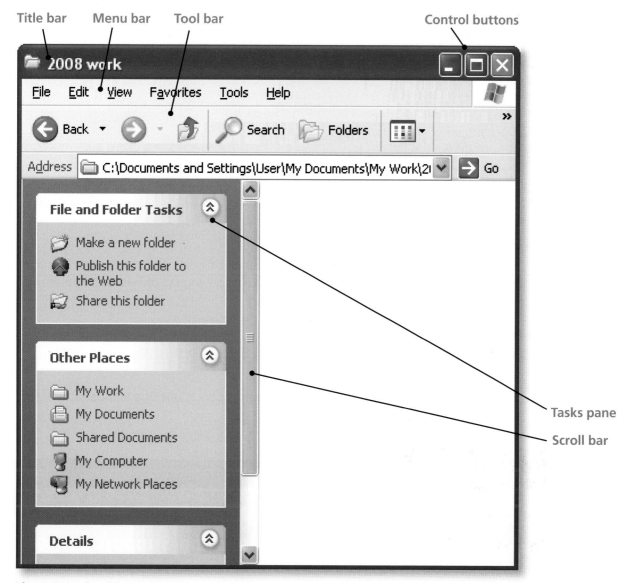

Fig. 1.6 Work with windows

resize a window

1 Make sure the window is **restored down**.

2 Position the mouse pointer over a **border**. It will show a black two-way arrow.

3 Click on and hold down the **mouse button** as you gently drag the border in or out.

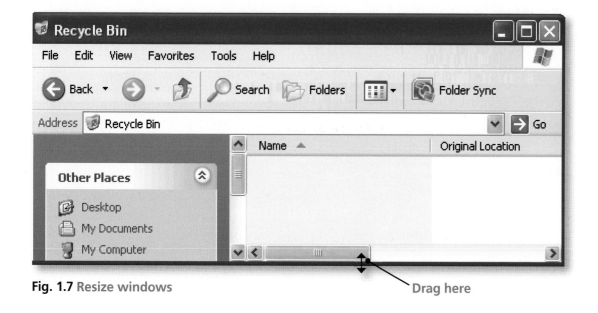

Fig. 1.7 Resize windows

Check your understanding 2

1 Open the **Recycle Bin**.
2 **Maximise** the window.
3 **Resize** the open Recycle Bin to make it very small.
4 **Minimise** the Recycle Bin to a button on the task bar.
5 Open any other icon, for example, My Computer.
6 Reopen the Recycle Bin.
7 Switch to My Computer.
8 Close all windows.

Using Help files

Windows XP machines have an on-board help system that will guide you through any new tasks you have to perform, or provide information or links to further sources of help such as those on the Internet.

use Help

1 Open the **Start Menu**.
2 Click on the link to **Help and Support.**
3 When the Help and Support Center window opens, click on one of a number of different categories to work down through lists of topics.
4 You can also type a word or phrase (**keywords**) into the top **Search** box.

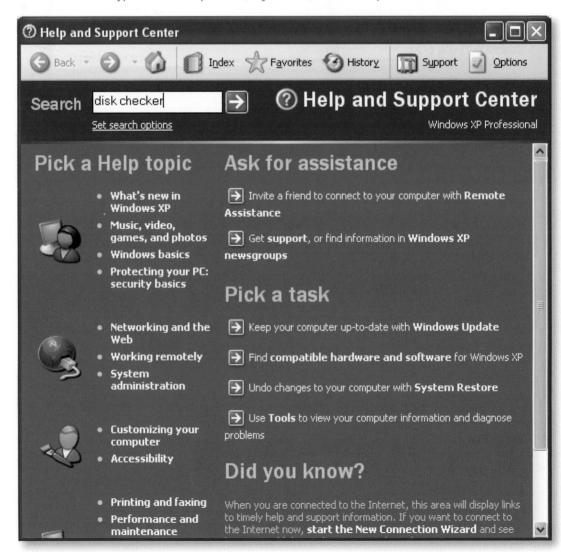

Fig. 1.8 Getting help 1

5 Click on the green arrow button next to Search to see relevant help topics. Click on any topic listed in the left-hand pane to view the details in the right-hand pane.

6 Return to earlier pages by clicking on the **Back** button.

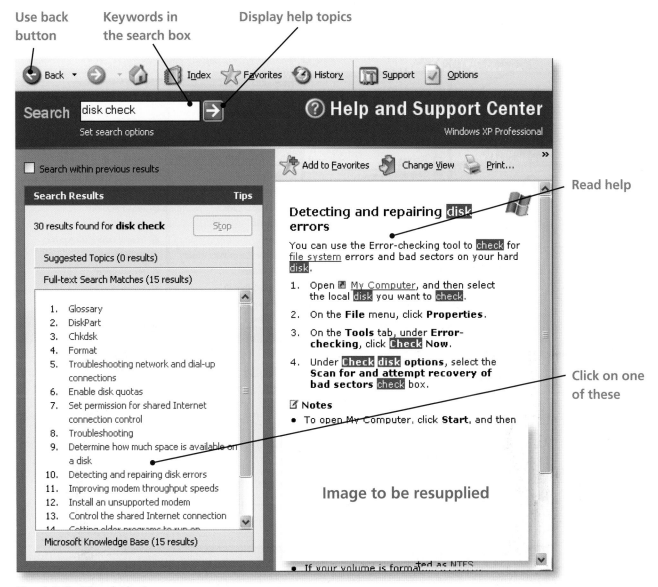

Fig. 1.9 Getting help 2

Launching programs

As programs are stored in folders, opening any program involves navigating to the folder in which it is stored and opening it up. You can then select it, click on its name or press the **Enter** key on your keyboard to open it on your computer.

For example, a useful calculator and the drawing/painting program Paint are both found in the **Accessories** folder, and system applications such as Disk Defragmenter are available from a subfolder within Accessories labelled **System Tools**.

find a program from the Start Menu

1 Click on the **Start** button to open the menu.

2 Hover over **All Programs**. This reveals the first level of folders containing programs on your computer.

3　Click on the relevant folder, for example, **Accessories**.
4　To locate the disk defragmenter, click on **System Tools**.
5　Click on the **Defragmenter** program.

First level folder

Paint

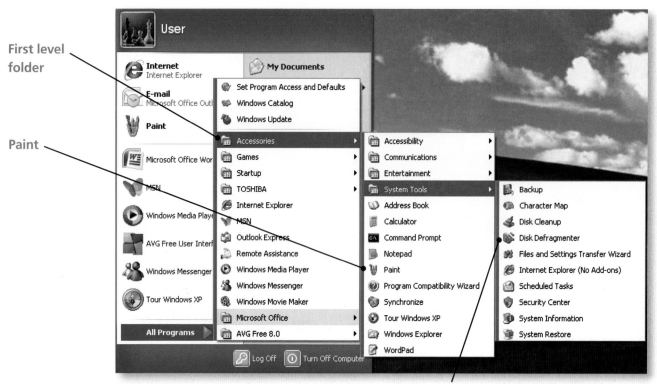

Fig. 1.10 Open defragmenter

Click to open target program

Closing programs

As all programs run within windows, closing the program involves closing the window. There are two methods:

● click on the **Close** button on the Title bar showing a cross
● open the **File** menu and select **Exit**.

Exit the program

Close the window

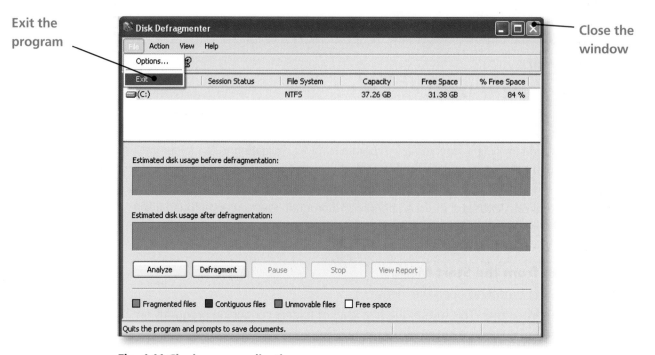

Fig. 1.11 Closing an application

If you have been working and have not saved any settings or entries, you will be prompted to do so before the program closes. If it was the only window open, you will return to the desktop. Otherwise, you will reveal windows that were already opened underneath and need to close these before you return to the desktop.

Application software

On the All Programs list accessed from the Start Menu, you will see both systems and application software. One folder is labelled Microsoft Office 2007, which contains a suite of programs. Programs used in this book include:

- **Word 2007** – a **word-processing** package used to work with text and produce documents such as letters, memos, reports or flyers

- **Excel 2007** – a **spreadsheet** program that enables you to work with numerical data such as balance sheets or budgets

- **Access 2007** – a **database** program where you can store, sort and search for records

- **PowerPoint 2007** – a **presentation** package that allows you to create slideshows

- **Outlook 2007** – a complex time-management program that includes a calendar, address book and **email software** needed for sending messages electronically.

One other program that you must be able to use is a **browser**. This enables you to view multimedia pages over the Internet. There are a number of browsers available that you could use, including Opera and Firefox, but the examples in this book are based on Internet Explorer 7.

There are, of course, hundreds of other programs you may come across that are not covered in this book. These include digital imaging programs for working with pictures, desktop-publishing software to produce professional-looking publications and music or video editing software for making your own music or videos.

Check your understanding 3

1 Launch and then close:
   a Word 2007
   b Internet Explorer 7
   c Paint (found in Accessories)

2 Which program would you use to help calculate your monthly expenditure?
   a Access
   b Java
   c Excel
   d Outlook

Previewing and printing

If you launch any program from the All Programs list, it will open in a window. You can now carry out tasks such as creating drawings, performing calculations or recording information and can then save the information or print out a copy.

Before printing, it is always advisable to view your work in **Print Preview**. The Windows operating environment offers **WYSIWYG** (what you see is what you get), which allows you to see exactly how the page will print out. You can then make any necessary changes before actually printing.

use Print Preview in an MS Office application

1 Click on the **Office** Button.
2 Hover over Print.
3 Select **Print Preview**.
4 Use any tools available such as Zoom in or out, Print from here or simply View the page.
5 Click on the **Close Print Preview** button to return to your work.

Office button

Print

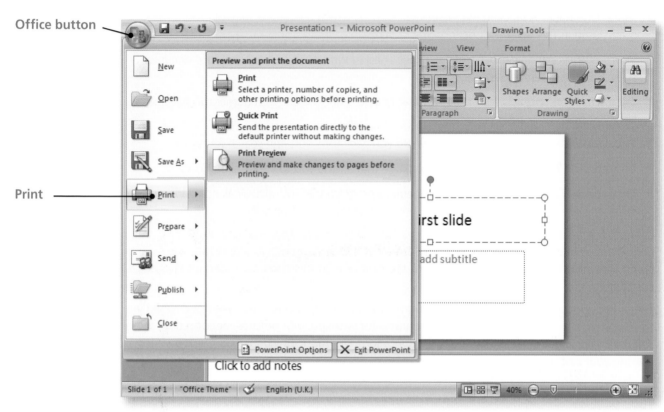

Fig. 1.12 Using Print Preview

Fig. 1.13 Within Print Preview

Printing

Having decided to print, you have two options:

- Print one copy of your work using the default printer and settings. In MS Office 2007 this is the **Quick Print** option.

- Change settings such as the number of copies or which items to print before sending the file to the printer. This is the **Print** option.

If you decide to stop printing once you have started, you need to cancel the command.

For instructions on using your printer, including troubleshooting and loading paper, see the manufacturer's guide.

cancel printing

1 Open the **Printer** window. Either double-click on a **printer icon** that should appear in your taskbar, or go to **Control Panel – Printers and Faxes** and open the **Default Printer** window.

2 On the **Printer** menu, click on **Cancel All Documents**.

3 Another option is to click on **Pause Printing** if you think you will want to resume printing shortly.

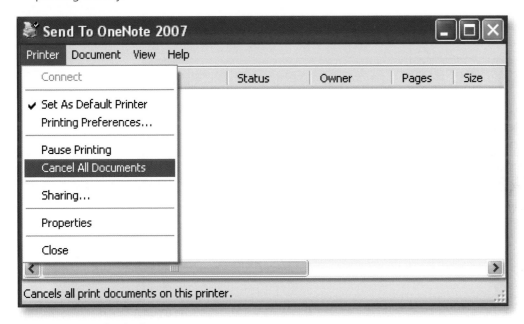

Fig. 1.14 Cancel printing

Switching off the computer

There are a number of options when ending a computer session. You can simply log off so the machine is ready for another user, you can restart the machine or you can switch it off completely. In all cases, it is important to follow the correct shut-down procedure. This is because temporary files will have been created, some settings may not have been saved, errors may have been detected and programs may be ready for installation. All these things need to be sorted out. This can only happen if you follow the procedure and do not simply switch off the power.

switch off completely

1 Open the **Start** menu.

2 Select **Turn Off Computer**.

3 Click on the **Turn Off** option.

4 (If updates to your system are being installed, you may see a message to this effect. Click on the correct button to allow installation to complete before the machine switches off automatically.)

5 In a few seconds, the computer will switch off.

Fig. 1.15 Turning off the computer

As an alternative, hold down the **Ctrl** and **Alt** keys and press the **Delete** key once. The Task Manager window will open and you can select the correct option from the **Shut Down** menu.

Fig. 1.16 Turning off via the Task Manager

3 File management

The hard disk of a computer houses all the programs you will need to use, organised into a hierarchy starting at the top level with Local Disk (C:). Programs are grouped into labelled areas referred to as **folders** (previously known as directories), and these in turn contain further folders or subfolders holding related programs.

For example, the folder Documents and Settings contains a subfolder named All Users that in turn contains a Start Menu folder containing further folders and shortcuts.

Files can also be stored on disks in other drives such as a CD or DVD drive.

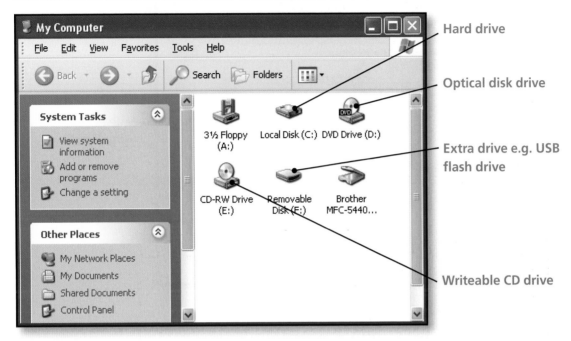

Fig. 1.17 Drives

Folders can be closed or open, revealing their contents. Once a folder contains subfolders, click on the + next to its name to show the contents or on the − to hide them.

Any documents, drawings, databases or charts that you create, as well as the instructions needed to run programs, are known as **files**. Windows machines help you manage your own files by providing folders in which to store them whenever you carry out a save. This means that you can group related files together so that they will be easy to locate in future.

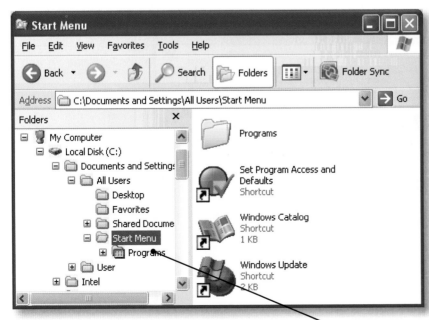

Fig. 1.18 Hierarchy of files on Local Disk (C:)   + shows it contains subfolders

Creating and working with folders

On Windows XP machines, one folder, My Documents, will have been set up for you already, but you can also create your own folders and move or copy files into different folders using the file management program **Windows Explorer**.

When viewing the contents of a folder such as My Documents, you will see that files display a small icon showing which program was used to create them, and folders are simple yellow boxes.

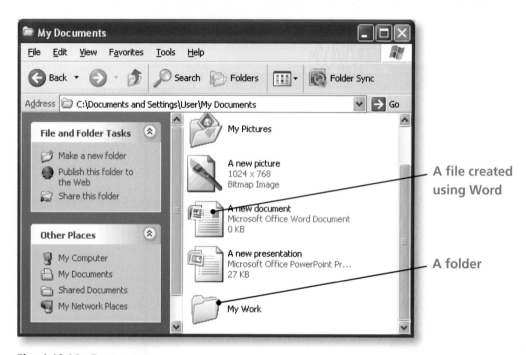

Fig. 1.19 My Documents

create a folder

1 Open **My Documents** from the Start Menu or a desktop icon.
2 Click on the link **Make a new folder** in the File and Folder Tasks pane.
3 When the folder appears, type a name for the folder into the highlighted box.
4 Click on the **mouse button** on-screen to confirm the naming.
5 If you make a mistake, click on the **Rename this folder** link.
   Or
6 Right-click and select **Rename**.

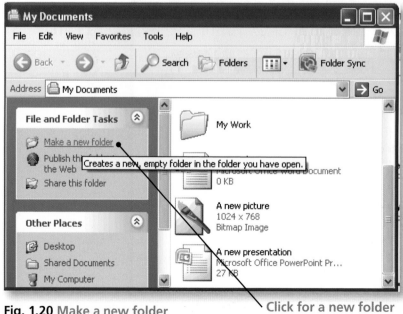

Fig. 1.20 Make a new folder

Or

7 Click on the folder name once to select the name.

8 Type in the whole folder name correctly or click in the box to correct characters.

Click to rename   New folder ready to name

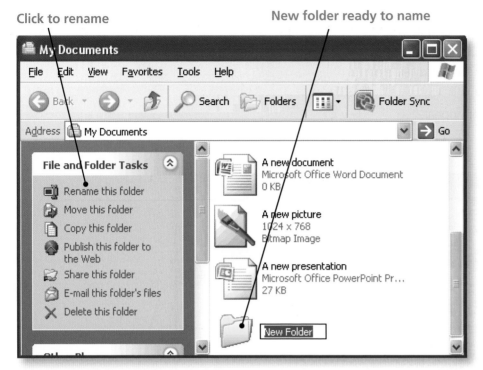

Fig. 1.21 Rename folder

create a subfolder

1 Open the 'parent' folder in which you want to create a subfolder.

2 Make a folder as above. The new folder will be created inside this opened folder.

3 To return to view the contents of the parent folder, or any folders further up the hierarchy, click on the up arrow. You will see the hierarchy or folder organisation in the Address box.

Parent folder   up arrow   Folder organisation

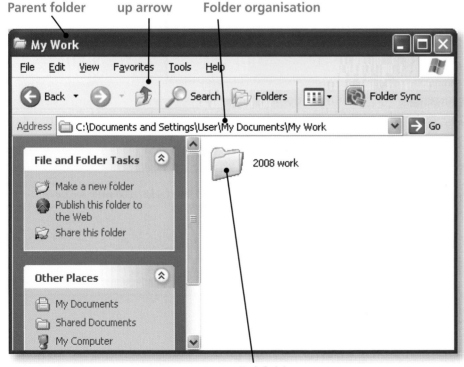

Fig. 1.22 Making a subfolder   Subfolder

You can also create folders when displaying a list of all the folders in your computer.

make folders using the Folders list

1 In My Documents, or any folder you have created, click on the **Folders** button.
   Or
2 Right-click on the **Start** button and select **Explore**.
3 This will display the folders on your machine.
4 In the left-hand pane, click on the disk or folder in which you want to create a new subfolder. It will turn blue to show it is selected.
5 Go to **File – New – Folder**.
6 Name the new folder that will appear.

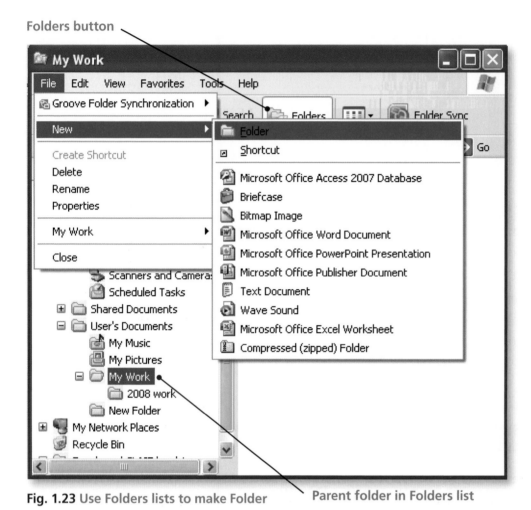

Folders button

Parent folder in Folders list

Fig. 1.23 Use Folders lists to make Folder

delete a folder

1 Open the parent folder or drive.
2 Select the folder you want to delete and press the **Delete** key on the keyboard.
   Or
3 Right-click and select **Delete** from the menu that appears.
4 Click to confirm when you see the warning message.
5 Remember that deleting a folder also deletes any files it contains.

Fig. 1.24 Delete folder warning

Check your understanding 4

1 In My Documents, make a folder named *Animals*.
2 Create three folders inside *Animals* and name them *Cats*, *Dogs* and *Horses*.
3 Create two subfolders inside *Dogs* named *Pedigree* and *Mongrels*.
4 Finally, delete the *Horses* folder.

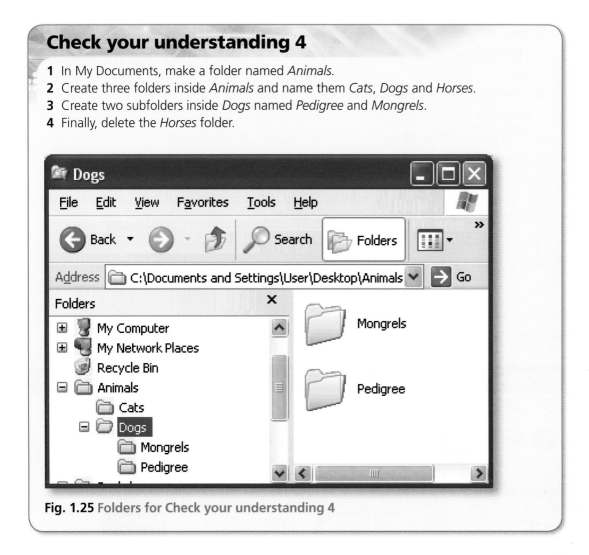

Fig. 1.25 Folders for Check your understanding 4

Moving or copying files

Having set up a folder structure, you can now save your work into suitable folders and move or copy files into different folders on the hard disk. You can also use the same techniques to transfer files to a different drive, for example to store them on a CD or flash drive.

Cut, copy and paste

One way to move or copy files is to make use of a temporary storage area in the computer's memory known as the **clipboard**. You can keep up to 24 copies of files in the clipboard at any time, as long as you do not switch off your computer.

Moving files into the clipboard requires you to **Cut** them out of the folder. Storing a copy of a file in the clipboard requires you to **Copy** it out of the folder. Moving or copying a file into a new folder requires you to **Paste** it out of the clipboard.

move or copy files into folders using the mouse

1 Open the folder containing the file(s) you want to move or copy.
2 Select the file(s):
   a To select several adjacent files, click on the first. Hold down the **Shift** key and click on the last. All files in between will remain selected.
   b To select non-adjacent files, click on the first. Hold down the **Ctrl** key and click on individual files. They will all remain selected.

3 To move the files, select **Cut** in one of the following ways:

   c Right-click on one of the selected files and click on **Cut** on the menu.

     Or

   d Open the **Edit** menu and select **Cut**.

     Or

   e Hold **Ctrl** and press **X**.

4 To copy rather than move the files, select the **Copy** option at this stage (**Ctrl + C**).

5 Now open the destination folder. To find it, you may need to go up through the folders hierarchy by clicking on the up button, or down through the hierarchy by opening folders and subfolders in turn that appear in the window.

6 Select **Paste** by right-clicking from the **Edit** menu or holding **Ctrl + V**.

7 The files will appear inside the open folder.

Selected files to be moved

Fig. 1.26 Moving files using Cut

Fig. 1.27 Paste in files

move or copy files using the Tasks pane

1 Select the file(s) to move or copy.
2 In the Tasks pane, select the **Move** or **Copy the selected items** option.
3 Locate and select the destination folder in the window that appears. (You may need to click on a + box to reveal the folders inside.)
4 Click on the appropriate **Move** or **Copy** button.

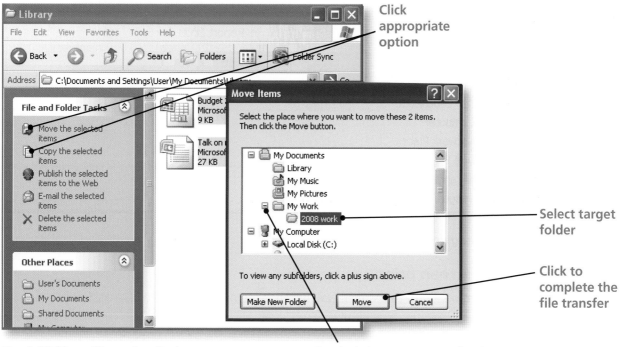

Fig. 1.28 Move files using Tasks pane

Click appropriate option

Select target folder

Click to complete the file transfer

Symbol shows you are viewing the contents of the folder

Drag and drop

Where target files and destination folders are visible on-screen at the same time, you can drag files into folders using the mouse. Unless both the original and destination folders are within the same folder or drive, this can only be done after you have displayed the folders list.

drag files into folders

1 Click on the **Folders** button.
2 Click on the folder in the left-hand pane that contains the files you want to move or copy. Its contents will be displayed on the right.
3 Select the files you want to move or copy.
4 Use the central bar to scroll up or down the folders list until you can clearly see the destination folder. (Do not click with the mouse as you will then reveal the contents of the wrong folder.)
5 Drag the selected files across the central divide from right to left towards the target folder. When it turns blue, let go and the file will be dropped inside.
   a If you drag using the left mouse button, files will be *moved* on the same drive, or *copied* onto a different drive.
   b You can copy them to a folder on the same drive by holding down the **Ctrl** key as you drag.
   c For more control, use the right mouse button. When you let go, you will be offered a menu and can select the **Move** or **Copy** option.

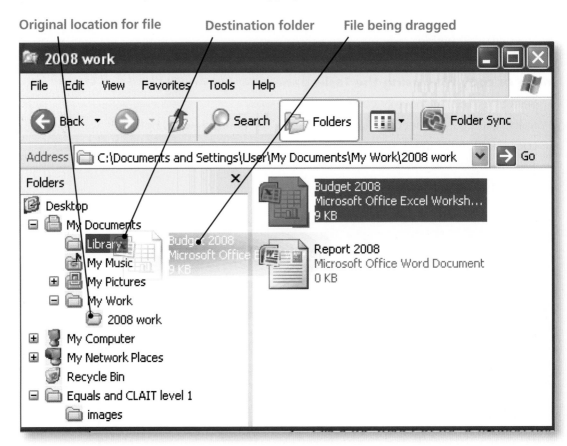

Fig. 1.29 Dragging files into folders

Taking a screen print

At some point during an assessment, you may need to provide evidence of tasks that you have performed – for example, selecting the correct icon, checking a particular option in a dialog box, creating folders or using print preview etc – where you cannot produce a normal printed copy. This is where you can use a special type of copy to take a picture of what is happening on-screen and paste it into a document that you can then print out.

take a screen print

1 With the items visible on-screen, press the key labelled **PrtSc** (Print Screen).
2 To take a picture of a single dialog box or active window, hold down the **Alt** key as you press.
3 Open a program that will display images – for example, Paint, Word or PowerPoint.
4 Hold the **Ctrl** key and press **V**, or select **Paste**.
5 A copy of the screen image will appear.
6 You can now save and print this page in the normal way.

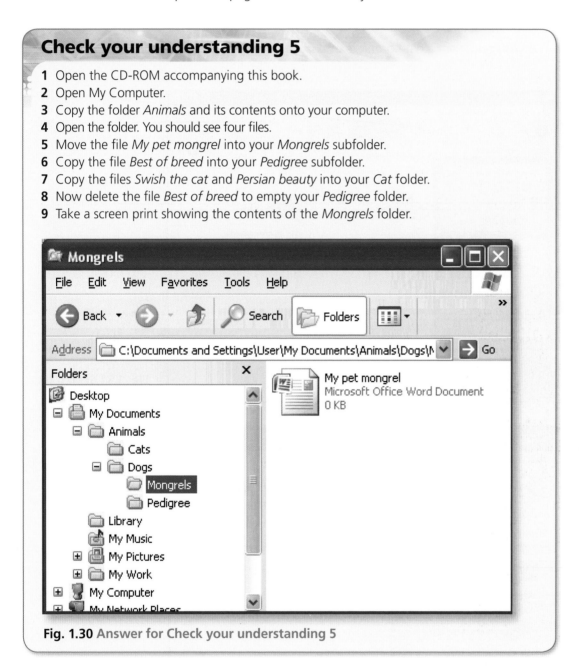

Check your understanding 5

1 Open the CD-ROM accompanying this book.
2 Open My Computer.
3 Copy the folder *Animals* and its contents onto your computer.
4 Open the folder. You should see four files.
5 Move the file *My pet mongrel* into your *Mongrels* subfolder.
6 Copy the file *Best of breed* into your *Pedigree* subfolder.
7 Copy the files *Swish the cat* and *Persian beauty* into your *Cat* folder.
8 Now delete the file *Best of breed* to empty your *Pedigree* folder.
9 Take a screen print showing the contents of the *Mongrels* folder.

Fig. 1.30 Answer for Check your understanding 5

Searching for files

If you need to find a file (or folder) on your computer, you can use the Explorer program to carry out a search. This allows you to search for a specific file by name or to look for all files of a certain type or that were created during a particular period of time.

use Search

1 Open a folder such as My Documents on the desktop and click on the **Search** button on the toolbar.
   Or
2 Go to **Start – Search**.

3 In the Tasks pane, select the appropriate starting point – for example, to look for a document or music file or for any files or folders.

4 In the next pane that opens, enter as much detail as you can about the file you are looking for. If necessary use the advanced search features.

  a You can type in its full name.

  b You can specify in which drive or folder it is located – click on **Browse** to work through your folder hierarchy to find the lowest level of folder.

  c You can enter part of the name – use an asterisk (*) to represent any unknown words or characters.

  d You can select a date or range of dates during which it was created.

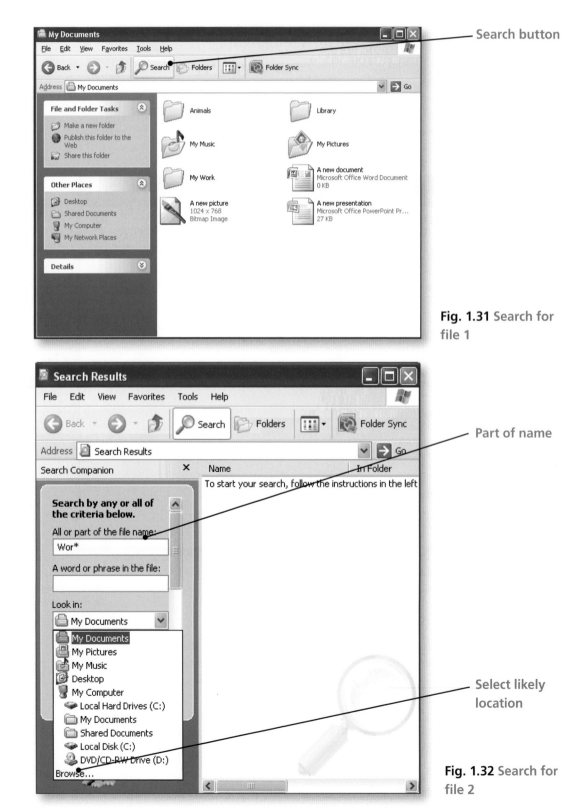

Search button

Fig. 1.31 Search for file 1

Part of name

Select likely location

Fig. 1.32 Search for file 2

5   When you have entered as much information about the file as you can, click on the
    Search button.

6   Files identified during the search will be displayed in the main window. You can now
    open them by double-clicking or carry out a new search.

    Note that you can view the files in different ways by clicking on the Views button
    e.g. selecting Details, Icons or List.

Fig. 1.33 Search for file 3

Check your understanding 6

1   Use the computer search facilities to find any files or folders named *Calculator*.
2   Now find the file *Persian beauty*.
3   Finally, find any files created or modified during the past week.

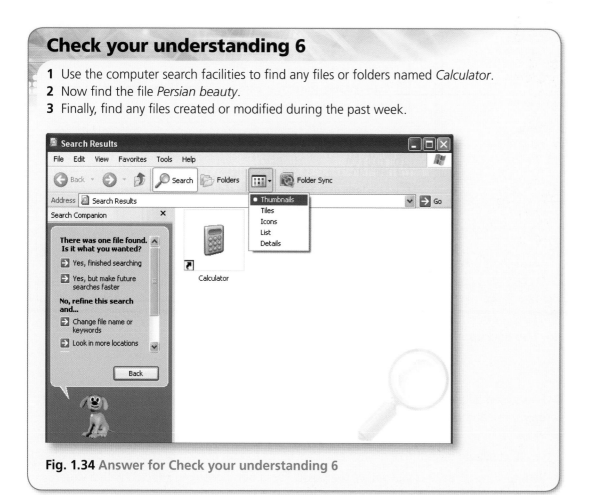

Fig. 1.34 Answer for Check your understanding 6

Data security

As well as saving files onto the hard disk, you can store data on removable storage media such as optical disks or portable flash drives. If the data is important to you, you will want to protect it from harm or loss.

To protect your data from physical harm, you need to handle disks carefully and keep them free from excessive heat, prolonged sunlight, damp, dust and sharp implements that may scratch the surfaces.

To protect sensitive or confidential information stored on your computer or removable disks, you need to take further precautions. Here are some methods that can be used:

- For high-security material, the computer and storage media should be kept in **secure rooms**, with no access allowed by unauthorised personnel.

- **Backup copies** should be taken and stored separately, so that there is always one copy of a file if the original is damaged or lost. In Microsoft Office 2007 programs, you can create backup copies easily:

  1 Click on the **Microsoft Office** button and then click on **Options**.

  2 Click on **Advanced**.

  3 Scroll to the **Save** section, and then select the **Always create backup copy** checkbox.

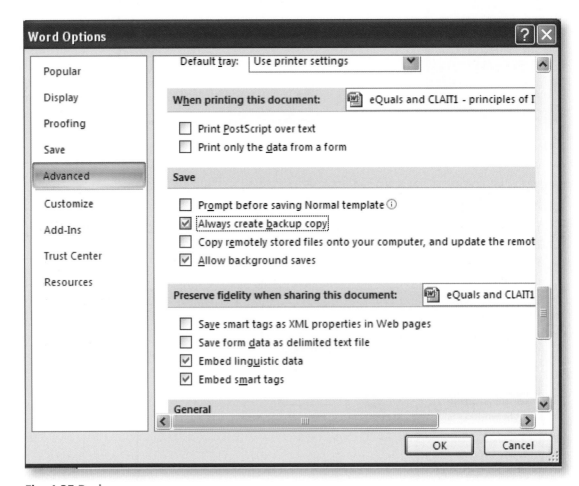

Fig. 1.35 Backup

- Files stored on a network should be protected by thorough **logging-in procedures** so that only those authorised to view the material can access it.

- There are **laws** that can be enforced to ensure files are not copied by others. For example, the law of copyright gives the originator exclusive rights to use, publish or copy their own material.

- Regular **virus checking** will reduce the possibility of files becoming infected with a virus.

- **Encryption** is a process used to 'scramble' information so that only authorised people with the key that can make it readable will be able to make sense of it.

- For those still using floppy disks, a sliding tab can be set so that the disk is **write-protected**. This means the data cannot be changed or erased. Some operating systems and flash drives also offer this option.

- When creating a file, you can set its properties to **Read-Only**, so that people cannot make changes to it.

Check your understanding 7

1 What law governs the use of someone else's original work stored on a computer?
  a Data protection   **b** Copyright   **c** Computer misuse
2 Name two things that could physically harm your disks.
3 Backup copies of files are made so that you can:
  a Save them to a disk
  b Have a copy in case the original is damaged
  c Reduce the amount of space they take up
  d Send them across a network
4 What is the procedure that helps protect data from unauthorised access over a network?
  a Cut and paste
  b Logging in
  c Backing up
  d Virus checking

---

4 Information networks

Most computer users will use a network at some stage. In schools, colleges, libraries and businesses you are likely to use a computer that is linked to others in the organisation so that files and resources such as printers and scanners can be shared. To search the World Wide Web for information or to send emails, you will also need to be connected to the Internet.

The **network operating system** is the software, such as Windows NT, required to connect all the devices on a network so that they can share resources and transfer files. It is usually in two parts: the **server**, which manages the files and programs and the **client**, such as an individual workstation, that makes the request.

Whenever you need to access an area on a network set aside for your exclusive use, such as an account with an Internet shop or your college work area, you will have to sign or **log in**.

Logging in

To log in, you will need to type two entities into a logging-in box:

- **User ID** or **Username** – this often takes a standard form such as your initials, surname and perhaps a number, so it may be easy for others to guess and is also often visible as part of your email address, for example, *jsherman25*

- **Password** – this is chosen by you and should take the form of a string of 6–8 characters, including numbers and upper- and lower-case letters, that you will be able to remember but that will **not** be easy for someone else to guess, for example, *we2xforD*

When logging in, the password characters will be represented by stars or bullet points so that no one nearby can see and remember them.

To protect your password:

- never tell it to others

- don't leave it written down

- don't use easy-to-guess words
- change it on a regular basis – you will often find a link for this on the log-in page or within the personal profile part of any account you have set up.

Fig. 1.36 Logging in

To protect your data further, take care not to stay logged in on computers in public areas.

Once you are logged in, you open folders and files in exactly the same way as you would when working on your own stand-alone computer at home. The only difference is that your data may be stored on a remote computer (server) set aside to store shared files and programs. This will have a different drive letter such as (S:) or (J:) and you will have to navigate there first of all.

At the end of any computer session when you are leaving the computer ready for another user, make sure you log off from your own area.

log off

1 Click on the **Start** button.
2 Click on **Log Off**.

Fig. 1.37 Log Off

> ## Check your understanding 8
>
> **1** What name is given to the process of accessing a secure network?
> **2** List two methods for keeping your password secure.
> **3** If you are working on a network, check which drive you save your work on.

5 Health, safety and good practice

When working with computers, it is important to follow common-sense procedures. These include:

1 Looking after the environment
2 Looking after the equipment
3 Taking care of yourself
4 Reporting and correcting faults and hazards as soon as possible.

The environment

To make sure that you do not have accidents, check that cables are secured safely and do not trail across the floor and also that there are no piles of paper, bags, coats or other items left lying around. There should always be a clear and safe route to any exit – in case of fire, for example.

Also, check that power points are not overloaded. If you are plugging in a monitor, high-performance computer, printer, speakers etc. it is important to check what load this puts on the system. Overload protection circuits can be used to shut off the computer power supply before a predetermined voltage-current load is exceeded.

Ideally, work in a clean, smoke-free and well-ventilated environment – this will be good for your health and will also limit the need for excessive cleaning.

When it comes to the global environment, it is important to conserve energy and consumables. This includes turning off computers rather than leaving them on standby; replacing CRT (cathode ray tube) monitors with more efficient LCD (liquid crystal display) screens; making use of monitor power-saving features or turning off monitors when not in use; recycling paper and upgrading machines where possible rather than simply throwing them away and buying new ones.

The computer

Computers can be damaged by a sudden increase in power so it is worth fitting power surge protectors. These prevent your computer from being damaged by a sudden voltage increase caused by lightning or other dramatic power surge.

As with all electrical equipment, you should take care to keep liquids and debris away from the machine and to keep it clean. Monitors, disk drives, storage media, keyboards etc. should all be cleaned regularly with proprietary cleaners and cloths.

Yourself

The three areas where problems can arise if you spend long periods working on a computer are:

- Physical strain on your back, arms and hands
- Problems with your eyes
- General fatigue.

An unpleasant condition known as **Repetitive Strain Injury** (RSI) arises if you work in one position for too long, holding yourself stiffly or gripping the mouse too hard. A simple way to avoid RSI is to take regular breaks and make sure you change position frequently.

There is a great deal of **ergonomic** equipment available that is designed specifically for computer users. This includes chairs that support your back; wrist rests for your hands; specialised types of mouse and footstools to keep you sitting comfortably whilst maintaining a good posture. You can also use screens to cut down on glare from the monitor or magnifiers if you find it hard to read screen contents.

Changing the settings on the computer can also help, for example you can adjust contrast and colours to make it more restful as you work.

It is important to set up your work area so that everything you need is within easy reach rather than requiring you to stretch awkwardly, and to stop working if you have a headache or feel particularly tired.

Check your understanding 9

1 List three health problems that can arise when using a computer.
2 Why use a power surge protector?
3 Suggest two energy-saving actions you can take.

6 Preparing to produce new documents

Word-processing applications such as Microsoft Word 2007 allow you to create professional-looking documents where you can enter, amend or move text easily as well as add emphasis to enhance the contents. Unlike simple text editors, modern word-processing software allows you to see how your documents will look when printed out through the concept of WYSIWYG (what you see is what you get).

Document types

Using a word-processing application such as Microsoft Word 2007 means you will be able to:

* make changes to your documents very easily
* have copies of your work readily available
* use various tools to enhance your text
* add and position images (graphics) to the best effect
* make use of utilities such as spellcheckers or a thesaurus to improve your work
* find particular words, or replace incorrect entries rapidly, using the Find and Replace tools.

You can produce a wide range of documents using a word-processing application. In many cases, there are templates available that show you what that type of document should look like. It is then easy to customise a template so that you create your own version of the document while leaving the original unchanged.

Each type of document is normally set out in a particular way so that it is instantly recognisable. For example:

Business letters

Business letters normally begin with the sender's address, perhaps in the form of a letterhead, then the recipient's address and the date. They begin Dear Sir or Madam (or Dear Mr or Mrs X) and this is usually followed by the subject of the letter. They finish with Yours faithfully (or Yours sincerely if the recipient's name is known).

Such letters are normally printed onto A4 paper that is in portrait orientation (see Figure 1.37).

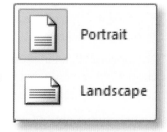

Fig. 1.38 Orientation

Memos

Memos are internal communications and normally have a top section showing four entries:

To – the name of the recipient

From – the name of the sender

Subject – the topic of the memo

Date

The main body of the memo then begins below this header.

Forms

Forms can be created offering boxes that people complete by writing in answers or placing a tick.

Reports

Reports are often very long documents that start with a main title and details of the writer. To make them easy to use, and in case pages get out of order, they should have a contents list, numbered pages and possibly brief details of the subject on every page.

Newsletters

Newsletters are commonly divided into columns, like newspapers, with pictures used to break up the text. They can go over several pages and stories are usually broken up so that later sections are continued on inner pages.

Invoices

Invoices are sent to customers or clients and show details of goods or services provided, together with payment that is owed.

Fax cover sheets

Fax cover sheets have space for the names of the sender and recipient, fax numbers, the date and the subject of the fax. It is a good idea to include the number of pages being sent, in case these become separated when the fax is received.

Advertising flyers

Advertising flyers are often smaller, perhaps printed on A5 paper. They can be in portrait or landscape orientation (see Figure 1.37), and may include borders, differently sized and enhanced text and graphics to increase their attractiveness.

Making documents readable

When creating documents, it is important to leave white space around graphics and text so that documents do not appear too cluttered or busy.

Word automatically sets a standard margin around the edge of the document, but this can be increased or decreased if it improves the readability or appearance of the page.

There are also various ways that text can wrap around a picture on the page, such as a photo or company logo – for example, tight up against it or leaving a small margin around the edge or at the top and bottom.

For 10,000 years cities have shaped the affairs of mankind. Now, more than half of the world's population is urban, dwelling in settlements that we identify as 'city' or 'town', some of them so extensive and so complex that they seem to transcend traditional notions of urban organisation.

The conference will deal with cities throughout the world, and proposals are sought for papers or panel sessions on any aspect of city life, form, ideology and culture. To find out more about the Anglo-American conference 2009, please visit the conference website.

Unfortunately if you sent 'cities@history.ac.uk' prior have not received it. We issue and can confirm the conference paper Please accept our inconvenience caused.  your submission to to 18th September we have resolved this address for submissions is now. apologies for any

Fig. 1.39 Text wrap round graphic

Document text

The style and appearance of the (**font**) text can make a significant difference to a document, and any changes you make are known as **formatting**. Whatever formatting you apply, the text should always be large enough to read clearly.

Some fonts are plain (for example, **Arial Black**). Others are child-friendly (*Comic Sans*) or fancy (𝔒𝔩𝔡 𝔈𝔫𝔤𝔩𝔦𝔰𝔥 𝔗𝔢𝔵𝔱). Some fonts resemble handwriting (for example, *Script MT*) or are even pictorial (Wingdings 2 ❩❸◎⑤ɑ◎⑤↩⑩🗐🗋).

Fonts can belong to one of three categories:

- **Serif fonts** have small lines (serifs) at the ends of the strokes – for example, `Courier New` and Times New Roman.

- **Sans serif** are plainer in style as they have no lines – for example, Arial and Tahoma.

- **Script fonts** such as *Script MS Bold* are similar to handwriting.

Font size

You can change the size of fonts, and the standard sizes range from

size 8   to

Titles are normally the largest, while headings, subheadings and the main text are progressively smaller and footnotes are the smallest.

Emphasis

Apart from altering its size, there are various ways to make your text stand out. These include using a colour, making it darker and thicker (**bold**), *italic* or <u>underlined</u>. This is known as adding **emphasis**. You can also place your text against a shaded background or within a border.

Paragraphs

Large blocks of text in a document can also be formatted and laid out in ways that make the content clearer or give it more impact.

- Each new topic should start a new paragraph. This means that the text begins on a new line and there is a clear line space between it and the previous paragraph.

- Words, lines or entire paragraphs can be positioned in different places on the page. For example, a block of text can be **indented** so that it starts a short way in from the left margin. You can also centre titles in the middle of the page, or line up an address with the right margin. This is known as text **alignment**.

- Columns of text can be spread across a page so that the content of each column lines up exactly with the entry above it, either by using **tabs** or by creating **tables**.

- List items can be emphasised and clarified by the use of **numbers** or **bullet points**.

7 Producing new documents

Using Word 2007

The application Word 2007 can be found from your Start – All Programs menu or you may have an icon on the desktop you can click on.

launch Word from the Program list

1 Click on the Start button.
2 Rest the mouse on All Programs.
3 If necessary, open a Microsoft Office menu.
4 Click on Word 2007.

Fig. 1.40 Launching Word

The opening screen

When Word opens, you will be presented with a blank document (temporarily labelled Document1) into which you can start typing. On-screen, the position where text will appear is marked by a flashing bar – the cursor. This is always set a short way in from the left-hand margin. As your typing reaches the right-hand margin of the page, the next word will be moved automatically to the start of the next line without you needing to take any action. This is known as word wrap.

Note that it is very important to use word wrap rather than clicking on Enter at the end of any lines within a paragraph, as it will affect the formatting you apply later.

Word 2007 windows

As you would expect on a Windows machine, the document opens within a window where you will see scroll bars for moving around the document, control buttons for maximising or closing the window and toolbar buttons and menu names. There is also a link to the Help pages in Word.

However, in many ways the Word 2007 interface is rather different from other windows you have already met.

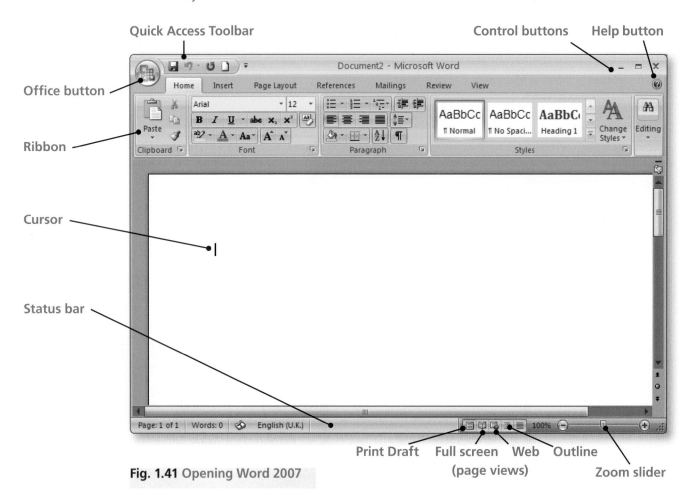

Fig. 1.41 Opening Word 2007

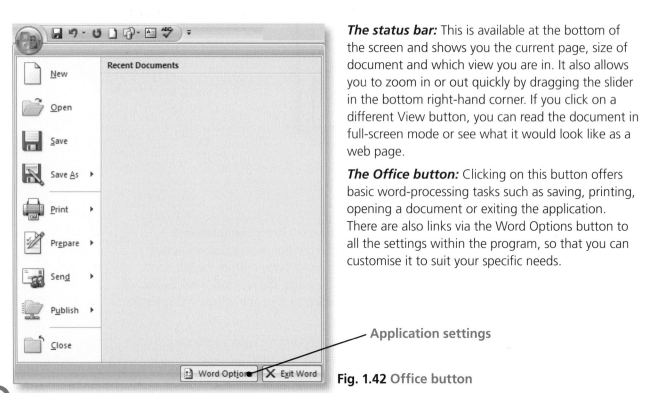

The status bar: This is available at the bottom of the screen and shows you the current page, size of document and which view you are in. It also allows you to zoom in or out quickly by dragging the slider in the bottom right-hand corner. If you click on a different View button, you can read the document in full-screen mode or see what it would look like as a web page.

The Office button: Clicking on this button offers basic word-processing tasks such as saving, printing, opening a document or exiting the application. There are also links via the Word Options button to all the settings within the program, so that you can customise it to suit your specific needs.

Fig. 1.42 Office button

The Quick Access toolbar: As the name suggests, commands are here to save you searching for them. If you click on the down arrow at the end of the toolbar, or right-click on any icon, you can add commands to this toolbar that you wish to use on a regular basis.

The ribbon: All the toolbar buttons and menus available in the program have been collected together into a **ribbon**. This offers seven different tabs on which similar commands and procedures are grouped together. To carry out an action, you must first select the appropriate tab and then either select one of the icons within a similar group or click on the small arrow button in the bottom right-hand corner to open up a relevant **dialog box** offering a wider choice. At any time, rest the mouse over an icon to learn about the command.

You will find that often as you move the mouse over a selection in a dialog box, such as a colour or style of text, you will be offered a preview of the effect in your document. This will help make selecting options much quicker.

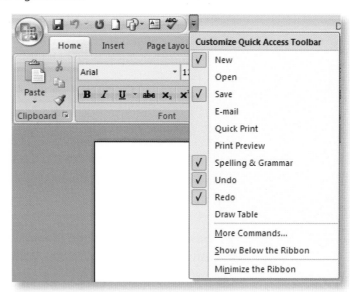

Fig. 1.43 Open Quick Access toolbar

The seven tabs are:

1   **Home** – this houses the commands related to font or paragraph formatting, and editing commands such as cut, copy and paste and finding or replacing entries.

Tab   Group of related icons/button commands   Click to open dialog box

Fig. 1.44 Home tab

2   **Insert** – here are links to objects you may want to add to your document such as tables, page numbers, pictures, symbols, shapes or new pages.

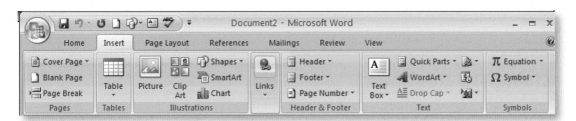

Fig. 1.45 Insert tab

3   **Page Layout** – this is the tab to open when you want to change margins, orientation and some paragraph features such as indentation and spacing.

Fig. 1.46 Page Layout tab

4 **References tab** (not needed for this level qualification) – is most valuable for large documents as here you can add a contents list, footnotes, indexes and bibliography.

5 **Mailings** (not needed for this level qualification) – is the tab for creating a mail merge (linking documents to a database of names and addresses).

6 **Review** – offers the chance to keep track of changes to a document and also to use spelling and grammar checkers and find translations or alternative words in a thesaurus.

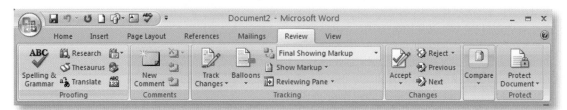

Fig. 1.47 Review tab

7 **View** – commands include different ways to view the page and change its magnification. Switch Windows will allow you to move between open files.

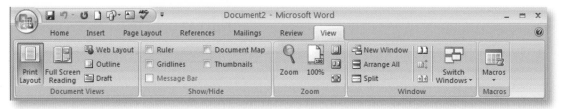

Fig. 1.48 View tab

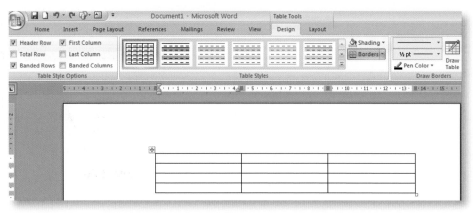

Fig. 1.49 Contextual icons

Contextual tools: You will find that as you work with various objects in a document, for example pictures or tables, a new Object Tools tab will appear offering extra, specialised tools to help you work with that particular object.

Using the keyboard

To create any word-processed document, text, punctuation symbols or numbers are typed in using the keyboard. The keyboard has rows of keys that display not only letters and numbers but also other labels or symbols. For example:

● **Caps Lock** – press this key before typing only upper-case (capital) letters. Press it again to turn it off before continuing with normal typing.

● **Shift** – hold this as you press a key to type a single letter as a capital or to type a punctuation symbol showing at the *top* of the key (for example, £ % , ? or +). Otherwise, the number or symbol showing at the bottom of the key will appear (for example, 3 ; # or \).

● **Enter** – press this key to move the cursor (text insertion point) onto the next line. Keep pressing to add more space in your document. When you start a new paragraph after a line space, this is known as a **paragraph break**. (Note that pressing Enter moves any text to the right of the cursor down with it, so make sure you are at the *end* of a line of text if you want to start a new paragraph.)

- **Space bar** – this is pressed to insert a space between characters or words. The convention is to leave a single space between each word and one or two consistently after a full stop.
- **Arrow or Cursor keys** – press one of these to move the cursor in the appropriate direction.
- **Esc** (Escape) – press this to abort an action (for example, printing a document).
- **Del** – this will delete any text to the right of the cursor.
- **Backspace** – this will delete text to the left of the cursor.
- **Page Up and Down** – press these to move through a long document as an alternative to using the scroll bar arrows or dragging the small box in the bar.
- **End** – move to the end of the line.
- **Home** – move to the beginning of the line.
- **Ctrl + Home/End** – move to the start or end of the entire text.
- **Alt** – hold this as you press particular keys to open different tabs.
- **F1–F12** (function keys) – these act as shortcuts to common actions such as getting help (F1) or finding a particular entry (F5).

Overtyping

If you want to type extra words into a line of text, you normally click to position the cursor in place and then start typing. The new text will be inserted into the document and the existing text will move to the right to make space for it.

Sometimes, new text can be set to *replace* existing text instead. This is known as overtyping. If set, you can go between the two typing modes by pressing the Insert key.

Undoing mistakes

One useful command is Undo. This steps back through actions you have taken and is very helpful if you make a silly mistake such as deleting the wrong entry.

undo or redo mistakes

1 Click on the **Undo** button to step back once – the button can be found on the Quick Access toolbar.
2 To step back through several actions, click on the **down arrow** next to the Undo button and select the actions.
3 If you go too far or change your mind, click on the **Redo** button.

Undo   Redo

Selected actions to undo

Fig. 1.50 Undo

Starting a new document

Once the application is open, you can start any number of new documents and keep them all open at the same time.

start a new document

1 Click on the **New** button on the Quick Access toolbar. (You can also hold **Ctrl** and press **N**.)
2 A longer method is to click on the **Office** button and then click on the **New** button.
3 In the window that opens, a Blank Document will be highlighted. Click on **Create** to open it on screen.
4 Each new document you open will be given the generic titles Document2, Document3 and so on, until you save and name them yourself.

New button

Fig. 1.51 New document

Closing

In Word, you can have several documents open at the same time. This means that closing the current document will leave the application and other documents open.

close a document

1 Click on the **Close** button showing a cross in the top right-hand corner.

   Or

2 Double-click on the **Office** button. (You will also find the **Close** option if you open the Office button menu first.)

exit Word

1 If only one document is open, clicking on its **Close** button will exit Word.

2 You can also click on the **Office** button and then click on **Exit Word**.

Check your understanding 10

1 Launch Word.

2 Start a new document.

3 Type in the following text:

   What will the temperature be on 21 December 2010? I can only spend £50 on a coat!

4 Leave several lines and then type your first name.

5 Change the date in the text to **20 November** and the amount to **£65**.

6 Add the following text as a new sentence after 2010: **I hope it isn't too cold.**

7 Now close the document without saving.

Saving documents

So that your work is preserved when you switch off the computer, you must save it onto the hard disk, a separate drive or suitable removable media such as an optical disk.

There are three types of save you can carry out:

- Saving a document for the first time: this involves giving it a name and saving it to a suitable location, for example, a folder such as My Documents.

- Saving changes to a document: it is important to do this regularly so that the latest version is retained. It is a 'quick' save as you will already have named your document and the save simply updates it by overwriting the original.

- Saving a different version of your document (often referred to as **Save As**): this retains the original, so the new version must either be given a different name or be saved to a different location.

Note that when saving a number of versions, it is important to keep names consistent and logical, so that working back through the documents will be straightforward.

save a document

1 Click on the **Save** icon on the Quick Access toolbar or open the **Office** button and click on **Save**. (A shortcut is to hold **Ctrl** and click on the letter **S**.)

2 In the dialog box that opens, select a location for the file so that it shows in the Save in: box. You can either click on the **down arrow** in the box or search for the location by opening folders showing in the main window. If you need to work up through the folder hierarchy, keep clicking on the **Up One Level** button. You can also select a location from the **My Places** bar.

Save button

Fig. 1.52 Save button

3 Amend the file name showing in the box or accept the wording that will appear automatically.

4 At this point, you can click on the **Create New Folder** button. This allows you to create a new folder inside the drive or folder showing in the Save in: box in which to save the file.

5 Click on the **Save** button or press **Enter** to complete the save.

6 You will return to your document and the new file name will now show in the title bar.

update a document by saving any changes

1 Click on the **Save** button or hold **Ctrl** and press **S**.

2 No Save As window will appear.

save a new version

1 Click on the **Office** button and click on **Save As**.

2 If you rest the pointer on the **Save As** button, this will open a new menu and you will be able to select from a range of file formats in which to save. (This is especially important if you want to send someone a copy of the document and they do not have the latest version of Word.)

3 In the Save As window that opens, amend the file name and/or change the location showing in the Save in: box.

4 Click on the **Save** button.

Automatic saves

To be absolutely sure you will have a copy if something goes wrong with the file you are working on, click on the **Office** button and go to **Word Options – Advanced**. Under Save, click in the **Always create backup copy** checkbox.

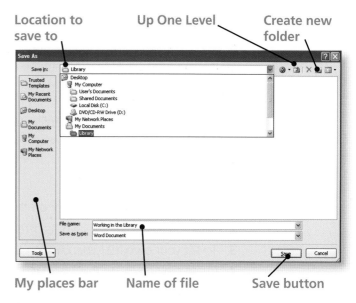

Location to save to   Up One Level   Create new folder

My places bar   Name of file   Save button

Fig. 1.53 Save As box

Fig. 1.54 Save As file formats

Check your understanding 11

1 Launch Word.
2 Type the words **Using salt dough** into a new blank document.
3 Save the file as *Salt dough* into a new folder named *Crafts*.

Page layout

At any stage, you can change the default margins, orientation or paper size of your document. All these options are available from the Page Layout tab.

Margins

The default margins that are set for a standard A4 page are 2.54 cm top, bottom, left and right. You can choose from a range of layouts or customise the margins by typing in your own measurements.

change margins

1   On the Page Layout tab, click on the down arrow below the Margins button.
2   Select from one of the layouts offered if they are suitable.
3   To set your own margins, click on the **Custom Margins** option.
4   In the dialog box on the Margins tab, click into a margin box and either type an exact measure or use the up or down arrows to change the measurements in tenths. (You will need to enter figures manually for hundredths.)
5   To set these margins for all future documents, you can click on the **Default** button and then confirm the changes.
6   Click on **OK** to close the box.

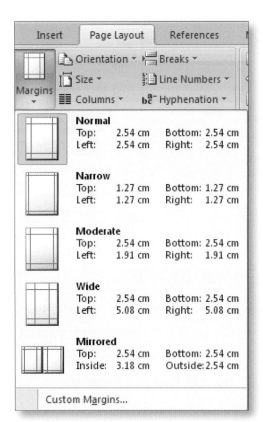

Fig. 1.55 Quick margins

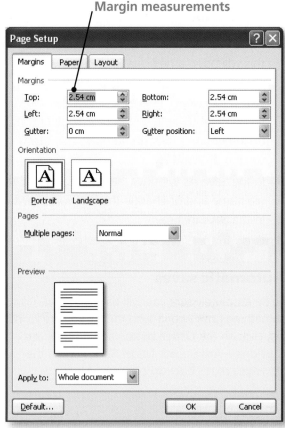

Margin measurements

Fig.1.56 Customise margins

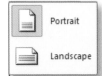

Fig. 1.57
Orientation

Orientation

The default orientation for Word documents is portrait. As some documents will need to be in landscape orientation, select this option from the **Orientation** button.

change orientation

1   On the Page Layout tab, click on the **Orientation** button and select **Landscape** or **Portrait**.
2   You will also find these options if you are customising margins.

Paper size

There is a wide range of standard paper sizes on which to print and you can also set your own measurements exactly.

set paper size

1 On the Page Layout tab, click on the **Size** button.
2 Choose an alternative size from the list. More sizes are available if you click on the down arrow in the scroll bar.
3 To type in your own measurements, click on **More Paper Sizes** and change entries in the width and height boxes.

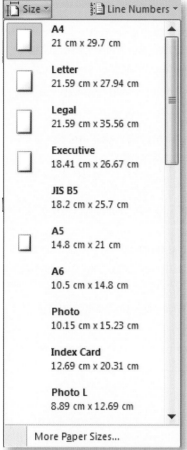

Fig. 1.58 Quick paper sizes

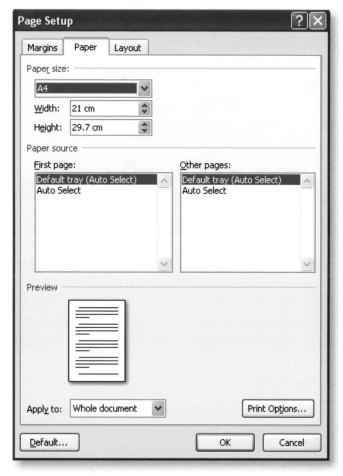

Fig. 1.59 Customise paper sizes

Check your understanding 12

1 Start a new document.
2 Set the paper size to A5.
3 Change to landscape orientation.
4 Change the margins so that left and right are now 2.00 cm.
5 Close the document without saving.

Default font

Fig. 1.60 Default fonts

This is what unselected text looks like

This is what selected text looks like

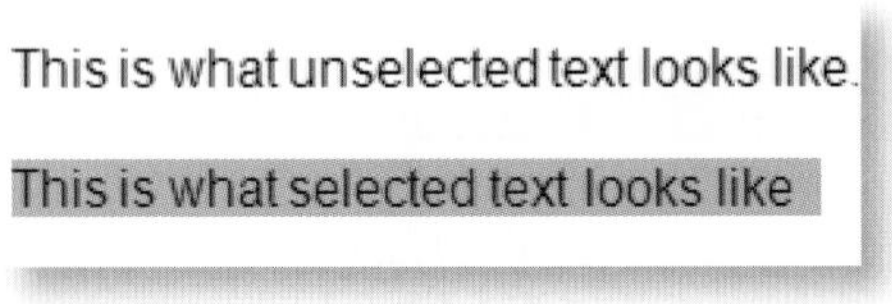

Fig. 1.61 Highlighted text

Selecting text

When you start entering text into a document, a particular font type, size and emphasis will have been set as the default. The settings will be visible on the Home tab.

You can set different font formats before you start typing, or you can change the text later. To do this, you have to select the text you want to change so that new settings will only apply to this specific part of the document. Selected text will appear highlighted in blue.

There are a number of different ways you can select text, using either the keyboard or the mouse.

select text using the mouse

1 Double-click on one word to select it.

2 Triple-click to select a paragraph.

3 Click in front of the first word, hold down the left mouse button and drag the pointer across the characters to select sections of text.

Note that if you overshoot, keep the mouse pointer held down and slowly move back up the text.

4 Position the pointer in the left margin. When it shows a right-facing white arrow, click to select one line or click and drag the pointer to select adjacent lines.

select text using the keyboard

1 Position the cursor in front of the first word, then hold **Shift** as you press an arrow key in the appropriate direction to select whole words or lines.

2 Position the cursor in front of the first word, move down the page using the scroll bar and hold **Shift** as you click after the last word to select a large block of text extending below the screen.

3 To select all the text, hold down **Ctrl** and press the letter **A** or click on **Select** in the Editing section of the Home tab and choose **Select All**.

4 To take off the highlight, click the mouse pointer anywhere on screen away from the left margin.

Using the floating toolbar

Fig. 1.62 Floating toolbar

Changing the font

There are 14 different boxes and buttons provided on the Home tab related to the font, and there are further options available if you open the Font dialog box. Once selected, the button will usually show as orange unless you are choosing alternatives from a list. Click on it again to take off the formatting, or click on a different button.

Note that, as you select text, a pale mini-toolbar appears floating above the text. Move the mouse up to it if you want to select any of the formatting options available. It offers just the more common fonts as well as paragraph options.

format font

1 Choose a different font type or face by selecting an alternative from the drop-down list in the **Font** box. To bring up a particular font quickly, start typing its name in the box to move to font names beginning with that letter.

Fig. 1.63 Font box

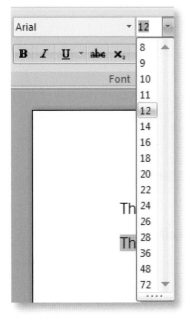

Fig. 1.64 Font Size

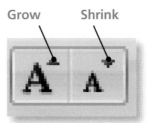

Grow   Shrink

Fig. 1.65 Shrink and Grow

Fig. 1.66 Clear format

2 Increase or decrease font size by selecting a different measure from the drop-down list, or enter your own preferred size over the highlighted number. You must confirm new sizes by pressing the **Enter** key.

3 Increase text size in steps by clicking on the **Grow Font** button.

4 Decrease text size by clicking on the **Shrink Font** button.

5 Return to plain text by clicking on the **Clear Formatting** button.

6 Add **bold emphasis** by clicking on the **B** button.

7 Apply *italic* formatting by clicking on the **I** button.

8 Underline the text by clicking on the **U** button. There are further options available, such as double underline, if you click on the down arrow next to the button.

The following are keyboard shortcuts for emphasis:

Ctrl + B for bold

Ctrl + I for italic

Ctrl + U for underline.

9 Apply a format such as ~~strikethrough~~ by clicking on the abc button.

10 Apply subscript with the button marked X_2 so that the character appears smaller and below the line – for example, in chemical formulae such as H_2O. First type the number or letter normally and then select and apply the formatting to that character.

Fig. 1.67 Emphasis

11 Apply superscript in the same way with the X^2 button – for example, in degrees of temperature such as 30°C.

12 Change case – for example, if you have typed all capitals by mistake, by clicking on the button labelled **Aa**. You will be offered a range of cases such as all capitals, all lower case or sentence case (first initial only).

13 Highlight the selected text by applying a bright colour.
You can choose alternative colours from the palette by clicking on the down arrow next to the button.

14 Apply a coloured font to the text, again changing the colours by selecting from the palette that appears when you click on the down arrow. The most recently used colour will appear as a bar underneath the letter A on the button.

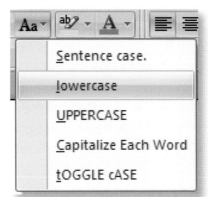

Fig. 1.68 Change case

Highlight   Font colour

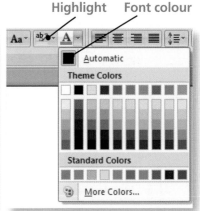

Fig. 1.69 Highlight and font colour

Check your understanding 13

1 Start a new document.
2 Type in the words: **Summer holidays are finally here**.
3 Check the default settings.
4 Change the font to a different type.
5 Increase the font size so that the text is twice as large.
6 Double underline the word **holidays**.
7 Make the word **Summer** yellow.
8 Clear all the formatting.
9 Close the file without saving.

Fig. 1.70 New example 13 format

Alignment

As you type, your text will line up on the left margin. This is known as **left alignment** and is the default setting. There are three other alignments that can be set:

Centre-aligned – text is centred on the mid-point of the page and is a common alignment for titles of reports or menu items.

Right -aligned – this aligns text with the right-hand margin and is often set for dates and addresses when writing letters.

Justified – this is the alignment applied to long documents to neaten up both left and right margins. Often, extra spaces are added and so a short line can look rather odd.

The alignment can be changed for individual lines or blocks of text, but you cannot have two different alignments on the same line. This means that to change from one alignment to the next you must first move onto a new line.

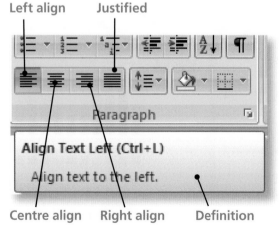

Fig. 1.71 Alignment buttons

set alignment

1 Click to place the cursor in the line or paragraph you want to realign, or first select a block of text.
2 On the **Page Layout** tab, click on the appropriate **alignment** button. A definition will appear below the ribbon and the selected button will appear orange.
3 You can also use keyboard shortcuts:
   Ctrl + E for centre-aligned
   Ctrl + R for right-aligned
   Ctrl + L for left-aligned
   Ctrl + J for justified

Check your understanding 14

1 Start a new document.

2 Type in the following text: **Holidays in Egypt**.

3 Leave a clear line space and then type in the main text as follows: **Egypt has a timeless appeal that has been drawing travellers for millennia. A highlight is to experience the journey down the river of the pharaohs, the Nile.**

4 Save the file as *Egypt*.

5 Now make the following changes to the text:

  a Centre the title on the page.

  b Colour the word **Egypt** blue wherever it appears.

  c Apply a Serif font, such as Times New Roman, size 16 to the title.

  d Format the main text to italic.

  e Change the title case to all capitals.

6 Add the following sentence: **The average temperature in the summer can be 30°C.**

7 Now use Undo to remove this sentence but retain capitals to the title.

8 Save the amended version of the document as *Egypt 2*.

9 Close the file.

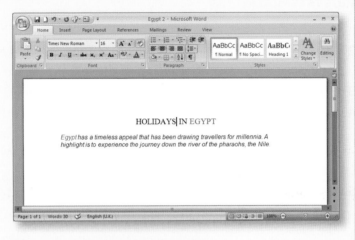

Fig. 1.72 New example 14 Egypt

Using tabs

Each time you click on the **Tab** key (labelled with two arrows, next to the letter Q) it moves the cursor across the page. The normal distance is in jumps of 1.27 cm or 0.5 in. If you fix the position it moves to (known as the **tab stop position**), you can use this facility to help you set out information in a document in neat columns. You do this by placing black symbols along the ruler exactly where you want the cursor to move to for each column.

As well as the tab stop position, you can also set the *way* in which columns line up (**tab alignment**):
- by their initial characters (Left Tab)
- by their last characters (Right Tab)
- centred on the tab position (Centre Tab)
- with decimal places in a column of figures lining up exactly (Decimal Tab).

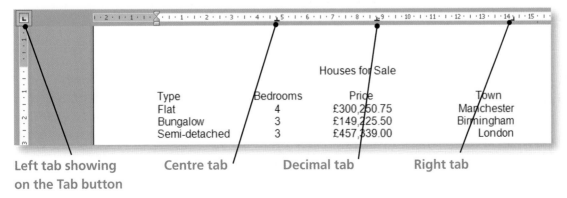

Left tab showing on the Tab button   Centre tab   Decimal tab   Right tab

Fig. 1.73 Columns with tabs

fix tab stops using the ruler

1   Make sure the horizontal ruler is showing. If it is not, either click on the **View Ruler** button at the top of the vertical scroll bar or click in the **Ruler checkbox** on the View tab.

Ruler checkbox

Fig. 1.74 View Ruler

2   Start by typing any column headings, spacing these by eye. It will be easier to get their position correct after typing all the text if they are not set using the Tab key.

3   Press **Enter** to position the cursor on the left margin.

4   Set the position for the first column. If you do not want a Left Tab, first click on the **Tab** button above the left scroll bar until it shows the correct type of tab symbol – for example, Right or Centre – then click on the ruler where you want the cursor to move to. The chosen symbol will appear.

5   Set the second type of column by clicking on the **Tab** button again if necessary and clicking in place on the ruler. Repeat the process until all the tab stops are on the ruler.

6   If you make a mistake, rest the pointer on the tab stop and then gently drag it up or down away from the ruler. When you let go of the mouse the symbol should disappear. You can also drag a tab stop to a different position on the ruler.

7   To type your document, either type the first entry so that the first column lines up on the left margin or press the **Tab** key and start typing where the cursor moves to. Press the **Tab** key again to move the cursor to the next column and repeat across the page.

8   When you have completed the first row, press **Enter** to move to the next line and start typing the next row of entries.

9   If you find you need a wider column, select **all** the text typed using tabs. Now drag the position for the incorrect tab along the ruler. A dotted line will show its progress and the column position will be readjusted.

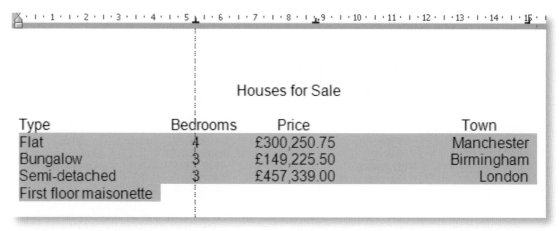

Fig. 1.75 Moving tab columns

use the menu

1 Type the headings and then press **Enter** to move to the first line for the column entries.
2 Type the first entry and then press the **Tab** key once to move to the next column. Repeat across the page. Your text will appear squashed but will be sorted out later.
3 Repeat for the remaining entries, pressing **Enter** each time to move to the next row. Then highlight all the column entries set with tabs.
4 On the Home tab, click on the arrow to open the **Paragraph** dialog box and click on the **Tabs** button.

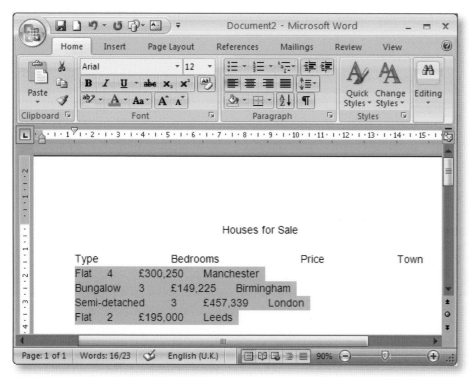

Fig. 1.76 Single tab between entries

Measurement along ruler for 2nd column

First column setting

5 In the Tabs dialog box, click in the Tab stop position box and enter the measure (figures only, no cm) for the first column – for example, Bedroom entries would be positioned in a column lined up at 4 cm along the ruler by entering 4. Click for **Centre**, **Right** or **Left** Tab and then click on the **Set** button.
6 Click in the box again (you will have to type over the entry that appears) and enter the position and tab alignment style for the next column. Repeat until all tab stop positions have been set.
7 Return to your document and check that the columns look right. If not, return to the dialog box and change any measurements or tab styles.
8 To remove unwanted tab stops, select them in the box and click on the **Clear** button.

Accept or change alignment

Set position

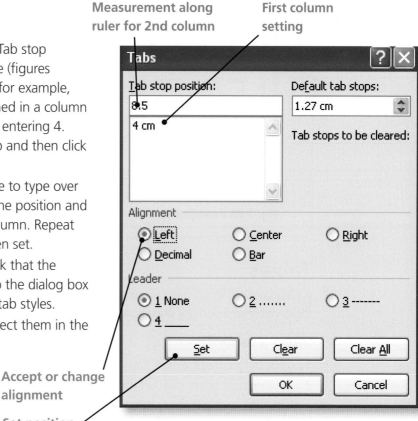

Fig. 1.77 Set tabs with menu

Check your understanding 15

1 Start a new document.

2 Enter the title **Christmas presents**.

3 Save the file with the same name.

4 Centre the title and apply upper case.

5 Now create the table set out below using tabs. Enter the column headings first.

6 Set the columns as follows:

Toy – on the left margin
Name – left tab at 3 cm
Age – centre tab at 7 cm
Price – right tab at 13 cm

Toy	*Name*	*Age*	*Price*
Teddy	*George*	*7*	*£14.95*
Doll	*Mary*	*8*	*£11.45*
Puzzle	*Petra*	*6*	*£3.50*
Book	*Helena*	*9*	*£12.99*

7 Format the column headings in bold and italic and make sure they are positioned correctly over the column entries.

8 Finally, move the Age column to 8 cm and adjust the heading position.

9 Save and close the file.

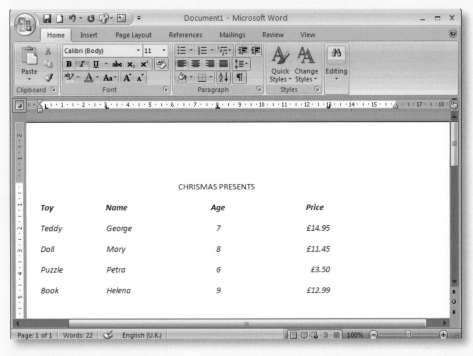

Fig. 1.78 Example 15 tabs

Tables

A different way to set out columns of text is to use a table. You can remove the gridlines or leave them visible and perhaps add emphasis with coloured borders and shading.

insert a table

1 Click on the page where you want the table to appear.

2 On the **Insert** tab, click on the **Table** button and drag the mouse across the **cells** (squares) to select the number of columns and rows. The table will appear when you let go of the mouse.

Or

3   Click on **Insert Table** and enter the dimensions into the boxes provided.

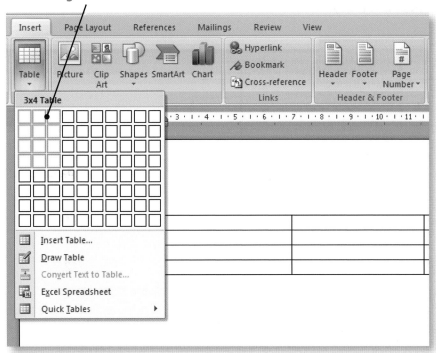

Fig. 1.79 Inserting a table

Table entries

Each cell is independent, so you can click into any cell to type, realign or format the entries.

make entries

1   Click in the first cell to enter text or numbers and then click with the mouse or press the **Tab** key or an arrow key to move across the row.
2   If you press **Enter**, you will move onto a new line within the same cell.
3   Move down columns by pressing an arrow key or clicking with the mouse.

insert extra cells

1   Click in the last cell and press the **Tab** key to add a new row.
    Or
2   Right-click on any cell and, on the menu that appears, click on **Insert** and then the appropriate option – for example, to insert a column to the left of the cell or a row above.

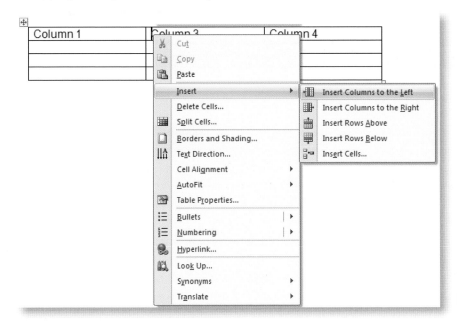

Fig. 1.80 Insert column in table

delete cells

1   To delete a row or column, click in a cell and then right-click.
2   On the menu, select **Delete Cells**. This will open the Delete Cells dialog box.
3   In the box, select the row or column option and then click on **OK**.

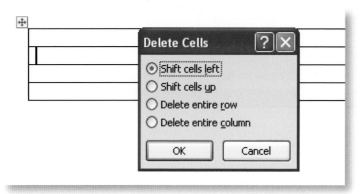

Fig. 1.81 Deleting table cells

4   To delete a whole table, first select it by clicking on the small square showing a cross in the top left-hand corner. (This is the **Move** handle and dragging it moves the whole table across the page.)
5   Then press the **Backspace** key.
    Or
6   Select the correct **Delete** option on the **Table Tools – Layout** tab.

Note that if you select the table and click on the **Delete** button, this removes the contents but not the actual table.

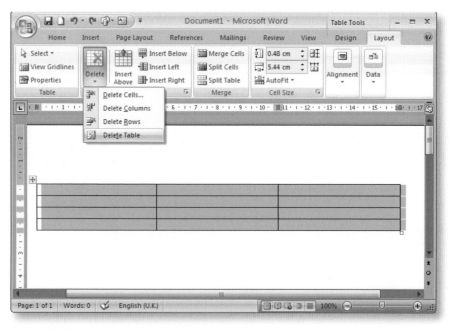

Fig. 1.82 Deleting a whole table

Formatting a table

Cell contents are formatted in the same way as normal text. For example, you can:

● apply a different font type and size
● add emphasis
● realign entries in particular cells.

As you often want all the headings or row labels formatted in the same way, select all the relevant cells first.

select an entire row

1 Move the mouse into the margin to the left of a row.
2 When it shows a right-facing white arrow, click to select the row or click and drag to select adjacent rows.

select an entire column

1 Position the mouse above the column.
2 When it shows a down-facing black arrow, click to select the column or click and drag to select several adjacent columns.

amend column widths

1 Click on the table to display the column width measurements on the ruler.
2 To amend widths manually, position the mouse in the ruler area at a boundary. When it shows a two-way arrow, click and drag across the ruler. A dotted line will show the new width measure.

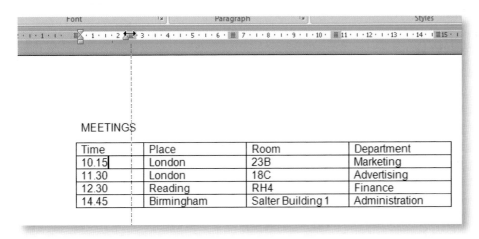

Fig. 1.83 Dragging a table column

3 To set widths exactly, click on the **Layout** tab under **Table Tools**.
4 In the Cell Size area, either enter figures into the size boxes or click on the **AutoFit** button. AutoFit Contents will let you fit the width to the size of the longest entry.
5 You could also click on the arrow in the bottom corner of the Cell Size area to open the **Table Properties** dialog box and enter exact measurements.

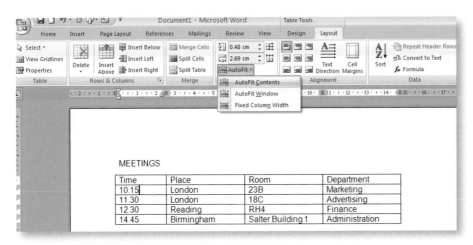

Fig. 1.84 Table layout

amend row heights

Use the vertical ruler or Layout tab as above.

add borders

1 Select the whole table or the cells you wish to border.
2 On the Table Tools tab, click on **Borders**. This offers a range of border styles such as grid, no borders or outside borders.
3 For more options, click on the bottom option labelled **Borders and Shading**.
4 In the box that opens, select a type of border, its colour, style and width and then click on **OK**.
5 There are also a range of AutoFormats offered on the tab that you can click on to apply.

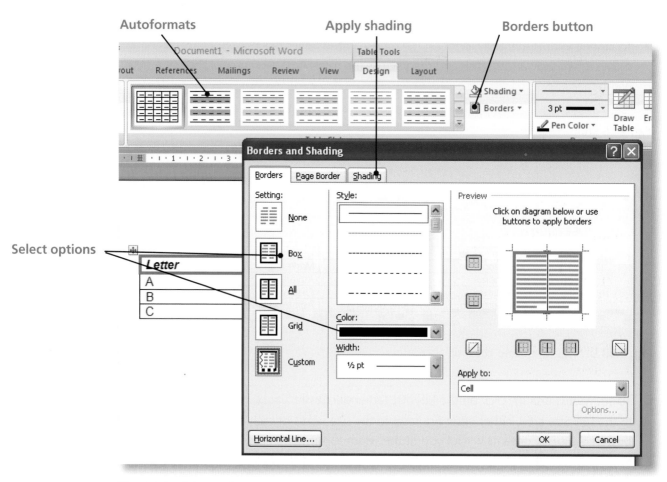

Fig. 1.85 Table borders

add shading to cells

1 Click on the **Shading** button on the toolbar and select from the palette of colours.
2 Click on **More Colors** for an extended range.
   Or
3 Click on the **Shading** tab in the Borders and Shading dialog box.

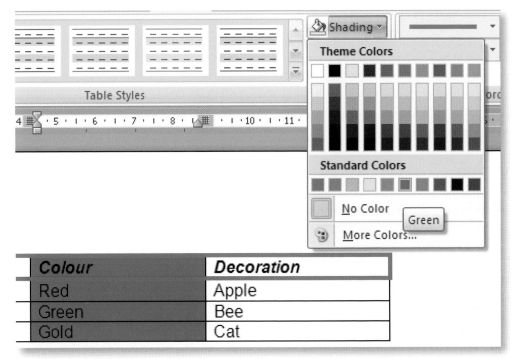

Colour	Decoration
Red	Apple
Green	Bee
Gold	Cat

Fig. 1.86 Shading table cells

Check your understanding 16

1 Create a table with four rows and four columns.
2 Enter the following headings in row 1:

Name

Colour

Season

Produce

3 Add entries as set out below:

Name	Colour	Season	Produce
Sunflower	Yellow	Summer	Seeds
Snowdrop	White	Spring	None
Rose	Pink	Summer	Hips

4 Save the file as *Flower table*.
5 Now make the following changes:
   a Insert a row below **Snowdrop** and add the following entry:
      Magnolia, **White**, **Spring**, **None**.
   b Format the column headings to bold, coloured blue.
   c Shade the cells containing flower details orange.
   d Remove all the borders.
6 Save and close the file.

Name	Colour	Season	Produce
Sunflower	Yellow	Summer	Seeds
Snowdrop	White	Spring	None
Magnolia	White	Spring	None
Rose	Pink	Summer	Hips

Fig. 1.87 Example 16 table

Working with paragraphs

When typing a document using the default settings, you usually find the document has a left alignment so that the text on each line lines up on the left margin. As you have already seen, you can change alignment but there are also other changes you can make, including setting special paragraph indents, changing line spacing and labelling list items.

Select a single paragraph when applying new formats by clicking anywhere inside, but click and drag to select several paragraphs.

Indentation

An indent is usually the text position that is set in from the left or right margin, and you can set these indents to an exact measure or change them by eye. They are often used to emphasise a section of text, for example, when including a quotation or to break up a block of text.

set an indentation using the toolbar

1   On the Home tab, click on the **Increase Indent** button, which shows an arrow pointing to the right. This will move the text in from the left margin by 1.27 cm.

2   Keep clicking on the button to move the text further inwards by this amount each time.

3   Click on the **Decrease Indent** button, which has an arrow pointing to the left to move the paragraph back towards the left margin.

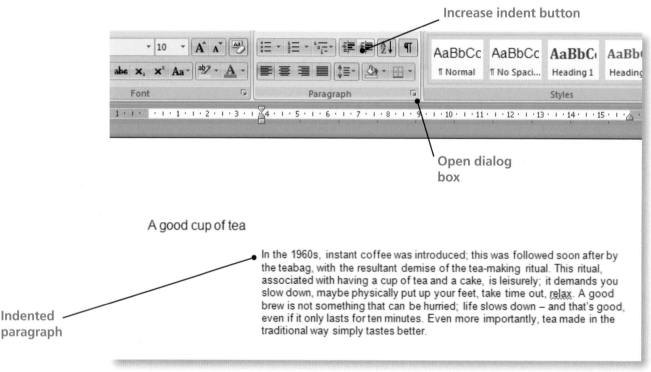

Fig. 1.88 Indent button

set indentations exactly

1   To indent from the right, or from both margins, click on the **Page Layout** tab and then change the measurements in the Left or Right Indent box by clicking on the up or down arrows.

Fig. 1.89 Indent boxes on Page Layout

2 You can also click on the arrow on the Home tab in the Paragraph group to open the dialog box and enter your measurements in the correct indent box(es).

3 Check the preview.

4 Click on **OK** to confirm the settings.

There are two special types of indent you can apply to a paragraph:

A hanging indent has the first line on the margin but the rest of the paragraph indented by a set amount.

  A first line indent is the reverse – the first line is indented but the rest of the paragraph lines up on the left margin.

apply special paragraph settings

1 Select the paragraph(s).

2 Open the **Paragraph** dialog box.

3 Click in the **Special** box. For normal typing, it will show (none).

4 Click on the down arrow and select the type of paragraph you want.

5 Set an exact measure if necessary in the **By:** box.

6 Check the preview and then click on **OK**.

Measurements changed

Special paragraphs

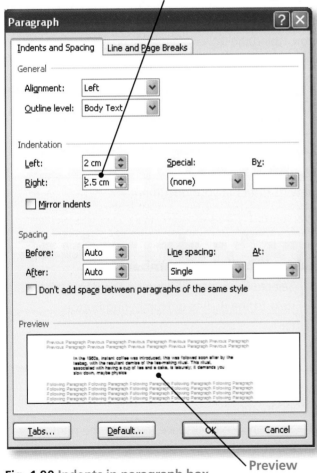

Fig. 1.90 Indents in paragraph box

Preview

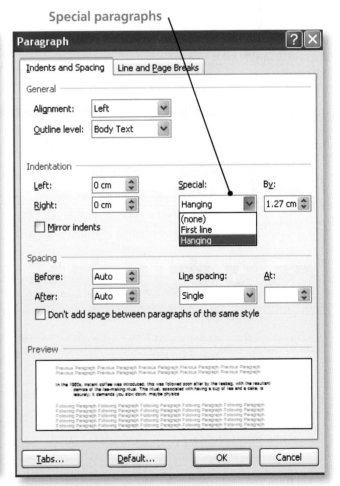

Fig. 1.91 Special paragraph settings

Line spacing button   Open dialog box

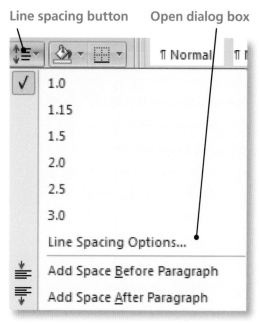

Fig. 1.92 Changing line spacing

Line spacing

You can set the space between lines to more than the normal, which is known as **single line spacing**. For example, **double line spacing** leaves a clear line space between lines of text and is useful if you want to allow room for someone to write comments on a word-processed document. For the purposes of this qualification you must be sure to check that you use single line spacing. As it's not the default setting, you may need to amend this in your documents.

change line spacing

1 Click on the arrow next to the Line spacing button and choose an alternative.

2 Use a keyboard shortcut:
   Ctrl + 2 = double line spacing
   Ctrl + 1 = single line spacing
   Ctrl + 5 = 1.5 line spacing

3 Open the Paragraph dialog box (from the ribbon or by clicking on **Line Spacing Options**) and change settings in the Line Spacing box. There is the option here to set a general measure such as 'more than… ' or 'exactly… '.

Bulleted or numbered lists

Long lists can be confusing, and it helps if each item in the list is identified by a number or a bullet point. You can do this before you start typing the list, or after selecting it. Once applied, a new number or bullet point will appear each time you press Enter.

apply numbers or bullet points

1 To apply bullet points, click on the **Bullets** button on the Home tab.

2 To number each item, click on the **Numbering** button.

3 If you want to change the default style of bullets or numbers, click on the down arrow next to the button and click on an alternative style.

4 Rest your mouse over an option to view its effect in your document.

5 Click on **OK** to confirm the choice.

Bullets   Numbering

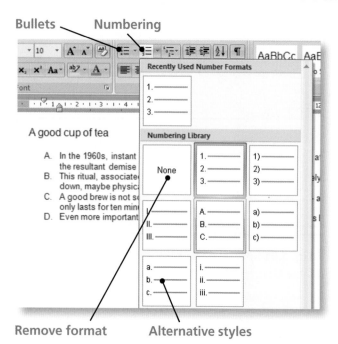

take off bullets or numbers

1 Select **None** after clicking on the down arrow next to the Bullets or Numbering button.
   Or

2 Select the list items and click off the button.

3 You can take off the setting for individual items in the list in this way, but may need to readjust indentation.

4 You can also backspace to delete the number or bullet for that line.

Remove format   Alternative styles

Fig. 1.93 Numbers and bullets

Check your understanding 17

1 Start a new document.
2 Type the following text as set out below:

'**To be or not to be**
That is the question.'

Everyone knows this quotation from *Hamlet***, but here are three more plays by**
   Shakespeare:

Macbeth
The Taming of the Shrew
Measure for Measure.

3 Save as *Plays*.
4 Indent the quotation by 3 cm from both the left and right margin.
5 Apply a hanging indent to the sentence starting **Everyone...**
6 Apply bullet points to the list of plays.
7 Change the style of bullets from the default.
8 Save and close the file.

"To be or not to be
That is the question."

Everyone knows this quotation from *Hamlet*, but here are three more plays by
Shakespeare:
➢ *Macbeth*
➢ *The Taming of the Shrew*
➢ *Measure for Measure*

Fig. 1.94 Example 17 plays

Borders and shading

As well as enhancing the borders of cells in a table, you can add borders and shading to text on the page. These settings can either apply to individual words, or extend across the whole of the line or paragraph.

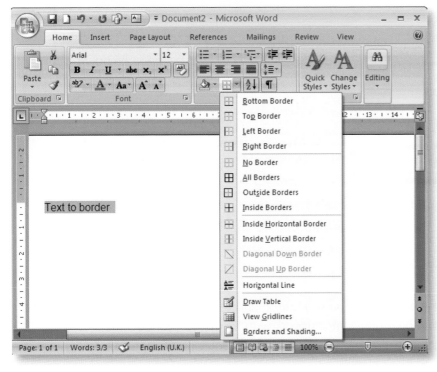

Fig. 1.95 Borders button

border text

1 Select the text and apply a border style such as **Outside Borders** after clicking on the down arrow next to the Borders button on the Home tab.

2 For more choice, click on the **Borders and Shading** option at the bottom of the menu.

3 In the main window, select a setting such as **Shadow** or **Box**.

4 Now choose from the range of styles, line widths and colours offered in the various boxes. The preview will show what the border will look like.

5 You could click on one of the buttons in the preview area if you wanted to remove the border from one or more sides.

6 Select whether to apply the border to text or paragraph and click on **OK** to confirm the settings.

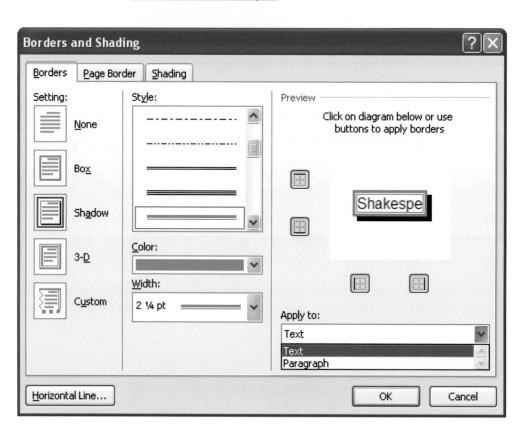

Fig. 1.96 Border text

Fig. 1.97 Chosen border style

shade text background

1 Select the text.

2 Click on the arrow next to the Shading button and select a colour. Colours are arranged in themes that may be modified if you work with themes in your document, or as standard colours that will stay the same even if you apply a different theme.

3 You will see the effect of the colour as you hover over your choice with the mouse.

4 Click on **More Colours** for a wider palette. When you click on a colour on the Standard tab, you will be able to compare it to the colour currently applied.

5 After you have clicked on **OK** to confirm your choice, the most recent colour chosen will now be displayed on the Shading button so that it can be applied again quickly in the future.

Note that you will not see the real effect of a colour change until you remove the highlight from your text.

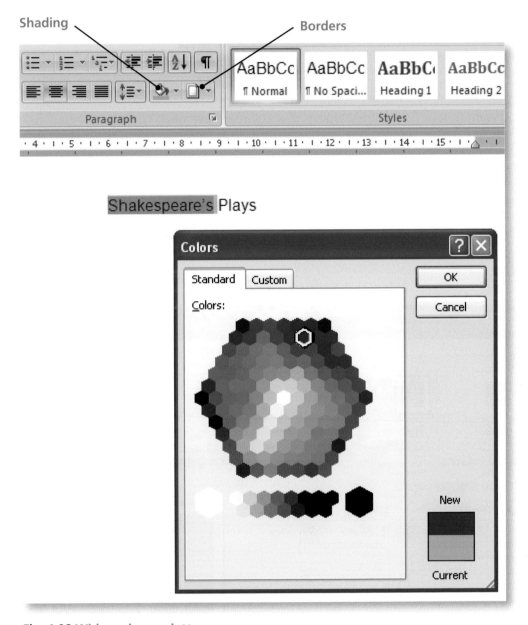

Fig. 1.98 Wider colour palette

Columns

With a large amount of text, it is often more sensible to arrange it in columns. Also, some text, such as in a newsletter or text covering a number of points, is best displayed in columns.

As with alignment, you must move to a new line before you can take off the column setting and return to normal typing (which is, in effect, a single column).

apply columns

1 Either apply the setting first, or type your document, select one or more blocks of text and then set the columns.

2 Click on the down arrow next to the Columns button on the Page Layout tab and select one of the column settings if you want two or three columns.

3 For more choice, click on **More Options**.

4 In the dialog box, select the number of columns and, if not of equal width, set the widths exactly.

5 Amend the spacing measure if you want extra space between columns.

6 You can add a vertical line between the columns by clicking in the line between checkbox.

7 If necessary, change the option to apply columns to the whole document or selected text.

8 Click on **OK** to return to your document.

9 If you want to return to normal typing after columns have been typed:

   a Click at the end of the text.

   b Click on **Enter** to move to a new line.

   c Open the **Columns dialog box**, select **One Preset** and then select **Apply to: this point forward**.

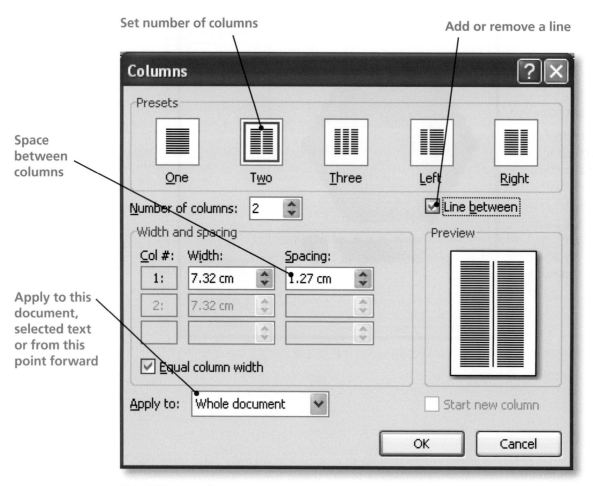

Fig. 1.99 Set columns

Within columns, you will need to decide which word should start at the top of the second or third column and set a column break at that point. Otherwise, Word 2007 will only start a second column when the text in the first column reaches the bottom of the page.

set a column break

1 Click in front of the word to start the next column.
2 On the Page Layout tab, click on **Breaks**.
3 Select **Column**.

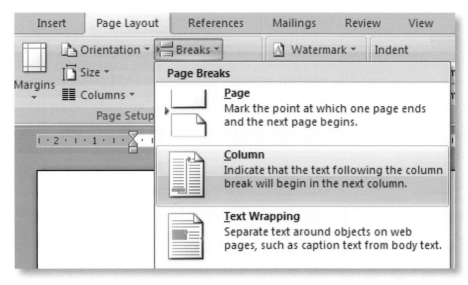

Fig. 1.100 Column break

Check your understanding 18

1 Start a new document and type the following text: **Flowers that I like**
2 Now type the following as a list:

Lilies
Daffodils
Tulips
Foxgloves
Roses
Sweet peas
Sunflowers
Lily of the valley

3 Centre the title on the page.
4 Select the title text and shade it pale green.
5 Add a double line paragraph border of any line width round the title so that it extends to both margins.
6 Set the list items but *not* the title in two columns.
7 Start the second column with **Roses**.
8 Now add a final sentence after the list that is *not* within a column but is typed normally across the page: **My favourite flower is the sunflower as it always makes people smile.**
9 Shade only the list items yellow.
10 Save the file as *flowers*.

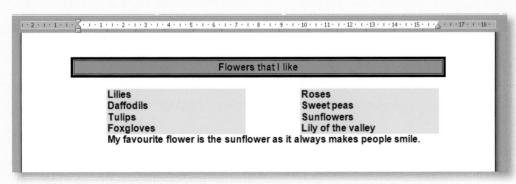

Fig. 1.101 Example 18 flowers

Copy, cut and paste

In the same way that files can be moved or copied between folders, you can move or copy parts of one document to another position or even paste them into another document altogether. During the manoeuvre, the copied or cut items are held safely in the clipboard.

Once you have carried out a move, make sure that the spacing is adjusted correctly.

move/copy and paste within a document

1 Select the text you want to copy or move.
2 Select **Cut** to move or **Copy** to copy – either right-click for the menu or click on the icon in the Clipboard section on the Home tab.
3 Move through the current document until you find the new position for your text. Click on-screen in the place for the text.
4 Select **Paste** and the text will appear.

move/copy and paste between documents

1 Select the text and choose **Copy** or **Cut**.
2 Move to the receiving document – you may need to open it or restore it from the taskbar, and you can even create a new document at this stage.
3 Click on the page where you want the text to appear.
4 Select **Paste**.

Page breaks

As you type a long document and you reach the bottom of the first page, your words will automatically continue onto a second or third page. The point at which the text moves onto a new page is known as a **soft page break**. This is because it will change whenever you delete or add extra text to the previous pages.

For those times when you want a particular word or title to start on a new page, you need to insert a **hard page break**. This ensures that the text will always start on its own page whatever happens earlier in the document.

set a hard page break

1 Click on the page in front of the first word you want to start on a new page.
2 Use the shortcut: hold **Ctrl** and press **Enter**.
   Or
3 Click on the **Insert** tab and select **Page Break**.
4 You can also click on the drop-down arrow next to Breaks on the Page Layout tab and select the Page option.
5 To remove a page break, click on the new page you have made and press the **Backspace** key.

Headers and footers

It is often the case that you want to add details to your document somewhere where they will not interfere with the main text layout. Common additions include the date, page numbers, author or file details.

You can add these to the margins at the top or bottom of the page where they are known as **headers** and **footers**.

add headers or footers

1 On the Insert tab, click on the drop-down arrow next to the Header button to add details at the top of your document.
2 Select a layout from the range of examples that will appear or click on the **Blank** option for the most freedom.

3 You will now be in the header area, and the document text will appear a lighter colour.

4 Enter the details that you want, such as your name, and format them in the normal way. You can move across the header area by pressing the **Tab** key or clicking the mouse, or press **Enter** to add extra entries on the next line.

5 The Header and Footer tools menu will appear and you can insert automatic entries such as the date, page numbers and so on, by clicking the buttons and selecting a style of insert.

6 If you will be delaying printing your document but want the correct date to appear, click on the **Update** checkbox.

7 To add the filename, you need to open the Field list available from the **Quick Parts** command. This can be found on the **Insert** tab or in the insert group under **Header & Footer Tools**.

   a Click on **Quick Parts**.

   b Click on **Field**.

   c In the Field names list, click on **FileName**.

   d If you want to include the path as part of the file name, select the **Add path to filename** checkbox.

8 Click on the **Go to Footer** button to add entries at the bottom of the page.

9 Return to your document by double-clicking on the pale document text or clicking on the **Close Header and Footer** button. You can re-enter the header or footer area by double-clicking on an entry if you decide to make any changes.

The file path is the map of your document on the drive, e.g C:\Documents and Settings\User\My Documents\CV.docx. The file name is CV.docx. While 7d above explains how to include the file path, paths should not be included in documents used in the CLAiT qualification.

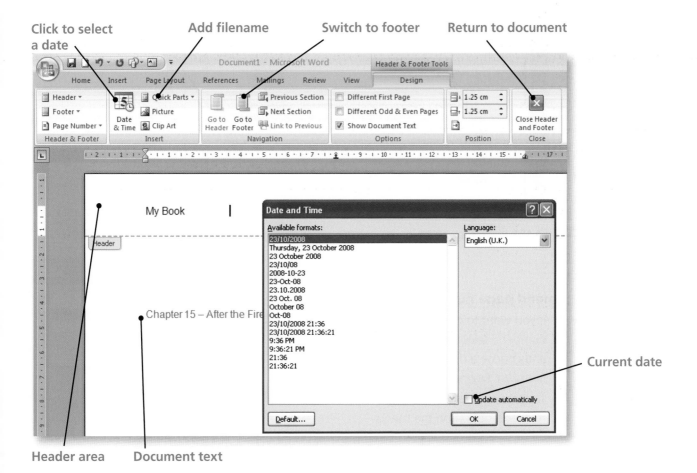

Fig. 1.102 Inserting a header

Page numbers

As well as inserting page numbers when you add headers or footers, you can also add them directly from the Insert tab. These will be updated automatically as you add pages to your document.

There are two main styles of number you may want to add: simple numbers or numbers including the total number of pages in the document, for example, Page 5 of 15.

There are a range of styles you can apply, and you can also choose where the numbers will be displayed.

add page numbers

1   Click on the **Page Number** button.
2   Hover over a position for the numbers and a sample of number styles will be displayed.
3   Scroll down the range of examples and select your preferred style.

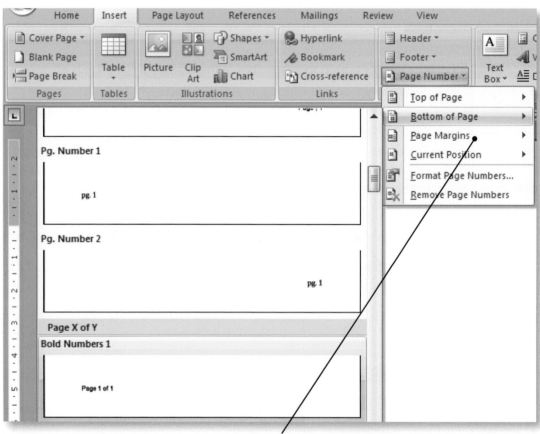

Fig. 1.103 Page numbers   Change or remove numbers

amend page numbers

1   If you want to change the appearance of the numbers, select **Format Page Numbers** and choose a different style from the **Page Number Format** box.

2   To remove page numbering, click on the **Remove** option on the menu.

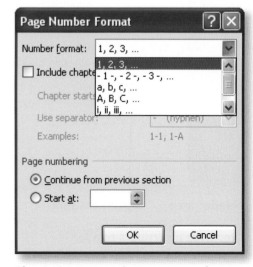

Fig. 1.104 Formatting page numbers

Check your understanding 19

1 Start a new document and enter the following heading and three paragraphs.

Italian cooking

There are two types of pasta dish you can make:
a One where the sauce is added to the cooked pasta at the last minute.
b A baked dish where pasta and sauce are cooked together in the oven, often covered in cheese or white sauce.

In both cases, you can use vegetables, meat, chicken or fish as the main ingredient.

Each dish has a recognisable name, for example, bolognese, carbonara or napoletana.

2 Save the file as *Cookery*.
3 Add a header that includes the text **cooking** and today's date.
4 Include page numbers and the number of pages in the footer.
5 Create a three-page document by inserting a page break after **sauce** and after **ingredient**.
6 Finally, update the header so that the text now reads **Italian cooking**.
7 Save and close the updated file.

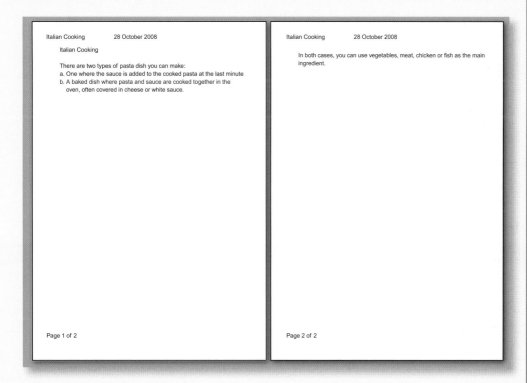

Fig. 1.105 Example 19 cooking

8 Editing existing documents

Opening a file

Having saved files with suitable file names, you will often have to find and open them again to make changes, print copies or otherwise work with them. This will require you to work up or down through your folder or drive pathways to locate the target file.

open a file

1 Click on the **Office** button and select one of the files listed in the **Recent Documents** pane, if appropriate, or click on **Open**.

Or

2 Hold **Ctrl** and press the letter **O**.

3 The Open dialog box will appear and a folder such as My Documents will appear in the Look in: box.

4 If the file you are looking for is not visible, but is somewhere else on your computer, such as on a CD or in a subfolder, you need to navigate to it in one of the following ways:

a Click on the drop-down arrow in the **Look in:** box to display other locations.

b Click on a location showing in the **My Places** bar.

c Double-click to open a folder showing in the main window to look inside. If you hover the mouse over the folder, it will display the contents.

d Click on the **Up One Level** button to work up through your folders.

e To open a file on a different drive, go up the folder pathway or click in **My Places** bar to display My Computer in the Look in: window. You will see the various drives available in the main window.

5 When the name of the file you want to open is showing in the main window, select it and press **Enter** or click on the **Open** button.

6 If no recent documents are listed on the Office buttons menu, click on the **Word Options** button. Click on **Advanced** and increase the number showing in the Recent Documents display box.

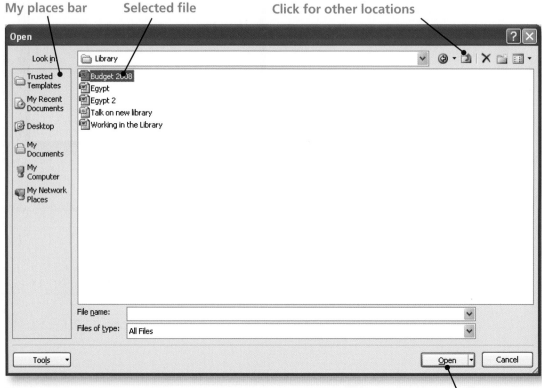

Fig. 1.106 Open files

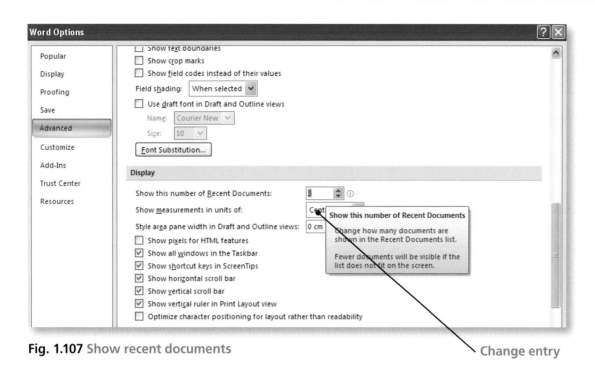

Fig. 1.107 Show recent documents

Change entry

Check your understanding 20

1 Open the file *Cookery* you created earlier.
2 Change to Landscape orientation.
3 Remove the last page break so that it is now a two-page document. Check that this is reflected in the footer page numbering.
4 Move the last sentence so that it becomes point c) on the first page.
5 Save a new version of the file named *Cookery 2*.

Italian Cooking   26 October 2008

Italian Cooking

There are two types of pasta dish you can make:
a. One where the sauce is added to the cooked pasta at the last minute
b. A baked dish where pasta and sauce are cooked together in the oven, often covered in cheese or white sauce.
c. Each dish has a recognisable name, for example bolognese, carbarona or napoletana.

Page 1 of 2

Fig. 1.108 Example 20 editing

Find and replace

When you are working with long documents, the Find and Replace tools available in Word 2007 are very useful if you want to locate a particular word or section quickly, or replace a misspelt or abbreviated word that has been used throughout the document.

find entries

1 On the Home tab in the Editing section, click on the **Find** button.
2 In the Find and Replace box that opens, enter the word or phrase you are looking for, either typing it exactly or just typing the first few letters.
3 Click on **Find Next** to find the first example of the word.
4 Keep clicking on this button to move through the document.
5 For a closer match, click on the **More>>** button and select the option to:
    a Search in a specific direction rather than through the whole document.
    b Match case – for example, to look only for words typed in capitals.
    c Search for unknown characters, by clicking on the **wildcards** checkbox. If you now use an asterisk * for missing letters, you will find all entries matching words spelt using the first and last letters.
    d Find entire words rather than parts of words.
    e Select a particular format or special character by clicking on the **Format** or **Special** buttons.
6 Click on the Find in button to search the headers and footers or text boxes.

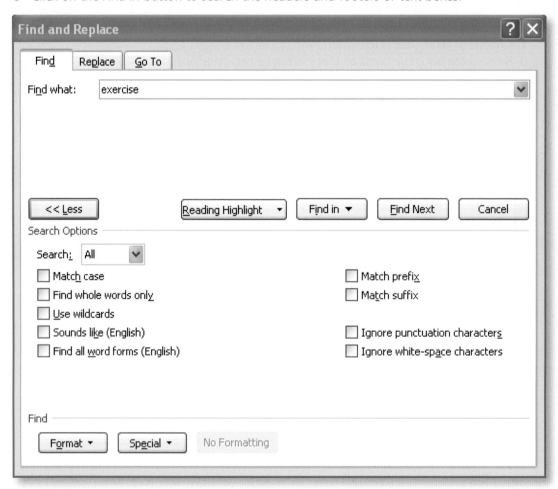

Fig. 1.109 Find box

replace entries

1 Click on the **Replace** button on the Home tab, or click on the tab in the **Find and Replace** box.

2 Enter the word(s) that are currently in the document in the **Find what:** box exactly as they are spelt.

3 Type the entry you want to replace them with in the **Replace with:** box.

4 Limit the search by clicking on **More>>** and clicking on any of the checkboxes.

5 Click on **Replace All** if you are happy for this to take place throughout the document.

6 Click on **Find Next** to check the first entry by eye. If you want it replaced, click on **Replace**. If you want it to remain, click on **Find Next** to move on to the next matching word.

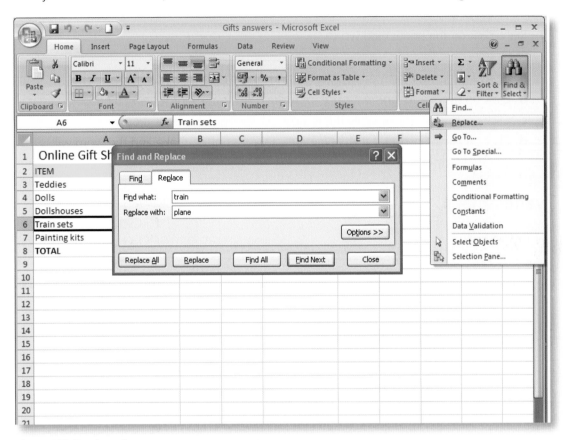

Fig. 1.110 Replace box

Word count

A useful tool, especially when creating work of a set length, is to be able to know exactly how many words your document contains.

know the word count

1 Look at the bottom of the screen on the status bar. It will show you:

- What page you are on
- The number of words in the document as a whole
  Or
- The number of any selected words, even if they are not on the same page.

Fig. 1.111 Word count

Spellchecker

Word 2007 has a spellchecker that compares all the words you type to those in its built-in dictionary, as well as a grammar checker that identifies where you have broken certain rules such as matching a singular noun with a plural verb.

Where an error is detected, the entry is underlined with a red (spelling) or green (grammar) line. You can:

- ignore it, for example if the word is spelt correctly
- learn more about the reason for the identification
- select a correct spelling from a list
- add words to the dictionary so they are not picked up again.

correct errors

1 Right-click on the underlined word.

2 For spelling:

    a If an alternative is offered, click on it to replace the misspelt word.

    b Click on **Ignore** to ignore it once, or **Ignore All** to prevent it being highlighted again.

    c Click on **Add to Dictionary** if it is a correct spelling you want recognised in future.

    d Click on **AutoCorrect** if it is a typing mistake you often make and the word will automatically be typed correctly in future.

    e Click on **Language** if it is a foreign word.

    f Click on **Spelling** to open the main spelling dialog box.

    g Click on **Look Up** for alternative words.

3 For grammar:

    a Click on **Ignore** to cancel the highlight.

    b Click on **Grammar** to open the dialog box.

    c Click on **About this Sentence** to understand the rule.

Fig. 1.112 Spellcheck a word

check a whole document

1 Right-click on a highlighted word and click on **Spelling** or **Grammar**.
   Or

2 Click on the **Spelling & Grammar** button on the Review tab.

3 Each underlined word will be displayed in turn and you can:

    a Click on an alternative if offered in the **Suggestions:** box.

    b Click on and manually change the entry showing in red.

    c Click on a **Change** option to update the document with the corrected word.

    d Click on an **Ignore** option to cancel such highlights in future.

    e Click on **Cancel** to close the box without working through all the errors in the document.

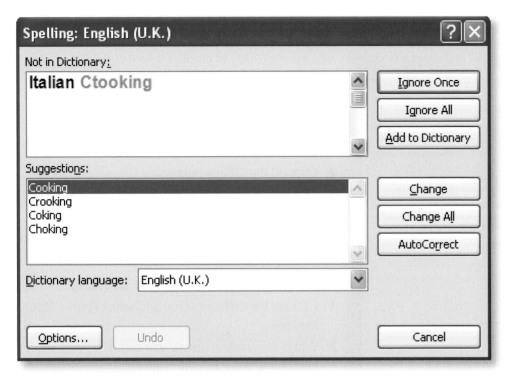

Fig. 1.113 Spell dialog box

Proofreading

The spelling and grammar checkers have limited value as many words can be spelt correctly but may still be used incorrectly. For example, letters can be missing (**train** and **rain**) or reversed (**lair** and **liar**), or can simply be wrong or in the wrong place. That is why it is vital for you to read carefully through all your professional documents for *meaning* rather than relying on the built-in checks alone.

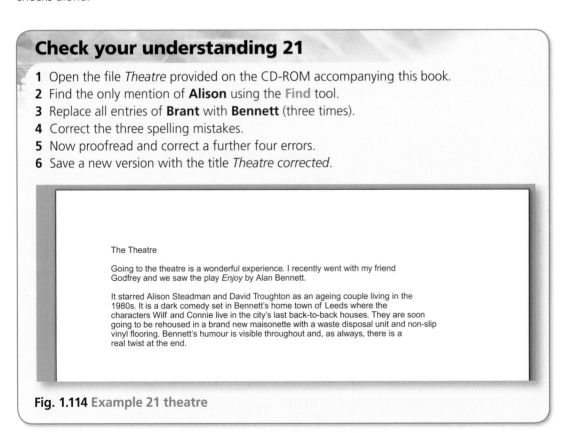

Check your understanding 21

1 Open the file *Theatre* provided on the CD-ROM accompanying this book.
2 Find the only mention of **Alison** using the **Find** tool.
3 Replace all entries of **Brant** with **Bennett** (three times).
4 Correct the three spelling mistakes.
5 Now proofread and correct a further four errors.
6 Save a new version with the title *Theatre corrected*.

The Theatre

Going to the theatre is a wonderful experience. I recently went with my friend Godfrey and we saw the play *Enjoy* by Alan Bennett.

It starred Alison Steadman and David Troughton as an ageing couple living in the 1980s. It is a dark comedy set in Bennett's home town of Leeds where the characters Wilf and Connie live in the city's last back-to-back houses. They are soon going to be rehoused in a brand new maisonette with a waste disposal unit and non-slip vinyl flooring. Bennett's humour is visible throughout and, as always, there is a real twist at the end.

Fig. 1.114 Example 21 theatre

9 Printing documents

Having created and saved a document, you are now ready to produce a hard copy.

This can be of the whole document, selected pages or particular objects or blocks of text.

Fig. 1.115 Print options

print one copy of the whole document

1　Hold **Ctrl** and click on the letter **P**.
　Or
2　Click on the **Office** button.
3　Rest the mouse on the **Print** option.
4　In the main window, click on **Quick Print**.

This will print one copy of the document from the default printer.

check your document before printing

1　Click on the **Office** button and select **Print – Print Preview**.
2　When the preview opens, you can work with the document in the following way:
　a　Zoom in for a closer view by clicking on the **Zoom** button and selecting a new magnification or entering an exact measure in the **Percent** box.
　b　In the Zoom box, select the number of pages you want to display at the same time.
　c　If a small section of the document has gone over to a new page, click on **Shrink One Page** to reduce font sizes, for example, as this may limit the number of pages.
　d　For long documents, click on **Next** or **Previous Page** to move through the pages.
　e　Click off the tick in the **Magnifier** checkbox if you want to work on the document in Print Preview. Otherwise, if you click on the document you will only be able to zoom in and out.
3　Go directly to **Page Setup** from this view to change orientation, margins, paper size and so on.

Open Zoom box

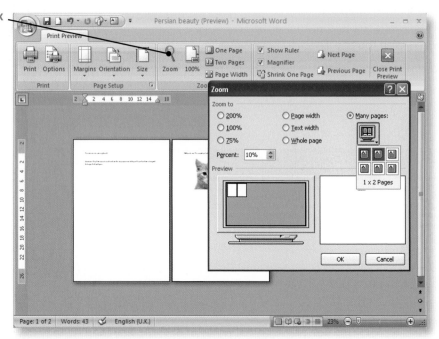

Fig. 1.116 Print Preview

4 Click on **Print** to open the Print dialog box.

5 Click on the **Close Print Preview** button to return to normal view.

set Print Options

1 Open the **Office** button and click on the **Print** option or hover over it and then select **Print**.

2 In the Print dialog box, change settings such as:

    a The name of the printer you want to use.

    b How many copies to produce.

    c Which particular pages to print – you can click on Current page to print the page your cursor is marking, a range of pages, the entire document or only highlighted text (Selection).

3 Click on **OK** to print.

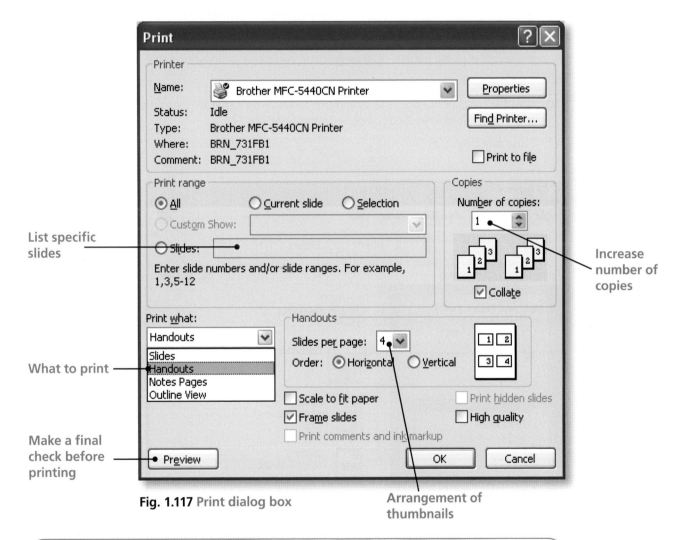

Fig. 1.117 Print dialog box

Check your understanding 22

1 Open the document you created in Check your understanding 14, *Theatre corrected*.

2 Add page numbers as a footer.

3 Check the document in Print Preview.

4 Increase magnification to 200%.

5 Set a hard break somewhere in the text so that it becomes a two-page document.

6 Change the orientation to landscape.

7 Print one copy of the last page only.

8 Now print two copies of page 1 only.

9 Close the file.

CLAiT Assignment

Task 1

1 Log-in to gain access to the data provided.

2 You need to organise your files and folders.

    a   Rename the folder *Amazon* to be *Bookshop*.

    b   In this folder create a new sub-folder called *Favourites*.

3 Copy the text file provided called *fiction* to the folder *Favourites*.

4 Move the text file provided called *comedy* from the folder *DVDs* into the folder *Favourites*.

5 Delete the folder DVDs and its contents.

6 Take a screen print as evidence of the folder called *Bookshop* and the contents of this folder.

7 Take a screen print of the sub-folder called *Favourites* and the contents of this folder.

8 In the footer of the page(s) displaying the screen prints, enter your name and today's date.

9 Save the screen print(s) within your filing structure.

10 Print the file(s) containing the screen prints. Make sure that all the contents of the folder and the sub-folder are clearly visible on the print(s).

11 Close any open files.

Fig. 1.118 Task 1, step 2

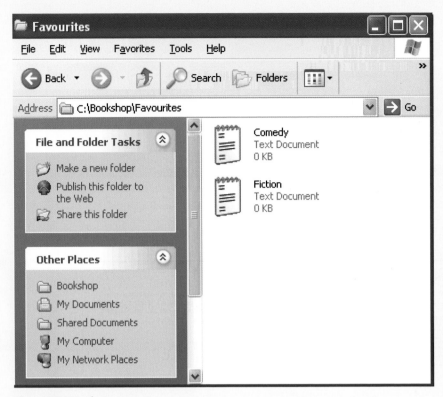

Fig. 1.119 Task 1, step 4

Task 2

1 Create a new word processing document.

2 Set the page orientation to landscape.

3 Set the **top**, **bottom**, **left** and **right** page margins to **3 cm.**

4 Set the font to a Courier font type.

5 Set the font size to **11.**

6 Enter the following text in **single line spacing**.

7 Make sure that the text is **fully justified**.

```
Famous People

Many people are fascinated by celebrities: particularly their
lifestyles, relationships and fortune. The average person doesn't
have the material things that celebrities do, and that makes some
people very envious. In particular, details of their personal
lives can take our focus off our own humdrum and even depressing
everyday living, at least for a while.

Fame also has a lot to do with the media. There are not many
papers or magazines in Britain that don't include regular stories
about celebrities. It is as if the media wants people to forget
about real and important issues and only concentrate on trivia.
That strategy could be termed irresponsible but they do it because
it helps sell their publications.
```

1 Check the file for any errors and carry out a spellcheck.

2 In the header, enter your **name**.

3 In the footer, insert an **automatic date** and an **automatic filename**.

4 Save the file using the filename *Famous People* in the sub-folder called *Favourites*.

5 Close the file.

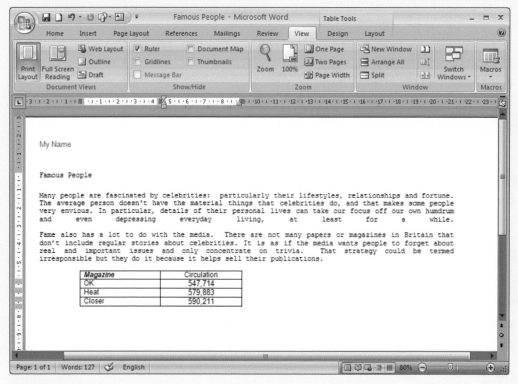

Fig. 1.120 Task 3

Task 3

1   Open your saved file called *Famous People.*

2   A table needs to be inserted at the end of the document.

3   Insert a paragraph break and a clear line space at the end of the final paragraph immediately after the text ending 'their publications'.

   a   Create a table with two columns and four rows.

   b   Enter the data below in the table:

Magazine	Circulation
OK	547,714
Heat	579,883
Closer	590,211

   c   Make sure all borders will be displayed for the table on the printout.

   d   Make sure all data in the table is fully displayed.

4   Format the heading **Magazine** to be bold and italic.

5   Centre the heading and contents of the **Circulation** column.

6   The remaining text and numbers must be left-aligned.

7   Save your file keeping the filename *Famous People*.

8   Print one copy of the file *Famous People*.

9   Close the file.

Task 4

1 You will need to make the amendments below in a file that has been provided for you.

2 Open the file provided on the CD-ROM called *Celebrities*; it is in your folder called *Bookshop.*

3 Save the file using the new filename *Depp* in your folder called *Favourites.*

4 Go to the paragraph that starts **In 1990.**

5 Insert the following text as a new sentence after **Al Pacino**: **He has also played in a number of family-orientated films such as 'Charlie and the Chocolate Factory' and 'Pirates of the Caribbean'.**

6 Go to the paragraph that starts **He made his film debut.**

7 Delete the text **by replacing Jeff Yagher.**

8 In the paragraph that starts **After a few years** move the following text to the first paragraph so that it forms the last two sentences: **After a few years in music, Johnny moved into acting. It is believed this was the result of visiting Los Angeles, California, where he met the actor Nicolas Cage.**

9 Apply bullet points to the following three lines of text:

   The Astronaut's Wife
   The Libertine
   From Hell

10 Apply **double line spacing** to the bulleted text only.

11 Indent the text **Less well known films are:** from the left margin.

12 Replace the word **productions** with the word **films** wherever it occurs (three times in all).

13 In the header enter **your name**, an **automatic date** and an **automatic filename**.

14 Check your text for accuracy.

15 Using the software facilities, carry out a word count in the file.

16 Enter the number of words on your printout at least two lines below the bulleted list. You may use any alignment for this.

17 Save the file with the filename *Celebrities amended*.

18 Print one copy of the file.

19 Close all files and folders.

20 Make sure you check your printouts for accuracy.

21 You should have the following printouts: **your screen print(s)**, *Famous People*, *Celebrities amended*.

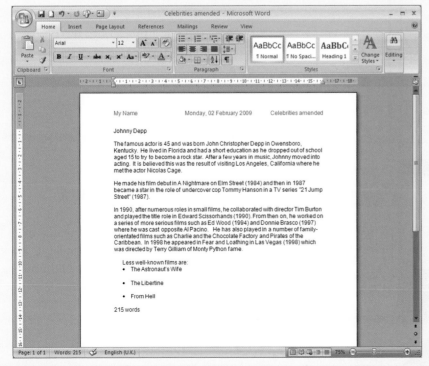

Fig. 1.121 Task 4

Creating spreadsheets and graphs

In this unit you will learn about using the application Excel 2007 to create spreadsheets. These are used to display numerical or financial information. They are set out in a grid of columns and rows and their structure allows you to enter or amend data and perform a wide range of complex calculations quickly and accurately. The application also enables you to display your data pictorially in the form of a chart or graph.

At the end of this unit you will be able to:

➔ identify, input and amend data in spreadsheet software accurately

➔ insert and replicate formulae in spreadsheets

➔ produce pie charts, line graphs and bar/column charts from given data

➔ use common formatting and alignment techniques in spreadsheets and graphs/charts

➔ save and print spreadsheets and graphs/charts.

1 Using a spreadsheet application

Fig. 2.1 Launch Excel

Opening the application

launch Excel

1 Click on the **Start** button.
2 If there is a shortcut to the program on the Start menu, click on the icon.
   Or
3 Rest on **All Programs**.
4 Click on **Excel 2007**, or first open a Microsoft Office folder.

Spreadsheet structure

When you open Excel, you will be presented with a blank grid of squares known as **cells**. The vertical columns are labelled with a letter and the horizontal rows are labelled with numbers. This labelling means that each cell can be identified by its column and row – for example, A5 or D17.

At any time, one cell will display a black border and its column letter and row number will be coloured orange. This is the **active cell** and is the cell in which any entry typed on the keyboard will appear. When a cell is activated, its name will be displayed in the **Name box** and its contents will appear in the **Formula bar**, a window above the cells. Take care to check your inputs regularly. Accuracy is important.

move to a different cell

1 Click on the cell you want with the mouse.

2 Press the **Tab** key to move to the right along a row.

3 Hold **Shift** as you press **Tab** to move to the left along a row.

4 Press **Enter** to move down a column.

5 Press one of the arrow keys to move in the appropriate direction.

6 Hold **Ctrl** and press the **Home** key to return to the first cell, A1.

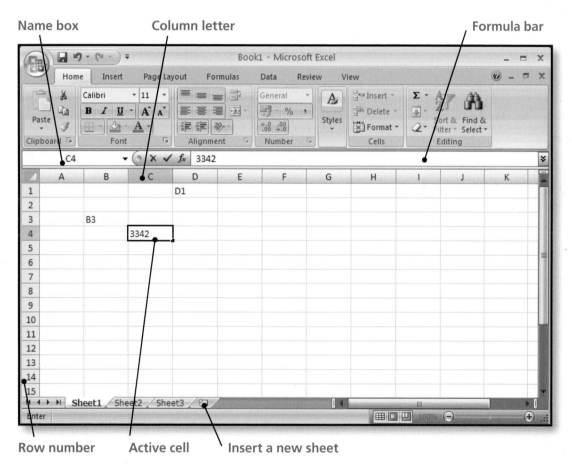

Fig. 2.2 Working with cells

File names

When you launch Excel, a new file will open on-screen. Spreadsheet files are known as **workbooks** and they usually contain a number of worksheets, which are labelled Sheet1, Sheet2 and so on, on tabs at the bottom of the screen. It is the entries on a particular *sheet* that make it a spreadsheet, although this is also the common name for Excel workbooks/files.

When you save a file, all the sheets will be saved at the same time, and you can add new sheets to a workbook by clicking on the **Insert Worksheet** tab.

As you only see the name of the entire workbook, not individual sheets, when searching for a file, it is important when saving to give each file a name that will help you find particular data easily. Although the spreadsheet you want to work on is often placed on Sheet1, you may have to look through other sheets to find it. Do this by clicking on the **Sheet** tab.

Saving

Excel files can be saved in a number of formats, including:

- as an Excel 2007 file, which cannot be read by earlier versions of the application
- compatible with earlier versions – for example, 97–2003
- as a different form of file such as CSV (comma delimited) or a web page
- as a template, so that the design can be used without changing the original.

For more information on saving and save as, see p. 38–9.

save a workbook

1   Hold Ctrl and press S.

    Or

2   Click on the Save button on the Quick Access toolbar.

    Or

3   Click on the Office button and then click on Save.

4   In the Save As: dialog box:

    a   Enter a name for the file.

    b   Select a suitable location by changing the folder name in the Save in: window.

    c   If necessary, click on the drop-down arrow in the Save as type: box to select a format other than Excel 2007 Workbook.

    d   Click on Save or press Enter.

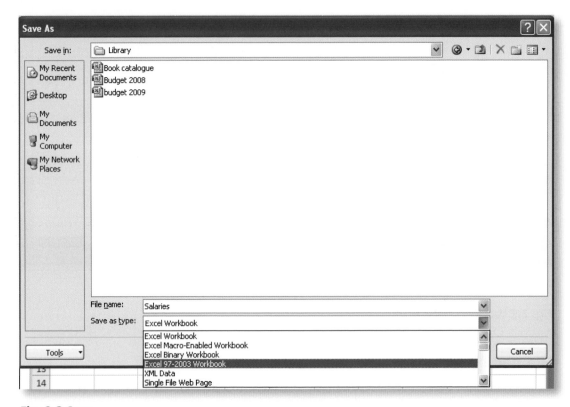

Fig. 2.3 Save

update a workbook

1   Hold Ctrl and press S.

    Or

2   Click on the Office button and select Save.

save a different version

1 Click on the Office button.

2 Select Save As.

3 Rename the file and/or select a different location or file type.

4 Click on Save.

You will also find that Microsoft Office 2007 applications have an automatic save or recover function. It saves the file regularly so that, if the program closes suddenly, your work will be recovered. The timing of these saves can be amended.

Timing for
automatic save

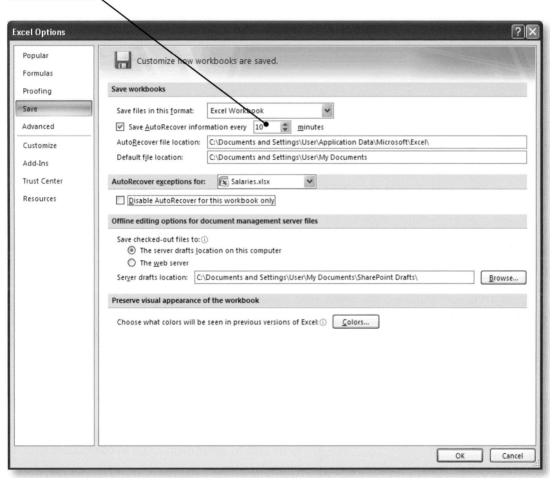

Fig. 2.4 Autosave

amend AutoRecover settings

1 Click on the Office button.

2 Click on Excel Options.

3 Click on the Save tab.

4 Increase or decrease the measure in the minutes box.

New workbooks

Once you have launched Excel, a workbook will appear ready for data entry. You can also create any number of extra workbooks and have these open at the same time.

create a new workbook

1 Hold Ctrl and press N.

Or

2 Click on the Office button and click on New – Create.

New files will be named Book1, Book2 and so on until saved and named.

With several workbooks open, you can switch between them easily.

move between open files

1 Click on the View tab.

2 Click on Switch Windows. All open files will be listed.

3 Click on the name of the file you want to display on-screen.

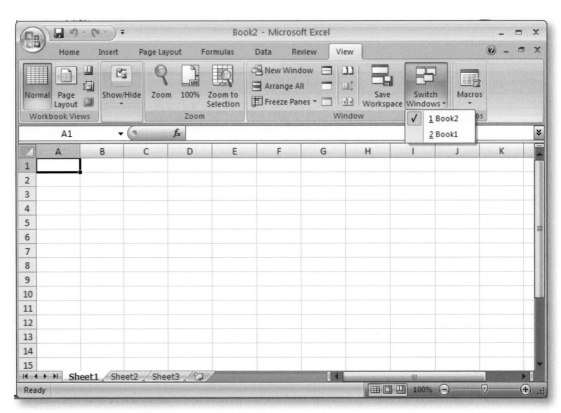

Fig. 2.5 Switching windows

Fig. 2.6 Recent documents

Opening workbooks

Having created and saved workbooks, you will need to be able to open them again to edit the contents or print a copy.

open a file saved previously

1 Hold Ctrl and press O.

Or

2 Click on the Office button.

3 If you have opened the file recently, it may be listed in the Recent Documents window. Click to open it.

4 Otherwise, click on Open.

5 In the Open dialog box, navigate to the folder containing the target file.

6 Select its name in the window and press Enter or click on Open.

Closing files

close a workbook

1 Click on the *lower* Close button in the top right-hand corner.

Or

2 Click on the Office button.

3 Click on Close.

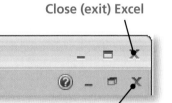

Close (exit) Excel

Close current file

Fig. 2.7 Close and exit

exit Excel

1 Click on the *top* Close button.

Or

2 Click on the Office button.

3 Click on Exit Excel.

Check your understanding 1

1 Launch Excel.
2 Save the workbook that opens as *Holiday costs*.
3 Create and save a new workbook named *Sales figures*.
4 Open the file provided on the CD-ROM named *Club income*.
5 Switch to *Holiday costs*.
6 Close all open files and exit Excel.

---

2 Creating a spreadsheet

In the same way that you would design the layout for a word-processed table, you must first decide on the best arrangement for the headings, columns and rows in your spreadsheet and then enter the data. Spreadsheets have a range of uses, and can be used to store numbers and text — as in schedules, for example. When setting up your spreadsheets, consider what they will be used for.

enter data into a cell

1 Click on the cell with the mouse, or move there using one of the navigation methods described earlier.

2 Type the entry in full.

3 Click on the next cell to continue entering the data.

4 Having entered text into one cell, the same text may be offered as you start typing a new entry into another cell within the same column. Press Enter to complete the entry automatically or continue typing if you do not want that text repeated.

5 If you find an entry extends beyond the edge of a column, do *not* split the data between cells. You will be able to widen columns to display all the data in full.

Note that cell contents will appear in the Formula bar as well as the cell.

edit the data

1 Click on the cell you want to amend.

2 Click in the Formula bar.

Or

3 Double-click in the cell to place the cursor inside.

4   Enter extra data in the normal way.

5   Use the **Backspace** and **Delete** keys to erase characters.

6   To confirm a change, either click in a different cell or click on the tick in the Formula bar.

7   Click in a cell and press the **Delete** key to remove the entire contents.

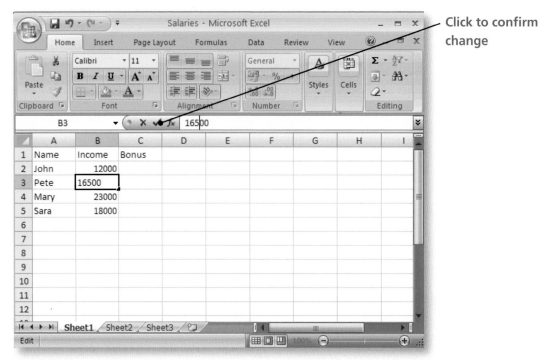

Click to confirm change

Fig. 2.8 Amend data

Check your understanding 2

1   Start a new workbook.

2   Save it as *Pets*.

3   Enter the text **Pet Shop** in cell A1.

4   Enter the following headings in row 2:
    Pet, **Price**, **Number**.

5   Now enter the data as shown in Figure 2.9:

6   Make the following amendments:

   a   The number of birds should be **21**

   b   The price of a mouse is **10.99**

7   Save as *Pets amended* and then close the file.

	A	B	C
1	Pet Shop		
2	Pet	Price	Number
3	Cat	35	7
4	Mouse	9	10
5	Bird	18.5	23
6	Snake	25	4

Fig. 2.9 Data for ex 2

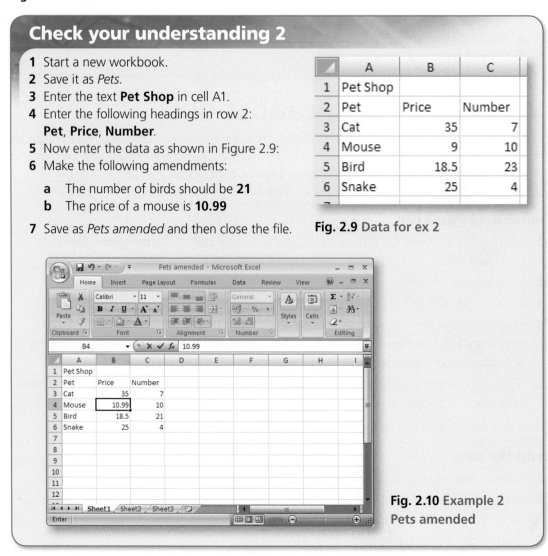

Fig. 2.10 Example 2
Pets amended

Formulae

At some stage, you will want to use a spreadsheet application to help you carry out various calculations. The instructions that are typed into a cell to produce a new value as the result of a calculation are known as **formulae**.

Simple formulae involve adding, subtracting, multiplying or dividing figures or using a combination of these. In Excel, formulae have to be typed in a specific way.

type in formulae

1 Click in the cell in which you want the calculation to be performed.
2 First enter the **= sign**. This identifies the instruction as a formula.
3 Enter the **first figure**.
4 Enter the correct **operator**. Excel recognises:

    + (add)   addition
    – (subtract) subtraction
    * (multiply) multiplication
    / (divide)   division

5 Enter the **next figure**.
6 Continue until all figures and operators have been entered.
7 To complete a calculation, you must confirm the formula. Either move to a different cell (for example, by pressing Enter), or click on the tick in the Formula bar.
8 When you activate any cell containing a formula, the resultant value will show in the cell but the formula you entered will be visible in the Formula bar.

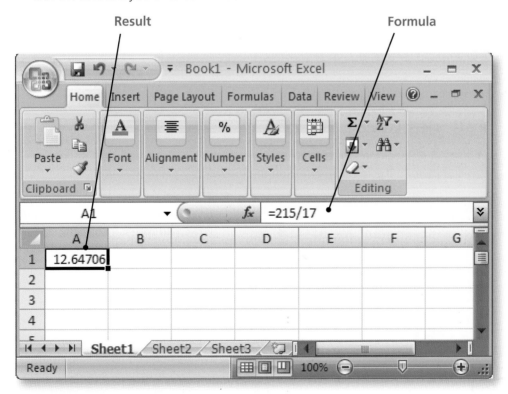

Fig. 2.11 Simple formula

Warning: Excel automatically places text on the left of a cell and numbers on the right. If numbers appear on the left, this means you have made a mistake (for example, by pressing the space bar or adding letters) and calculations cannot be performed.

Note that if you see ##### appear when completing a calculation, it means that the results have produced a figure with too many decimal places to display in the cell. If you widen the column (explained later) you will see all the figures.

Check your understanding 3

1 Start a new workbook.
2 In cell A1, use the correct formula to add 25 and 7.
3 In cell B1, use the correct formula to divide 600 by 45.
4 In cell C1, use the correct formula to multiply 5 by 15 and then add 6.5.
5 Close the file without saving.

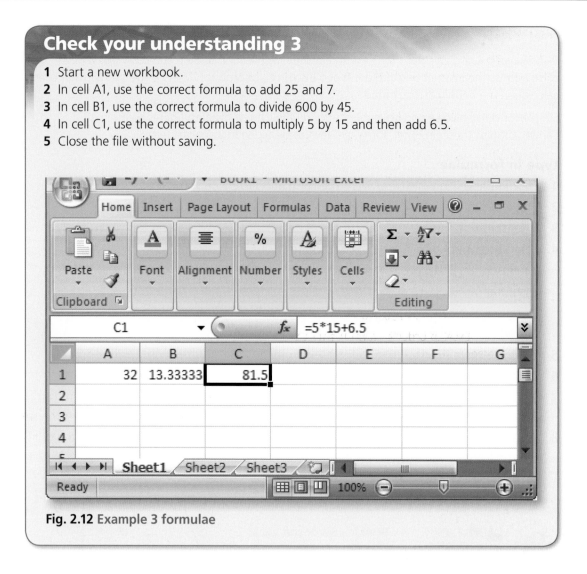

Fig. 2.12 Example 3 formulae

Using cell addresses

When using figures in your calculations that are already present on the spreadsheet, there are several ways to add them to the formula, including the following:

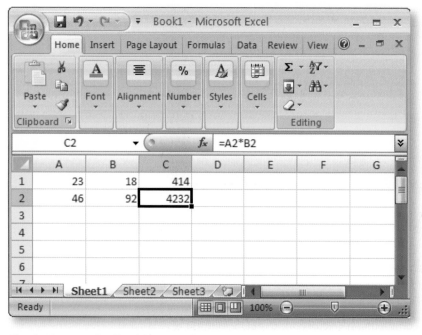

- Type in the figure again. The disadvantages of doing this are that you could type it incorrectly, and if the spreadsheet data is updated, you will have to repeat your formulae using the new figures.

- Enter the addresses of the cells *containing* the figures. If the figures are changed, the formulae will be updated automatically.

In the example below, instead of typing = 46 * 92, the formula becomes:

  = (cell containing first figure) * (cell containing second figure)

You can enter the cell names using the keyboard, or click in each cell with the mouse to add its name into the formula.

Fig. 2.13 Use of cell address in formula

BODMAS – DIV ÷MULT → AD →SUB

When creating complex formulae, you need to be aware that Excel follows the mathematical rules of BODMAS. This means that calculations are carried out in the following order:

1 Any part of the formula contained in **B**rackets
   e.g. =4+221/**(25-12)**-600 = 4+221/**13**-600

2 any part of the formula displaying an **O**rder/power
   e.g. =52-**10⁴** +6/7 = 52-**10000**+6/7

3 **D**ivision or **M**ultiplication working from left to right
   e.g. = 4+**65/6.5** +11-**4*15**+= 4+**10**+11-**60**

4 **A**ddition or **S**ubtraction working from left to right

This means that, if you want an addition or subtraction carried out *before* a multiplication or division, you need to put that part of the formula in brackets.

Functions

As there are many types of calculation performed on a regular basis, certain formulae have been built into Excel in order to carry them out quickly. They include totalling a range of figures, creating averages, identifying the highest (maximum) or lowest (minimum) figure within a range of figures, or counting the number of cells containing an entry.

Predefined formulae that carry out set calculations are known as **functions**.

To view all the functions within Excel, or to get help with a particular function, click on the button labelled **fx** in the **Formula bar**.

Click for function box

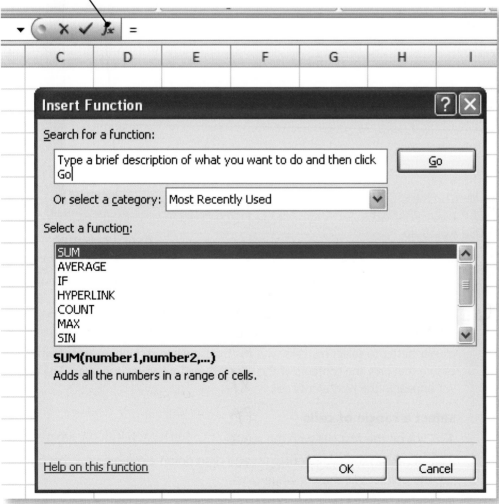

Fig. 2.14 All functions

Totals

When adding up two or three figures, it is easy to enter the following formula:

=A1+A2+A3

Where more than three figures are involved, it is quicker to use the **Total** function.

The formula to total a range of cells is:

=SUM(first cell in range: last cell in range),
e.g. =SUM(A3:E3)

total a range of figures

1   Click at the bottom of a range of cells, or in the cell to the right of a row of figures.

2   Enter the function exactly (using either upper or lower case for SUM but including the colon and brackets).

Or

3   Click on the **AutoSum** button to enter the formula automatically.

4   Press **Enter** or click on another cell to complete the calculation and display the total.

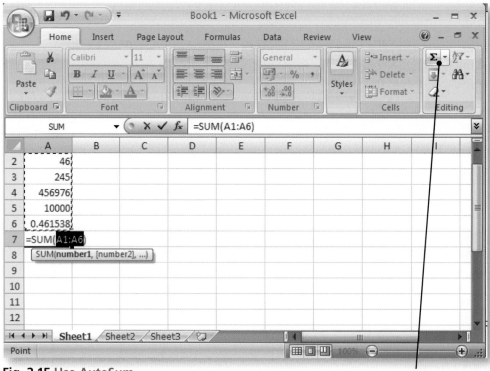

Selected range of cells

Fig. 2.15 Use AutoSum

AutoSum button

Fig. 2.16 Selecting cell range

Selecting a range of cells

To make sure the correct range of cell addresses is entered into a formula, it is usually better to select the cells with the mouse. Then clicking on **AutoSum** will ensure that only the contents of the selected cells are added together. The result will appear in the next empty cell.

select a range of cells

1   Click on the first cell with the mouse.

2   Hold down the **mouse button** and drag down a column or across a row. The pointer will show a white cross.

3   All the selected cells will show a black border, although the first cell in the range will appear white rather than a very pale blue.

Average

calculate the average within a range of cells

There are two methods:

- Total the cells and divide by the number of entries.
- Use the **Average** function. The formula is:

  =AVERAGE(first cell in range: last cell in range)

use the Average function

1 Enter the function from the keyboard.

  Or

2 Select the cells.

3 Click on the drop-down arrow next to the AutoSum button and select **Average**.

4 Press **Enter** or click on a new cell to display the value in the next empty cell.

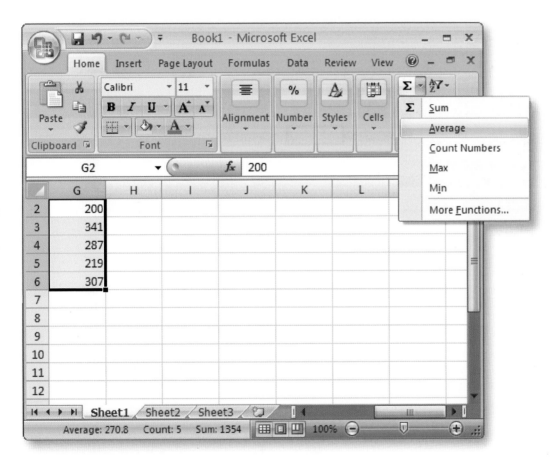

Fig. 2.17 Average function

Maximum, minimum or count functions

To display the highest figure in a range of cells, you can select the **Max** option from the drop-down arrow next to the AutoSum button or enter the following formula:

  =MAX(first cell in range: last cell in range)

To display the minimum, select **Min** or use the formula:

  =MIN(first cell in range: last cell in range)

To count the number of cells showing a numerical entry (not blank or containing text), select **Count** or use the formula:

  =COUNT(first cell in range: last cell in range)

Check your understanding 4

1 Start a new spreadsheet.

2 Enter the figures shown in Figure 2.18.

3 Now carry out the following calculations using functions:

    a In cell E1, total entries in row 1.

    b In cell A5, display the average for entries in column A.

    c In cell C5, display the maximum figure in column C.

4 Save the file as *Functions*.

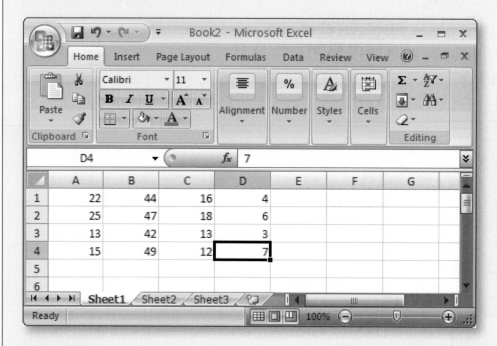

Fig. 2.18 Figures for ex 4

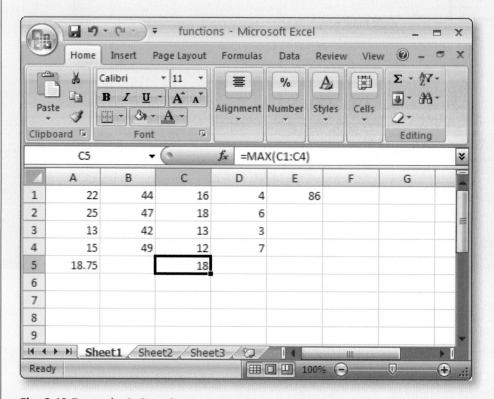

Fig. 2.19 Example 4, Step 3

Copying formulae

It is often necessary to repeat calculations such as totalling or averaging across a number of columns or rows. To do this quickly without having to re-enter the formulae each time, you can copy one formula across and it will reflect the column or row that it is copied to. This is because Excel uses relative cell references.

So, for example, if the formula =SUM(A1:A6) is copied across row 7, the next formula will reflect the fact that it is now adding the cells above it in column B and the next will add those in column C, etc.

	A	B	C
1	2007 figures	2008 figures	2009 figures
2	200	600	367
3	350	566	387
4	469	756	376
5	236	833	322
6	480	455	401
7	=SUM(A2:A6)	=SUM(B2:B6)	=SUM(C2:C6)

Fig. 2.20 Relative cell reference

copy formulae using the mouse

1 Click on the cell containing the formula you want to copy.
2 Position the pointer over the bottom right-hand corner of the cell where there is a small black box – the **fill handle**.
3 It will change to a small black cross.
4 Hold down the **mouse button** and drag the pointer across the column or down the row.
5 When you let go of the mouse, the cells will fill with the appropriate formulae.

A7			f_x	=SUM(A2:A6)	
	A	B	C	D	
1	2007 figures	2008 figures	2009 figures		
2	200	600	367		
3	350	566	387		
4	469	756	376		
5	236	833	322		
6	480	455	401		
7	1735		+		

Fill handle   Pointer for copying

Fig. 2.21 Copying formulae with mouse

copy formulae using the menu

1 Select all the cells to receive the formulae. Make sure you include the cell containing the formula to be copied.
2 Click on the **Fill** button on the Home tab.
3 Select the appropriate direction.
4 The formula will be copied.

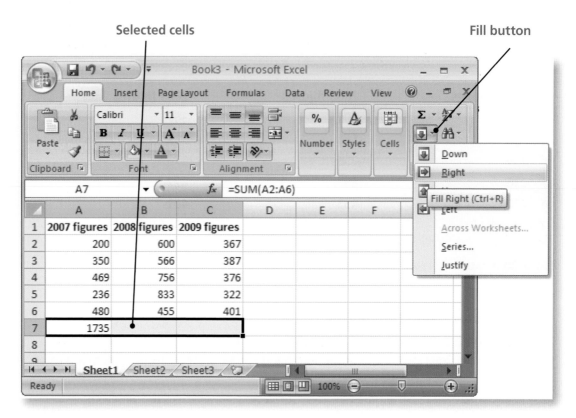

Fig. 2.22 Fill menu

3 Formatting a spreadsheet

There are many ways you can change the look of spreadsheet data to help clarify the contents but without changing the underlying values.

If you click on a column heading letter or row number, you will select the *entire* column or row. Only do this when working on the column/row (for example, to change measurements or remove an entire column/row), or to format a large number of columns/rows at the same time. Otherwise, select the cells by dragging with the mouse before formatting.

If you click on the grey square to the left of A and above 1, you will select the entire worksheet.

Aligning cell contents

It may be easier to read down columns of data if the contents of some cells are realigned. Perhaps a heading needs to be centred over data, or more space added between close columns of figures.

realign cell contents

1 Click on a cell or select a range of cells.
2 Click on the appropriate alignment button on the **Home** tab.
3 Horizontally you can choose from left-, centre- and right-aligned. You can also align cell contents vertically at the top, middle or bottom of a deep cell.

Vertical
alignment

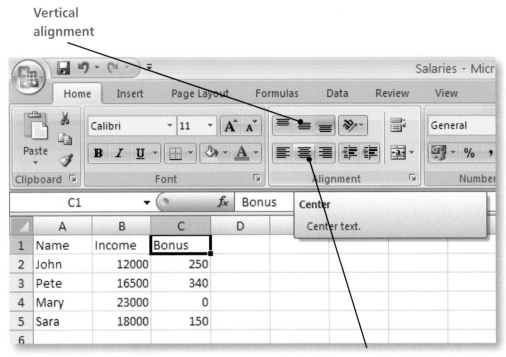

Fig. 2.23 Align cell contents

Horizontal alignment

Cell widths and height

The contents of a cell of a standard size may not be displayed properly if more data is entered into adjacent cells. To correct this, you can widen a column or increase the height of a row.

widen columns manually

1 Position the pointer between header letters on the right-hand boundary of the column you want to widen.

Actual measure   Position for pointer   New boundary shown by dotted line

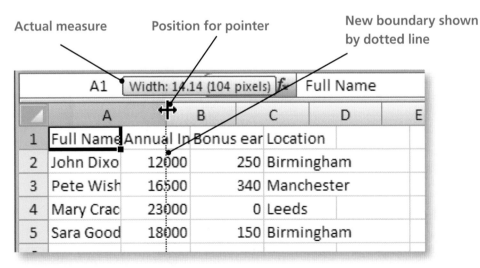

Fig. 2.24 Widen by dragging

2 Double-click to set the width to that of the longest entry.

Or

3 Set the measure yourself using the mouse. When the pointer changes to a two-way arrow, hold down the **mouse button** and drag the boundary out to a new width.

4 The actual measurement will be shown and the position for the new boundary will appear as a dotted vertical line.

increase row height

1 Position the pointer over the *lower* boundary of a row header number.

2 When it shows a two-way arrow, drag this down to increase row height.

widen columns using the menu

1 Select the column by clicking on its header letter, or click on a single cell.

2 On the Home tab, click on the drop-down arrow next to the Format button.

3 Under **Cell Size**, select a width option:

   a Column Width to enter an exact measure.

   b AutoFit to widen the column to fit the longest entry.

   c Default Width to return to the Excel standard column measurement.

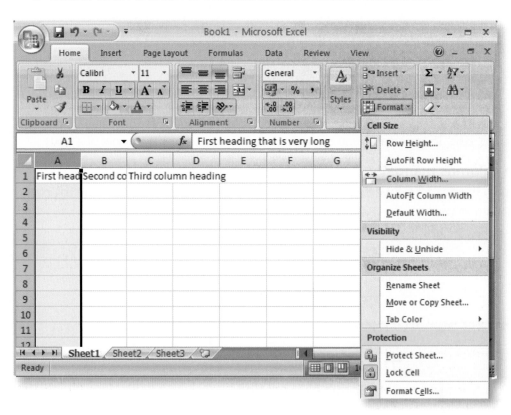

Fig. 2.25 Column width menu

increase row height using the menu

1 Click on a cell or the row header number.

2 On the Home tab, select **Format – Cell Size – Row Height** to enter your own measure.

3 Select **AutoFit Row Height** to adjust the height to fit the deepest entry.

Formatting fonts

The same fonts and formatting tools are available in Excel as in Word, and so you can enhance your spreadsheet by applying a range of font types and styles.

To select several non-adjacent columns or rows, in order to apply the same format, hold **Ctrl** as you select further cell ranges.

format fonts

1 Click on a cell or select a range of cells that you want to format.
2 On the Home tab, click in the **Font** box to select a different font such as Arial, Comic Sans, Courier and so on.
3 Click in the **Font Size** box to increase or decrease the size of entries.
   Or
4 Click on the **Increase** or **Decrease Font Size** buttons to step through font sizes.
5 Apply bold, italic or underlining by clicking on one of the **emphasis** buttons.
6 Click on the **Font Colour** button to select a different colour for your data.
7 Click on the **Fill Colour** button to shade the cell background.
8 Click on the **Borders** button to add a border round the selected cells.
9 For more options, right click a cell or click on the button in the bottom corner of the Font group to open the **Format Cells – Font** dialog box.

Font formatting buttons

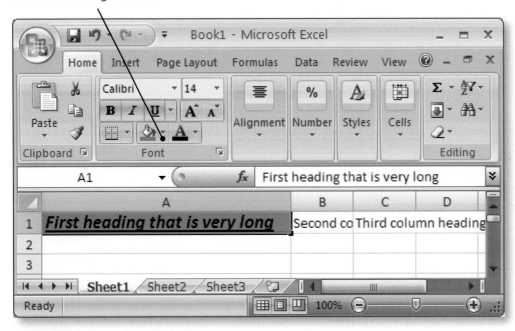

Fig. 2.26 Formatting font

Formatting numbers

When you enter figures into a spreadsheet, they are unformatted (a 'General' format is applied) and you will either see exactly what you enter or a default setting such as a date style will be applied. Without changing actual values, you can change the display of figures on a spreadsheet in a variety of ways, including:

- changing the number of decimal places that are visible
- adding symbols such as £ or $ to currency entries
- showing percentages
- adding separators (commas) between thousands
- showing the date or time in a different way.

format figures using the toolbar

1 Select the cell(s) and then click on the appropriate button on the Home tab in the **Number** area.
2 Each time you click on a cell and set a different format, the entry in the **Number Format** box will change to reflect this – for example, you may see General, Number, Date, Percent and so on.

3 All drop-down lists will have a link to the main **Number Format** dialog box where you can set more precise formats.

a To change the display of decimals, click on the **Increase Decimal** or **Decrease Decimal** buttons as appropriate.

b To show whole numbers only (**integers**), set decimals to zero.

c To add the £ symbol, click on the **Currency** (Accounting Number) format button. Click on the drop-down arrow to select an alternative to the £.

d Click on the **Comma Style** button to add separators to long numbers.

e Click on the **%** button to multiply a decimal by 100 and display the percentage symbol.

f Excel should recognise a date or time, so click on the cell and then click on the drop-down arrow in the Number Format box. A range of options will be available, such as short date (13/06/09) or long date (13ᵗʰ June 2009).

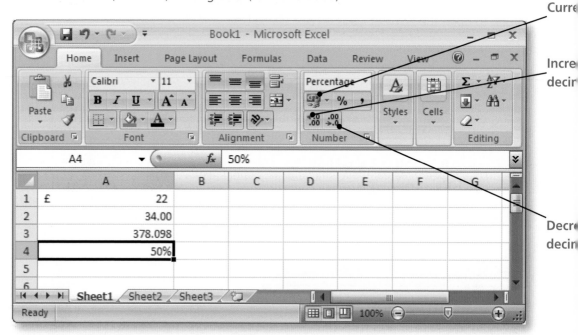

Fig. 2.27 Number formats

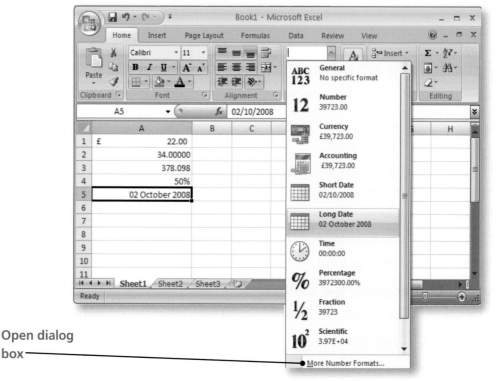

Fig. 2.28 Date format

format figures using the dialog box

1 Select the cells you want to format and then open the dialog box.
2 Click on the appropriate **Category**.
3 Increase or decrease the number of decimals you want to display.
4 To remove a currency symbol that has been applied, click on the **Currency** category and change the symbol entry to **None**.
5 Click to add a 1000 separator.
6 Click on **OK** to close the box.

Note that it is important *not* to select the text heading for a column of figures when applying number formats, as you will not be able to check the preview of how the figures will be displayed.

To retain numbers starting with 0, or where numerical entries won't be used in calculations (for example, telephone numbers or stock codes), you need to identify that they are not ordinary numbers. Do this by starting the entry with an apostrophe (') or by selecting **Text** as the category.

Entries that combine numbers and text (for example, postcodes) are known as **alphanumeric** entries.

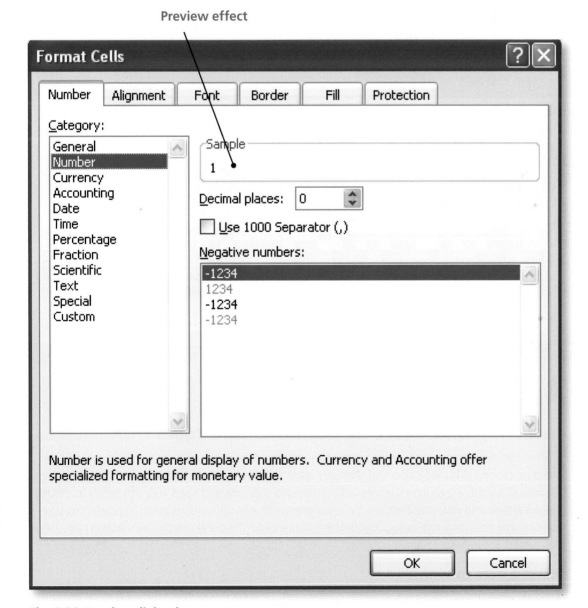

Fig. 2.29 Number dialog box

Check your understanding 5

1 Open the spreadsheet *Gifts* provided on the CD-ROM accompanying this book.
2 Increase the font size for the main heading to size 16.
3 Widen all columns as necessary to display the entries fully.
4 Shade the column heading cells in row 2 yellow.
5 Work out the overall income for *Teddies* (**Price** x **Sales**).
6 Copy this formula to work out the overall income for all other items.
7 Apply a number format to the **Price** and **Overall Income** entries to show a £ symbol and two decimal places.
8 Format the word **Total** in bold.
9 Right align the **Sales** heading only.
10 Calculate the total income for all sales in cell D8.
11 Format this cell only to integer format (no decimals).
12 Shade the total figure blue.
13 Save as *Gifts answers* and close the file.

Fig. 2.30 Example 5 Gifts answers

4 Editing spreadsheets

Inserting and deleting columns and rows

It often happens that partway through creating a spreadsheet you realise you need some extra columns or rows. You may also find that you want to remove redundant data without changing the overall layout. Excel allows you to add or remove columns and rows very efficiently as column header letters and row numbers will be reassigned and any calculations will be updated to take the new cell positions into account. However, you should still check that recalculations have been performed accurately.

insert a new column

1 Click on a cell or select the column to the *right* of where you want the new column to appear – for example, column D in Figure 2.31.
2 Right-click and select **Insert**.

Or

3 On the Home tab, click on the **Insert** button.

4 A new column will appear and header letters will be adjusted automatically.

5 Keep clicking on the button to add further columns to the left.

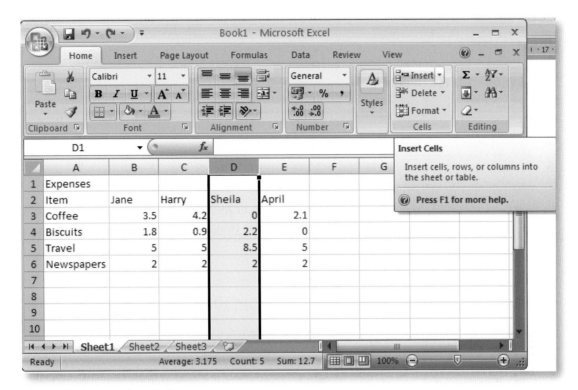

Fig. 2.31 Insert column, 1

New column D

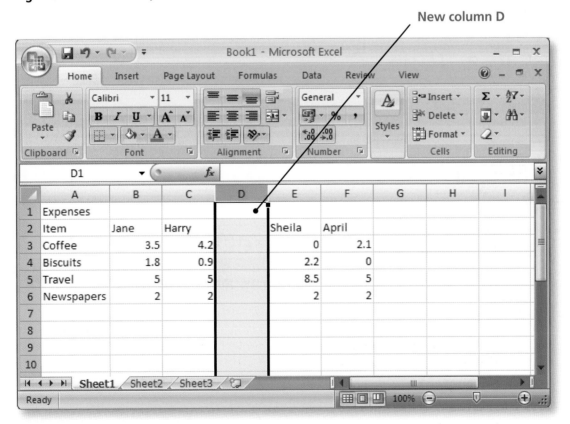

Fig. 2.32 Insert column, 2

insert rows

1 Select the row *below* the position for the new row.
2 Right-click or click on the **Insert** button and new rows will be added above.

delete a column or row

1 Select an entire column or row by clicking on the header letter or number and right-click the mouse.
2 Select **Delete**.
3 If you have only selected a single cell, click on the correct option in the dialog box – for example, to delete an entire row.
4 Click on **OK**.

  Or

5 Click on the **Delete** button on the Home tab.
6 If you have only selected a cell and not the entire column or row, choose from the drop-down list or you will simply delete the cell contents.

Warning: do not simply select the contents of a column or row with the mouse and press the Delete key, or you will remove the contents but leave the columns or rows unchanged.

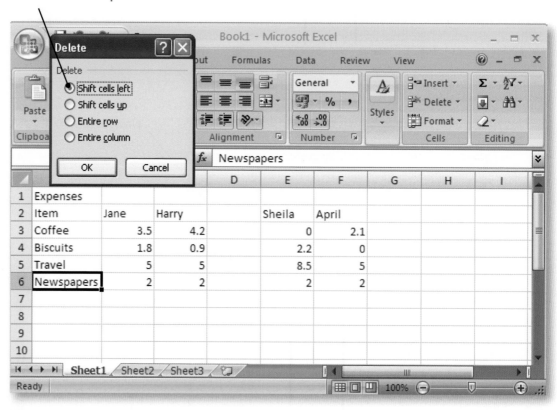

Fig. 2.33 Delete column or row

delete cell contents

1 Select the cells with the mouse.
2 Press the **Delete** key.

Moving and copying cell contents

There are three main ways that the contents of a cell or range of cells can be moved or copied:

- dragging with the mouse
- copy or cut and paste
- replicating using the Fill handle or Fill menu.

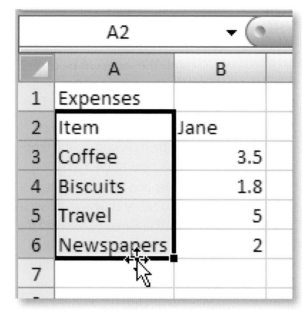

Fig. 2.34 Move arrow

move or copy using drag and drop

1 Select the target cell(s).
2 Move the mouse pointer up to the boundary of the selected cells. It will change to a white arrow showing four black arrows at its tip.
3 Hold down the button and drag the cells to a new position.
4 When you let go of the mouse the cells will drop into place.
5 If you hold down **Ctrl** as you drag, the contents will be copied and not moved and the arrow will display a + sign.

use cut, copy and paste

1 Select the target cells.
2 Right-click and select **Cut** (**Ctrl + X**) to move them or **Copy** (**Ctrl + C**) to copy them. These options are also available on the Home tab.
3 The contents will be placed in the Clipboard.
4 Move to the target area, worksheet or new workbook and click in the **first** cell to receive the cell contents.
5 Right-click and select **Paste** (**Ctrl + V**).
6 Flashing dotted lines (a marquee) will appear round the selected cells, these will disappear if you are moving the contents but will remain after copying. Remove them by pressing the **Esc** key.

replicate cell contents to adjacent cells

1 Click on the cell containing an entry you want to copy.
2 Move the pointer to the fill handle in the bottom right-hand corner of the cell.
3 Drag down the column or across the row when the pointer shows a black cross.
   Or
4 Select all the cells including the cell containing the original content, click on the **Fill** button on the Home tab and select the direction to copy to.
5 Formulae will reflect the relative cell references, but text or figures will be copied exactly.

Excel recognises certain entries such as dates, days of the week or years and, if you copy from one of these, the copies will automatically increment in steps. You can also create your own series. Excel recognizes dates such as the days of the week or the months, so if you replicate one of these it completes the series automatically. You can also use the fill facility to create series of numbers that increase or decrease in steps.

Copy down from here

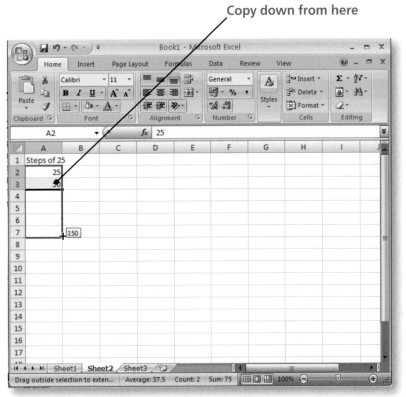

Fig. 2.35 Fill series

create a series

1 To increment dates, enter the first one and then replicate in the normal way using the Fill handle or Fill button to continue the series.

2 To increment numbers, enter two consecutive numbers – for example, 5, 10.

3 Select *both* cells and replicate from the second. The series will be copied – for example, in steps of 5.

   Or

4 Use the menu by entering the first figure and then clicking on the drop-down arrow next to the Fill button.

5 Select **Series** and type in the steps you want to use and where the series will stop. If you have not selected the cells receiving the series you should also select the direction for the fill.

6 Click on **OK** and the series will be created.

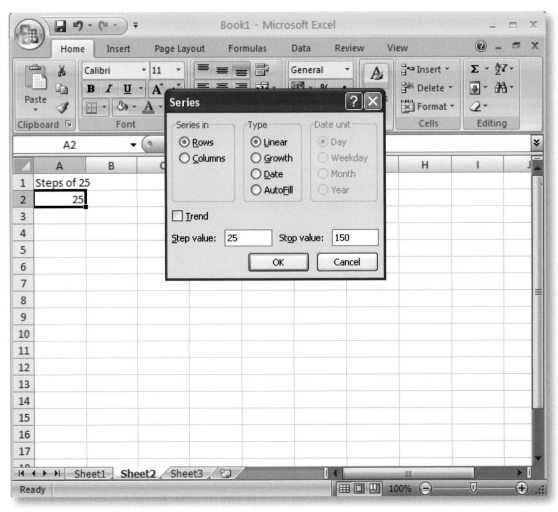

Fig. 2.36 Fill series with menu

Check your understanding 6

1 Open the spreadsheet *Golf* provided on the CD-ROM accompanying this book.
2 Complete the date series in row 3 so that the headings cover **January to April**. Use a function to work out the monthly totals.
3 Copy the title **Gladington Golf Club** to cell A13.
4 Format the copied title to a different font type and smaller font size.
5 Move the row heading and monthly totals in row 8 to cells A14 to E14.
6 Insert a new row between **Club house** and **Donations** and add the heading **Chairman's contribution**.
7 Enter the figure £50 for each month.
8 Check that totals have been updated.
9 Make sure all entries are fully displayed.
10 Right align the month column headings.
11 Delete column B and then use **Undo** to add it again.
12 Format all prices to currency with the £ symbol but no decimal places.
13 Add shading and emphasis as you like to improve the appearance of the spreadsheet.
14 Save as *Golf completed*.

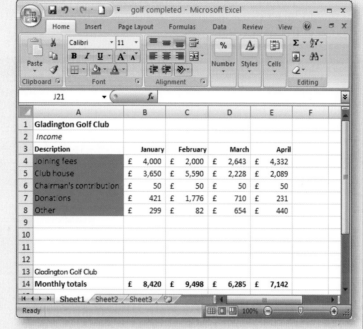

Fig. 2.37 Example 6 Golf completed

Sorting cell contents

Any column can be sorted so that entries are in a different order – for example, alphabetically, by decreasing prices or by increased weights. However, most spreadsheets contain related data in adjacent columns. Where this is the case, it is important *not* to sort one column on its own as you would no longer be able to make sense of the data. You will find that, if you try to sort a single column, you will see a warning message.

carry out a simple sort

1 Select the column or several columns if they contain related data.
2 Click on the **Sort & Filter** button on the Home tab.
3 Select **A–Z** for an alphabetical or increasing-order sort, or **Z–A** for a decreasing-order sort.
4 With several columns selected, the sort will be carried out on the left-most column only.

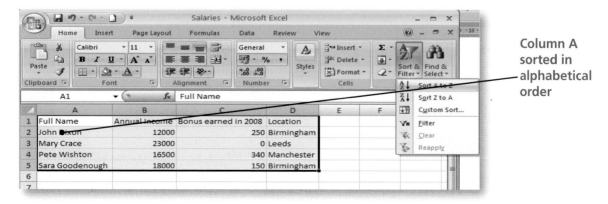

Column A sorted in alphabetical order

Fig. 2.38 Single A–Z sort

carry out a more advanced sort

1 Select all the data including the headings.
2 Click on the **Custom Sort** option on the **Sort & Filter** button, or first click on the **Data** tab.
3 In the **Sort by**: box, select the first level of sort – for example, by name or location.
4 Now select what to sort on – for example, values or formatting.
5 Choose the order – for example, A to Z or Z to A.
6 You can carry out a second order sort on a different column by clicking on **Add Level**.
7 Complete all the boxes and add a third level sort if needed before clicking on **OK**.

Note that if you do not select the headings, the sort order will identify column letters.
You should take off the tick in the 'My data has headers' box to make sure headings are not included in the sort.

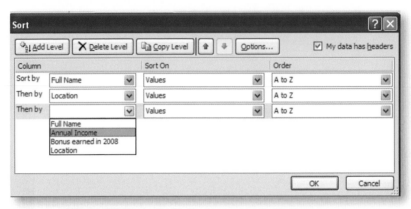

Fig. 2.39 Sort box

Check your understanding 7

1 Open the file *Houseboats* provided on the CD-ROM accompanying this book.
2 Sort the boats so that they are in increasing order of Final price.
3 Save as *Houseboats sorted*.

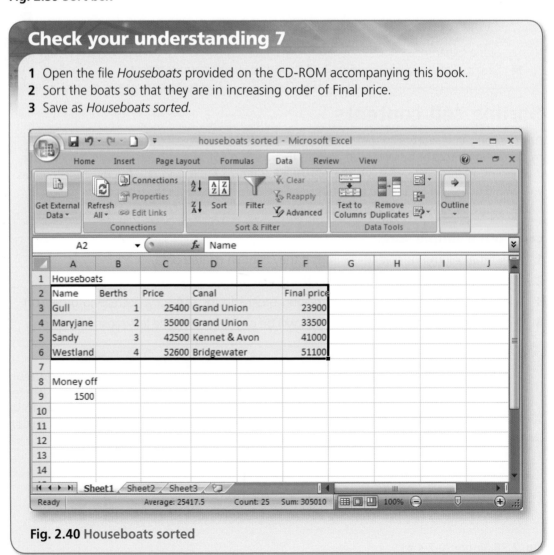

Fig. 2.40 Houseboats sorted

Find and replace

As with all Office programs, Excel 2007 offers a quick way to find and/or replace data when you want to locate details or make changes to your spreadsheet.

use find and replace

1   Click on the **Find and Select** button on the Home tab.

2   To locate an entry, click on **Find**.

3   The search will find any matching data in cells. If you want to restrict the search to a complete entry, click on **Options** and place a tick in the checkbox labelled 'Match entire cell contents'.

4   Enter the data you are looking for in the **Find what:** box and click on **Find Next**.

5   The first matching entry will be highlighted.

6   Keep clicking on **Find Next** if you want to find further matching entries.

7   To replace an entry, click on the **Replace** option or the labelled tab in the **Find and Replace** box.

8   Enter the data you want to change in the **Find what:** box.

9   Enter the new data you want to replace it with in the **Replace with:** box.

10 If you are sure the process will be applied correctly, click on **Replace All**.

11 Otherwise, click on **Find Next**, check by eye and if you want the change made, click on the **Replace** button.

12 To retain an entry, click on **Find Next** and the search will continue across the spreadsheet.

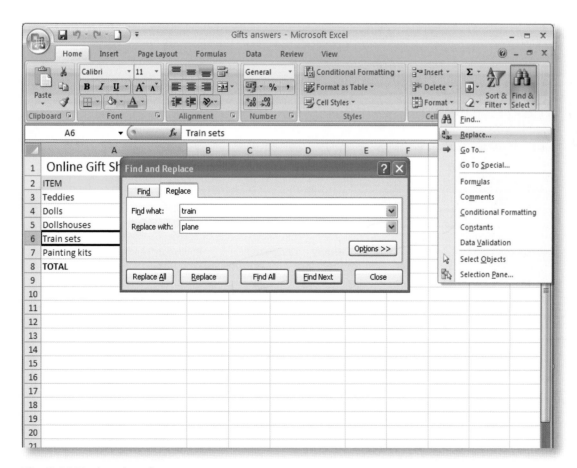

Fig. 2.41 Find and replace

> ## Check your understanding 8
>
> 1 Start a new spreadsheet.
> 2 Enter the following numbers down column A: 15, 20, 25, 30, 35.
> 3 Use **Find** to locate the first number with a 2 in it.
> 4 Use **Replace** to replace the number 15 with the number 10.
> 5 Now replace the number 35 with the number 350.
> 6 Close the file without saving.

5 Printing spreadsheets

As with word-processed documents, you can change orientation and margins, add headers or footers to worksheets to help identify printouts, and print all the sheets, individual sheets or parts of any sheet in a workbook.

Only the data you have entered on a spreadsheet will print out if you use the quick print option, but it may extend over several pages or just onto a new page. To make sure you only print the data you want, use the print preview facilities and make changes before you actually print.

In normal view, dotted lines show what will print on the first page.

To scroll across a wide spreadsheet, use the navigation arrows at the bottom right of the screen.

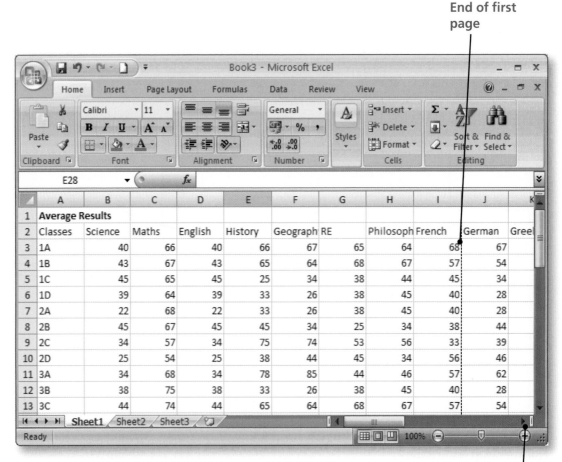

Fig. 2.42 What prints

change page layout in normal view

1 Click on the **Page Layout** tab.
2 Click on **Margins** to select from a range of styles.
3 Click on **Orientation** to go between Portrait and Landscape.
4 Click on **Size** to change the paper size you are printing onto.
5 Click on the **Print** option under **Gridlines** or **Headings** to print gridlines and row and column headings.

For a more detailed examination of page layouts, see page 40.

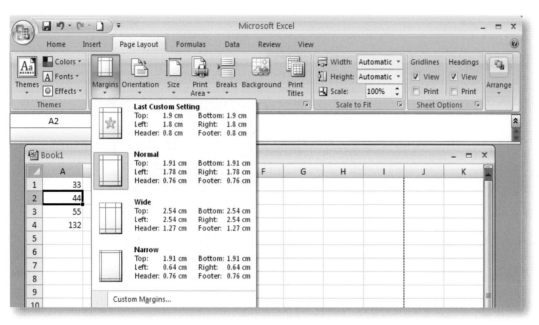

Fig. 2.43 Page Layout tab

use print preview

1 Click on the **Office** button.
2 Rest on the **Print** option and select **Print Preview**.
3 Click on **Zoom** to see the page in detail.
4 Click on **Next** or **Previous page** to move through a large spreadsheet.
5 Click on **Page Setup** to open the dialog box and make the following changes.
   a On the Page tab, click to change from Portrait to Landscape orientation.

Fig. 2.44 Print Preview

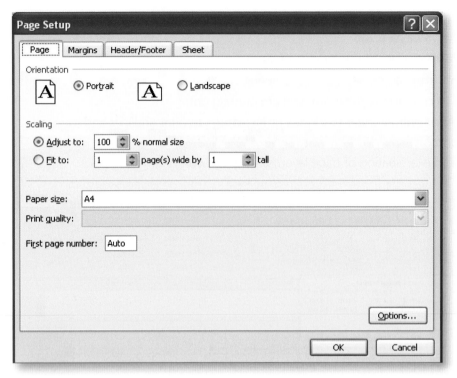

Fig. 2.45 Page Setup

b Click in the **Fit to:** radio button and set the number of pages (for example, 1) to reduce font sizes and print on a single sheet of paper.

c Change to a different paper size by selecting or typing in customised measurements.

d On the Margins tab, set different margins or centre the data horizontally and vertically on the page.

e On the Sheet tab click in the checkbox to add or remove visible gridlines.

f Click in the **Row and column headings** box to display these (A, B, C… and 1, 2, 3…) as well as your data entries. Displaying row and column headings on your printouts will make the documents easier to use, especially when dealing with complex spreadsheets and large amounts of data.

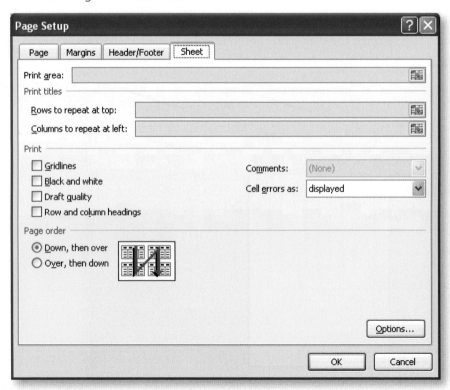

Fig. 2.46 Sheet tab

insert a ready-made header or footer

1 Click on the Insert tab.

2 Click on the Header & Footer button to display the Header & Footer Tools.

3 Click on the Header button for a choice of entries at the top of the sheet, or Footer button for an entry at the bottom.

4 Click on Go to Header or Go to Footer to set the position, and then click on one or more of the options to add page numbers, the date, file name and so on.

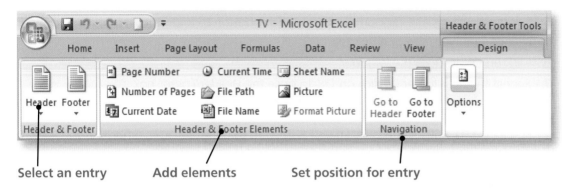

Select an entry   Add elements   Set position for entry

Fig. 2.47 Header and footer tools

add headers and footers using the dialog box

1 Open the file in Print Preview.

2 On the Page Setup – Header/Footer tab, select a ready-made header or footer if they are appropriately worded.

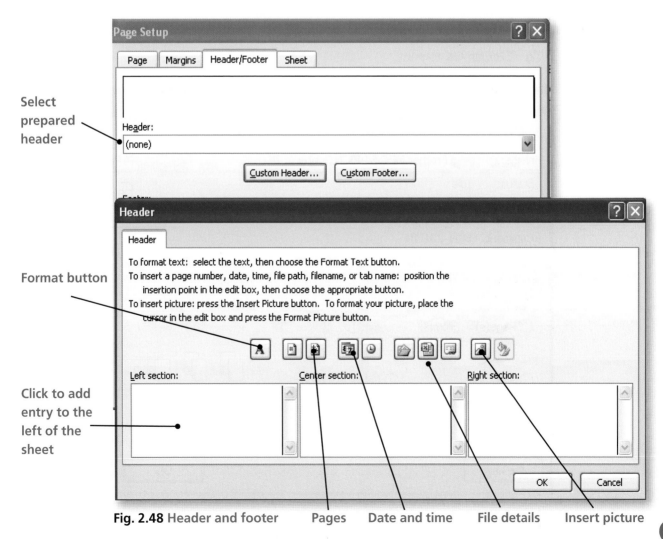

Fig. 2.48 Header and footer   Pages   Date and time   File details   Insert picture

3 To create your own header, click on the **Custom Header** button.

4 In the dialog box, click in one of three panes to add entries on the left, centre or right of the page. You can type text or click on a button to add an automatic entry. These include:
   - page numbers and numbers of pages
   - date and time
   - file pathway, file name and sheet name
   - pictures.

5 Select any entries and click on the **Format Text** button to open the **Font** dialog box and change font type, size or emphasis.

6 Click on **OK** to close the window.

7 Repeat to add a footer or click on **OK** to close the Header/Footer box.

print

1 First select part of a spreadsheet if you only want to print one area, otherwise you will print the whole sheet.

2 Click on the **Office** button.

3 Rest the mouse on **Print** and select **Quick Print** for one copy of the entire worksheet.

4 Click on **Print** to open the **Print** dialog box and then change any of the following settings:

   a Under Print what, click on **Selection** to print a selected range of cells.

   b Click on **Entire Workbook** to print all the sheets.

   c Click on **Active sheet** to limit the printout to the current sheet.

   d Under Print range, click on **Pages** and enter the actual pages you want to print.

   e Increase the number of copies you will produce.

   f Click on the drop-down arrow in the **Name** box to send the data to a different printer.

   g Click on **OK** to print.

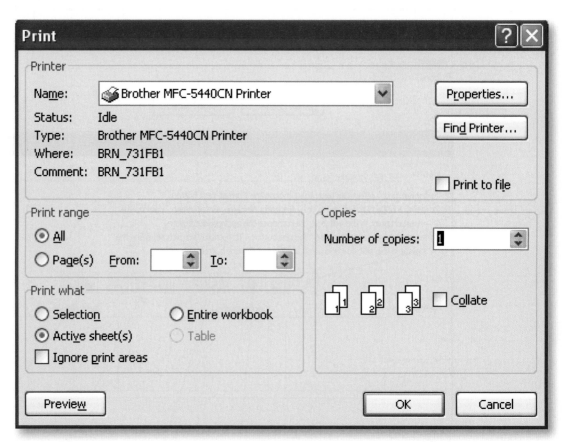

Fig. 2.49 Print box

Printing formulae

For examination purposes, you may need to produce a printout displaying the formulae used rather than the values. Take care when printing as your spreadsheet will become wider to accommodate the extra data displayed.

print formulae

1 Click on the Formulas tab.
2 In the Formula Auditing section, click on Show Formulas.
3 To hide them, click on the button again.
4 You can also show/hide formulae by holding Ctrl and pressing ¬ (next to 1 on the keyboard).
5 Print as normal.

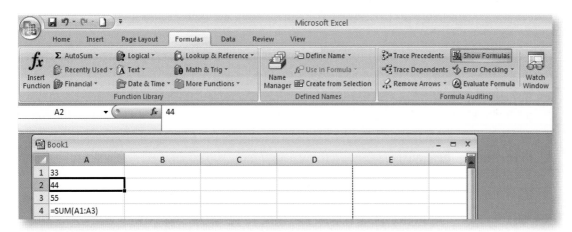

Fig. 2.50 Show formulae

Check your understanding 9

1 Open *Houseboats sorted*.
2 Check in print preview.
3 Add a footer that includes the page number on the right and the file name on the left.
4 Change to landscape orientation.
5 Make sure the spreadsheet will print out showing gridlines.
6 Print one copy.
7 Now remove the gridlines and just print out the data in cells A1:B6 to include row and column headings.
8 Save as *Houseboats with footer* and close the file.

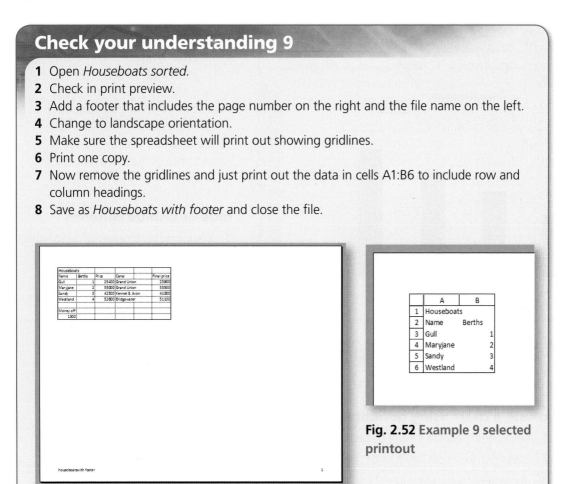

Fig. 2.52 Example 9 selected printout

Fig. 2.51 Example 9 footer

6 Charts and graphs

A range of charts and graphs can be produced in Excel very easily using the **Chart Tools** options. Charts can be 2D or 3D and they can come in a variety of styles including pie, bar, column or line. When created, charts can be added to the same sheet as the data or they can be placed on their own worksheet.

Charts are based on selected data and so you must always have a spreadsheet open on which to base the chart. If including data in **non-adjacent** columns or rows, hold **Ctrl** as you select the second or further ranges and they will all stay selected. An alternative is first to **hide** all columns between those being selected. Hiding is different to deleting or clearing, both of which remove data. Although invisible, hidden columns and rows can be restored — unhide, descibed below.

There are a number of graph and chart types to choose from, and each type is best used to display certain types of data. The list below features some of the more common types, but is not exhaustive.

- **Area charts** – these are often used to show changes over time. You could use an area chart to show the increase in the number of women graduating from university since 1945.

- **Bar charts** – these allow you to make comparisons between individual items. You could use a bar chart to record the frequency of absences on different days of the week, and discover whether more people are off ill on a Monday or a Tuesday.

- **Line charts** – these are best used to show data trends. You could use a line chart to review the changes in your company's recorded profits over the past 10 years.

- **Pie charts** – these show proportions in relation to a single set of data. You could use a pie chart to illustrate the relative contribution to the annual sales total made by each person on a team.

- **Scatter charts** – these show the relationships between different sets of data. You could use a scatter chart to show the different birthdays of everyone on your team, and then identify the month with the highest concentration.

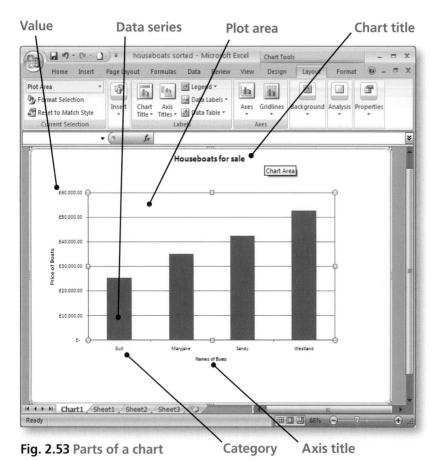

Fig. 2.53 Parts of a chart

hide or unhide columns

1 Click on the **Home** tab and select **Format** in the Cells group.
2 Select **Hide and Unhide** in the Visibility section and select **Hide Columns or rows**.
3 Return here when you want to reverse the option.

create a chart using default settings

1 Select the data on which to base the chart, including any column headings.
2 Press the function key **F11** at the top of the keyboard.
3 A column chart will appear on its own sheet.
4 To make any changes, right-click on the chart area or select chart elements and format as outlined below.

create a chart in steps

1 Select the spreadsheet data.

2 Click on the Insert tab.

3 Select the type of chart, such as Column or Pie, and click on one of the chart styles.

Note that for the assessment, you should not use a 3D or stacked chart.

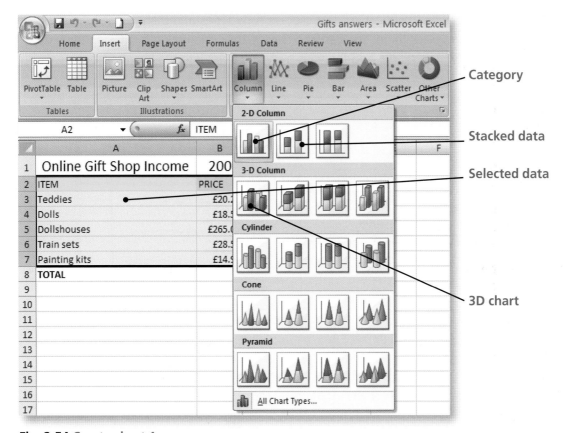

Fig. 2.54 Create chart 1

4 A simple chart will appear on the same sheet. Whenever it is selected the Chart Tools options will be available.

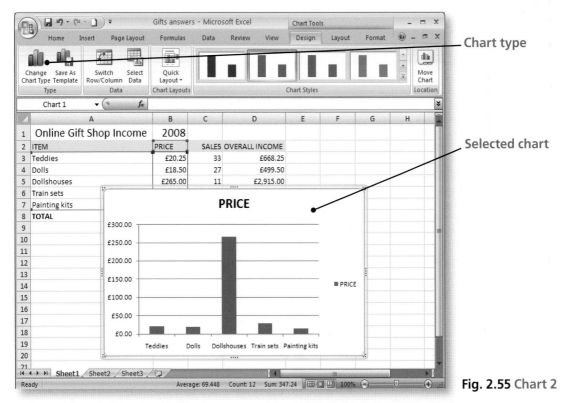

Fig. 2.55 Chart 2

5 Click on the **Layout** tab to add or amend information such as axis titles, or a graph legend (the key to the data).

a Click on **Chart Title – Centred Overlay Title** and replace the default title by typing into the **Formula bar**. To add the new title to your chart, click on the tick. You can also do this by clicking on the title to select it, typing in your new title, and pressing **Enter** to apply the new title.

b To add axis titles to your chart, first click on **Axis Titles** and then decide where you would like to place them. You can also change their orientation by making them run horizontally or vertically. Add the titles by typing them into the **Formula bar**.

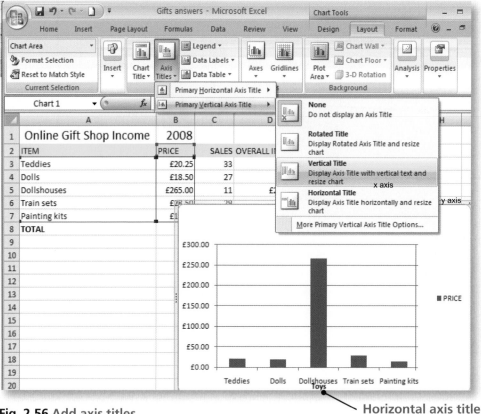

Fig. 2.56 Add axis titles

Fig. 2.57 Amend data label

c To move the legend, click on **Legend** and select where you would like it to appear.

d You can add details such as values, percentages or categories to the bars, columns or pie chart slices. To do this, click on **Data Labels**. To remove labels currently in place, click on **Data Labels** and select **None**.

e If you want to add to or amend the labels, you can click on **Data Labels – More Data Label Options** or you can right-click on the label you would like to amend and select **Format**.

f Click on **Move Chart** on the Design tab if you want the chart on its own worksheet. You will be able to enter a sheet name, or leave the default as Chart1, Chart2 and so on each time you create a new chart.

Note that the data on which the chart is based will still be available – usually on Sheet1 of the workbook. Return there by clicking on the sheet tab.

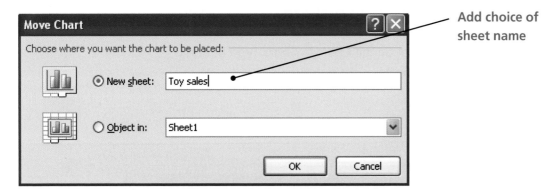

Add choice of sheet name

Fig. 2.58 Move chart

Check your understanding 10

1 Open the file *Magazines* provided on the CD-ROM accompanying this book.
2 Create a pie chart showing the price of all the magazines.
3 Change the title to **Price of Home Magazines**.
4 Add data labels to show magazine name (category) and price.
5 Save the file as *Magazines completed*.

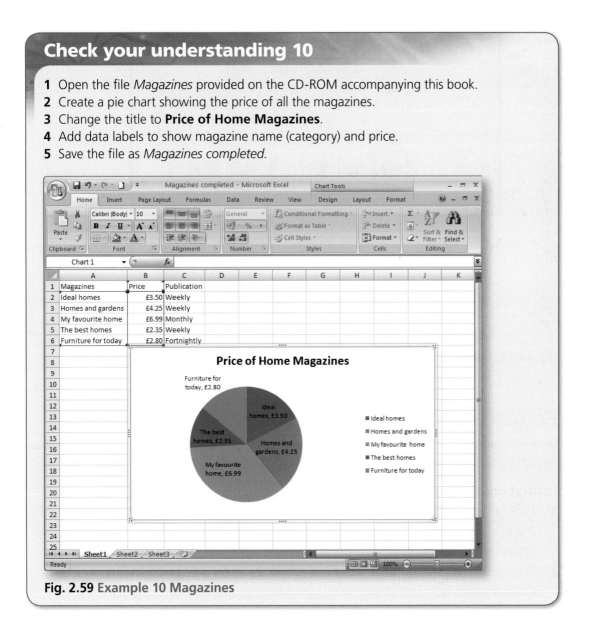

Fig. 2.59 Example 10 Magazines

Changing chart type

Having created a chart, you may decide the data would be better displayed with a different type of chart or graph. Change the chart directly, rather than starting again from scratch.

change chart type

1 Select the chart.
2 Right click on the plot or chart area and select Change Chart Type.
  Or
3 On the Design tab, click on the Change Chart Type button.
4 Choose a different chart from the display and click on OK.

Click to change chart

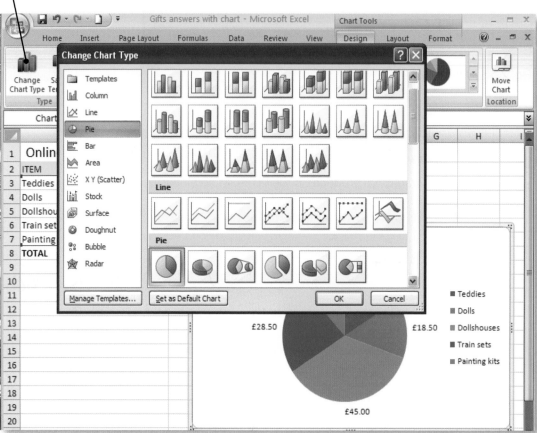

Fig. 2.60 Change chart type

Formatting chart elements

Once you have created a chart and added elements such as chart or axes titles, you may want to format them to improve the clarity or appearance of the chart.

format chart elements

1 Click on the aspect of the chart you would like to change, such as the legend, a title, the line of a line graph or pie slice. Alternatively, you can select that element from the drop-down box on the Format tab.
2 Once you have selected the element you would like to change, you then have two options:
  a You can use the normal font or colour editing options on the Home tab.
  b You can right-click on the element to bring up a reduced menu which allows you to – for example – to open the Font dialog box, add Data Labels or select different fill colours.

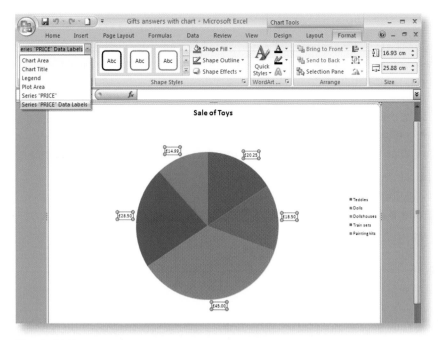

Fig. 2.61 Format chart

3 You can also select any part of the chart and click on **Format Selection** to open a relevant window where you can 'fine tune' the formatting, or use links on the **Format** tab – for example, to amend line colour and width for elements such as the plot area.

Format
selected item

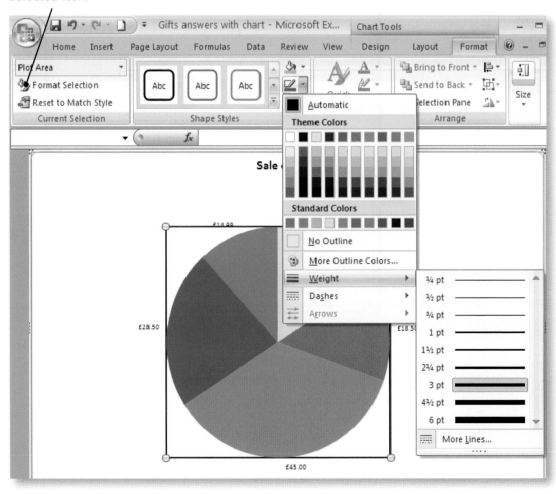

Fig. 2.62 Format chart areas

Scale

The upper and lower axes limits will have been set automatically when you created the chart. If you want different limits, you must change the scale. Axes limits are not automatically set when using pie charts. Pie charts, being round, do not have axes.

change scale

1 Right-click on the axis and select **Format Axis**.
2 In the main window, click on the **Fixed** button for the Axis Options Minimum and enter a new figure.
3 Repeat if necessary to change the maximum.
4 Change the Major unit if necessary.
5 Click on **Close** to return to the chart.

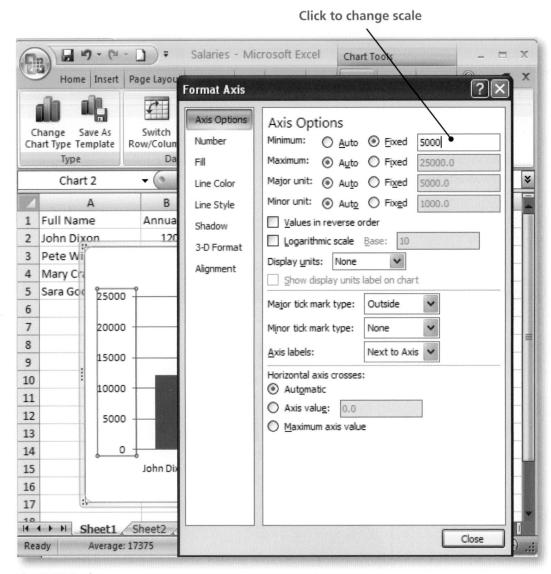

Fig. 2.63 Scale

Check your understanding 11

1 Start a new spreadsheet and enter the following data:

	A	B	C	D
1	SAVINGS			
2	Month	Peter	Sally	
3	Jan	£23	£23	
4	Feb	£34	£33	
5	Mar	£15	£39	
6	Apr	£21	£49	
7	May	£44	£59	
8	Jun	£32	£48	
9				

Fig. 2.64 Savings data

2 Create a line chart displaying the data.
3 Now change the scale so that the minimum is £20 and the maximum £60.
4 Close the file without saving.

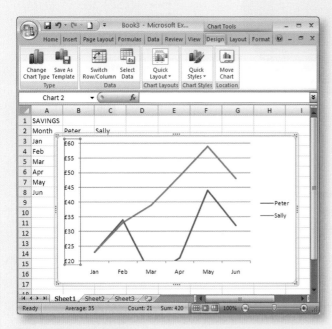

Fig. 2.65 New scale

Printing a chart

- To print a chart that is on its own worksheet, open the sheet on-screen and then print as normal.

- To print a chart alone that is on the same sheet as the data, make sure the chart is selected before printing. Note that if you print a chart in this way, the size of the chart could mean the labels or axes will not display fully. Use print preview to check this, and amend font sizes if necessary.

- To print a worksheet showing chart and data, deselect the chart before printing.

The type of data you are working with will determine the best graph or chart type to use. Different amounts and types of data will be best displayed in an assortment of graphs and charts, so experiment with a variety before working out which type is best for your data. Remember also that the various chart types will look different when printed.

Always check in Print Preview before printing, to make sure you are printing correctly.

Check your understanding 12

1 Open the spreadsheet *TV* provided on the CD-ROM accompanying this book.
2 Create a pie chart to show the viewing figures.
3 Move the chart so that it is on its own sheet. Rename the sheet if you prefer – for example, **TV viewing chart**.
4 Change the chart title to read **TV viewing figures**.
5 Add data labels to show values and percentages.
6 Increase the size of the data label and legend fonts, and apply a bold emphasis.

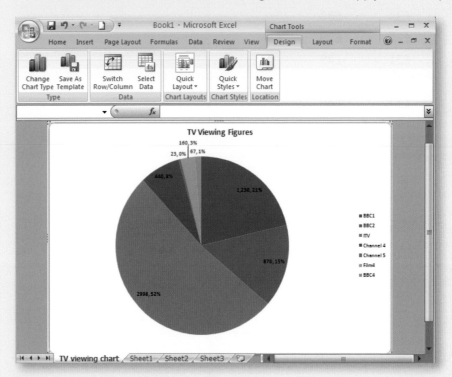

Fig. 2.66 Example 12, Step 6

7 Print a copy of the chart on its own.
8 Change the chart type to a column chart.
9 Remove the data labels and legend.
10 Add axis titles to explain the data – for example, **Channels** and **Viewing figures**.
11 Save and close the file.

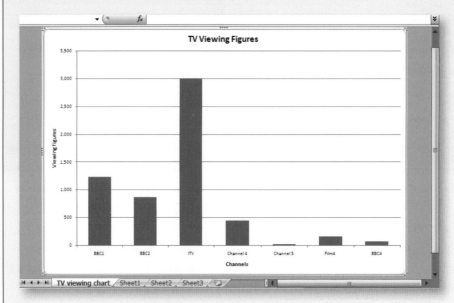

Fig. 2.67 Example 12, Step 8

Using a chart to compare data

When you are comparing one or more sets of data, you simply select the appropriate data ranges before creating a chart in the normal way.

When printing, it can sometimes be difficult to distinguish between similar lines or columns and so you need to take one or more of the following steps to ensure the data is clear:

- Take extra care that chart labels are used correctly
- Colour data sets differently
- Display a legend
- Change the weight or style of one set of lines or markers

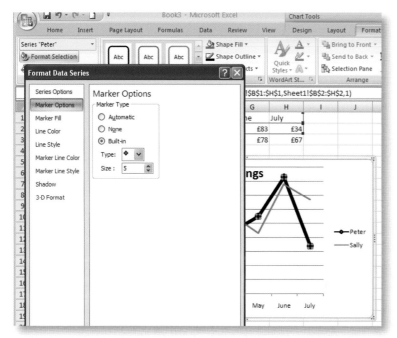

Fig. 2.68 Distinguishing data

- Especially if printing in black and white (you can choose this option from Page Setup on the Chart tab), check in Print Preview that the data sets look different. With column or bar charts, you could even see what effect it would have to apply a fill texture rather than solid colour. (Previous versions allowed a pattern fill but this is not available in Excel 2007.)

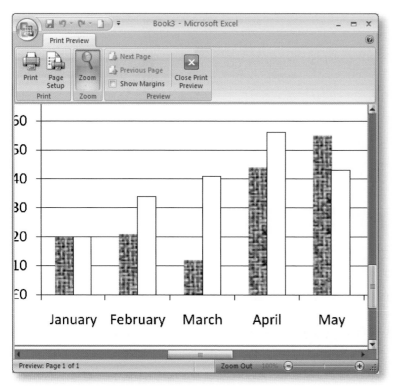

Fig. 2.69 Texture added for printing charts

121

CLAiT Assignment

TASK 1

1   Create the following spreadsheet. Set the page to **landscape** orientation and key in the data set out below:

Garden Centre						
Item	Code	Wholesale price	Retail price	Number sold	Income	Profit
Small pots	127	0.5		357		
Ceramic pot stands	342	1.2		221		
Large pots	542	16		89		
Fertiliser bags	45	2.75		506		
Bulb compost	211	2.2		377		
Gloves	33	2.5		52		
Shears	88	15		18		
Snail pellets	65	3		315		

2   Add your name and today's date as a header.

3   Save the file as *Garden Centre*.

4   In the Retail price column, use a formula to work out the retail price for Small pots. These are 15% more than the wholesale price. (The formula will be 1.15 x Wholesale price.)

5   Replicate this formula down the column to work out the Retail price for all items.

6   Now enter a formula to work out the Income for Small pots. (Retail price x Number sold.)

7   Replicate this formula down the column to work out Income for all items.

8   Update the spreadsheet to save these changes and print a copy (Figure 2.70). Make sure all data is displayed in full and gridlines and row and column headers will print out.

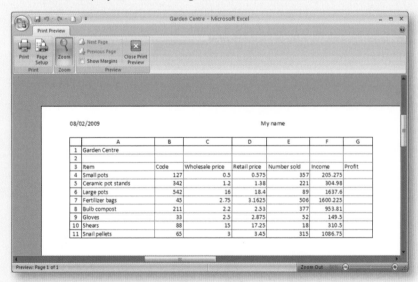

Fig. 2.70 Garden centre

9   Now make the following changes:

   a   Bulb compost has run out. Delete this row without leaving empty cells.
   b   Increase the Wholesale price for Large pots to 17.50.
   c   Format all column headings to bold.
   d   Format the title to bold, font size 16.
   e   Centre-align all row headings.

10 Add a new row headed TOTAL and use a function to work out the total number sold.

11 Format all prices to currency, to two decimal places.

12 Format all numbers to integer (0 decimals).

13 Add a single line border to emphasise the column headings.

14 Save as *Garden Centre2*.

15 Now use a formula to work out the Profit for Small pots (Retail price - Wholesale price x Number sold). Use brackets where necessary.

16 Replicate the formula down the column to work out Profit for all items.

17 Print a copy of the spreadsheet showing the formulae. Make sure all the data fits on one page (Figure 2.71).

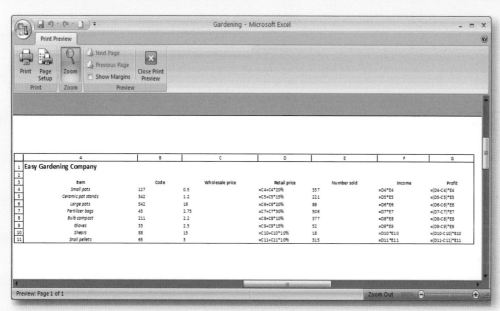

Fig. 2.71 Formulae

18 Insert a new column to the right of the Retail price column headed VAT. Use a formula to work out the Vat on all items at 15%.

19 Print a copy of the updated spreadsheet and save it as *Garden Centre2* (Figure 2.72).

	A	B	C	D	E	F	G	H
1	**Garden Centre**							
2								
3	Item	Code	Wholesale price	Retail price	VAT	Number sold	Income	Profit
4	Small pots	127	£0.50	£0.58	£0.09	357	£205.28	£26.78
5	Ceramic pot stands	342	£1.20	£1.38	£0.21	221	£304.98	£39.78
6	Large pots	542	£17.50	£20.13	£3.02	89	£1,791.13	£233.63
7	Fertilizer bags	45	£2.75	£3.16	£0.47	506	£1,600.23	£208.73
8	Gloves	33	£2.50	£2.88	£0.43	52	£149.50	£19.50
9	Shears	88	£15.00	£17.25	£2.59	18	£310.50	£40.50
10	Snail pellets	65	£3.00	£3.45	£0.52	315	£1,086.75	£141.75
11	TOTAL					1558		
12								

Fig. 2.72 Garden centre 2

20 Print another copy, this time displaying the formulae.

21 Finally, print a copy of all details just for the first three items, showing row and column headers (Figure 2.73).

22 Save and close the spreadsheet file.

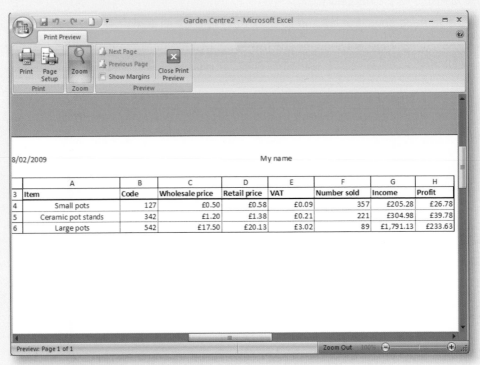

Fig. 2.73 Selection

TASK 2

1 Open the spreadsheet *Stallholder* supplied on the CD-ROM accompanying this book.

2 Create a line graph comparing income from two sources only: cake sales and burgers for the 6 months.

3 Make sure the months are displayed on the x-axis.

4 Give the graph the title *Cakes and Burgers*.

5 Add the x-axis title Months.

6 Add the y-axis title Income.

7 Retain a legend.

8 Add data labels to each line.

9 Change the y-axis scale so that it ranges from £200 to £1900.

10 Add a footer with your name and today's date.

11 Make sure the data will be easily distinguished when printed out.

12 Print out just the graph.

13 Save as *Stallholder with chart* and close the file.

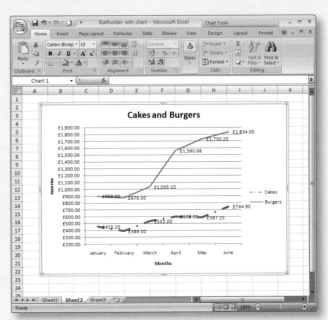

Fig. 2.74 Chart

Database manipulation

This unit covers the basic features of the database application Access 2007. You will learn when to use databases, how to create them and how to use them to store, sort or search for information.

At the end of this unit you will be able to:

➡ enter data in an existing database and present and print data

➡ create simple queries/searches on one or two criteria and sort data

➡ produce appropriate pre-defined reports from databases using short cuts

1 What is a database?

A database is a collection of data about people or things. It is used to store information in a systematic way so that it can be manipulated easily. You will have come across many examples of databases, including address books, catalogues and student registers. Do not confuse databases with spreadsheets, which can also be used to store data. The two systems are used for different purposes. For more information on spreadsheets, see Unit 002.

In Access, information is stored in **tables** and the details relating to a single person or item held in any table are collectively known as a **record**. Within each record, the information that is entered under a different heading or category (the **field name**) is known as a **field**.

Field name

Record

Name	Age	Gender	Location
Tom	3	Male	Liverpool
Sara	2	Female	Birmingham
Ali	3	Male	Liverpool
Molly	4	Female	London

'My Relatives' table

Field

Fig. 3.1 Fields

Data types

For each field, only one specified type of data is allowed. This is because Access can only perform calculations or searches based on recognised data types. You are most likely to use the following data types.

● **Text** – for entries such as names and addresses, or for any mixture of letters and numbers (alphanumeric entries) such as postcodes, stock codes or emails that may include figures not used in calculations. The length of any entry is limited to 255 characters.

● **Number** – for numbers such as ages, items sold or sizes.

- **Currency** – used for financial entries such as costs and prices, which usually display appropriate currency symbols like £ or $.

- **Date/Time** – for dates and times where you want to be able to perform calculations such as finding an earlier or later day in the month.

- **Memo** – this data type is applied to long textual entries such as descriptions or notes.

- **Yes/No** – used where a simple answer is all that is required.

- **AutoNumber** – this counts each record and assigns the next consecutive number automatically.

Although not required for the qualification, it is helpful for your understanding of databases to know how to create a file and design a table, and so these skills are included in this chapter.

Primary key

In any professionally designed database, it is important to be able to identify each record – for example, to distinguish between people with similar names or items with similar functions. Access 2007 automatically creates an ID field for this purpose. To make sure that every record has a unique identifier, this field is assigned a **primary key**, which means an error message will appear if you try to enter duplicate data. The primary key also plays an important role when you create relationships between different tables.

You can assign a primary key to any field, and suitable fields that will not contain duplicated data include ISBN book numbers, stock codes or National Insurance numbers.

You will not need to assign or use primary keys for this level of qualification, and so you may prefer to remove the ID field altogether.

2 Starting to work with Access

Unlike most Microsoft Office applications, you do not start work on a blank page in Access as soon as it opens. Instead, you must first create the database file in which all your data will be stored.

Note that sometimes a table of data rather than the file is referred to as a 'database'. In fact a database table is an **object** within the file.

create a database file

1   Click on a shortcut icon or go to **Start – All Programs – (Microsoft Office) – Access.**

2   On the opening Getting Started page, click on **New Blank Database**. (Make sure your window is maximised or you may not see this.)

Create a new file

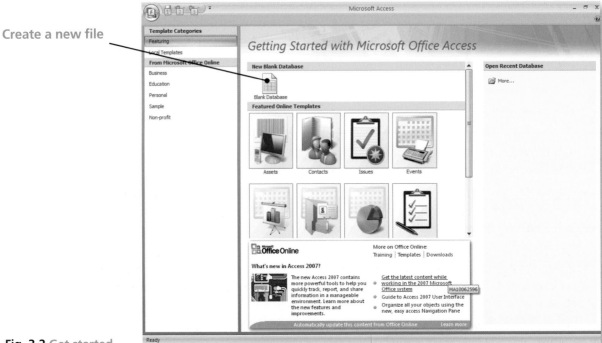

Fig. 3.2 Get started

3 When the Blank Database pane opens, click in the box and give the file a suitable name. The extension *.accdb* will be added automatically to show it is an Access 2007 database.

4 To change the location for storing the file, click on **More** and browse for a suitable directory/folder. At this stage you could create a new folder to hold the database.

5 Click on **Create** and the new file will open on-screen.

Click browser for folder
storage location

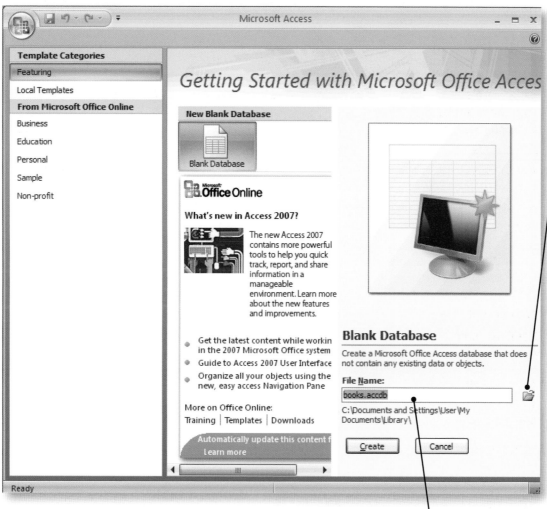

Fig. 3.3 Create new database

Name the file

Creating tables

When your new database file appears, the ribbon will show the Table Tools commands related to a table of data temporarily labelled Table1 that will have been set up ready for you to customise. It will contain a single field – ID with an AutoNumber data type.

A database file can hold any number of different tables, but these should all have some relationship to one another. For example, a **Library** database file could contain tables related to *Staff, Books, Customers, DVDs* and *Borrowing.*

You can view a table in two different ways: displaying the information it contains (Open or Datasheet view) or viewing just the underlying structure (Design view). When Access opens you are presented with the Datasheet view ready to add or search through the records contained in the table.

Before you can enter any records you must set up the design of your table properly. There are three important decisions to make when designing your own tables:

- appropriate headings (field names) under which the data will be stored
- the type of data that will be stored in each field
- a name for the table that will indicate the type of information it contains.

To design a table, you need to be in **Design view**.

Go to Design view

Empty table ready to customise

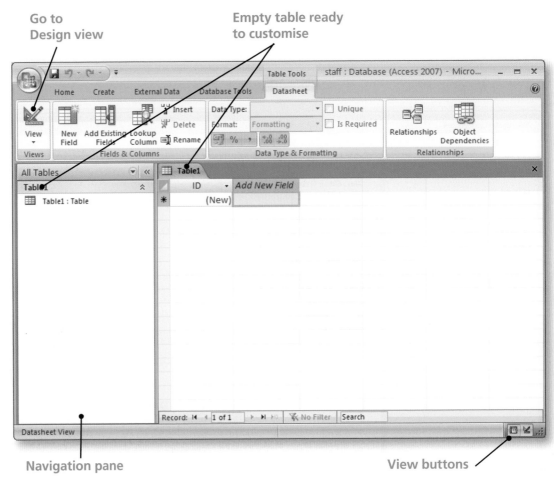

Navigation pane

View buttons

Fig. 3.4 Opening view

Fig. 3.5 Name table

design a table

1 Click on the **Design** button on the ribbon or in the bottom corner of the screen to move to Design view.

2 A **Save As:** box will appear and you must enter a name for your table. Choose one that relates to the information the table will contain but that is *not* the same as the database file name.

3 In Design view you will see the tab on the left displaying the table name and three columns in the main window labelled Field Name, Data Type and Description.

4 Click in the first empty cell below ID in the Field Name column and enter the name for your first field – for example, *First name*. (You may find some field names, such as *Name* or *Date*, will be rejected. In these cases simply find an alternative.)

5 Press the **Tab** key or click in the next column and select a data type. Text will appear automatically, but click on the drop-down arrow to select an alternative.

Properties of *First name* field

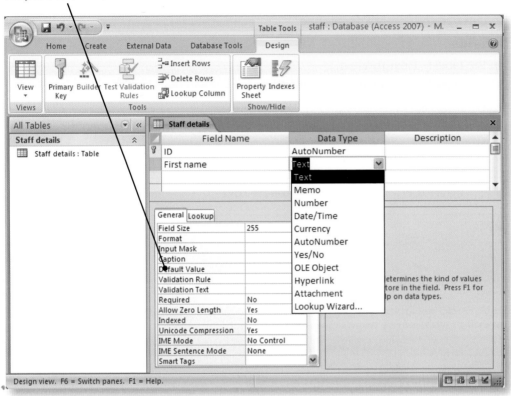

Fig. 3.6 Add field names

Note that if you click in the cell and type in the first letter of the data type, such as N for number or C for currency, the correct entry will appear.

6 The Description column is available to you as the table designer, in case there are any comments you wish to include about a particular field.

7 Each time you add a field name and data type, the properties of that field will be displayed below.

8 To continue designing the table, click in the next empty Field Name cell and type in the next field name – for example, *Surname*. Select a data type and continue adding fields until all the field names have been added.

9 When your table is complete, click on the **Datasheet view** button to start entering records. You will first have to click on **Yes** to save the changes you have made to the table.

Go to Datasheet view   Exit Access

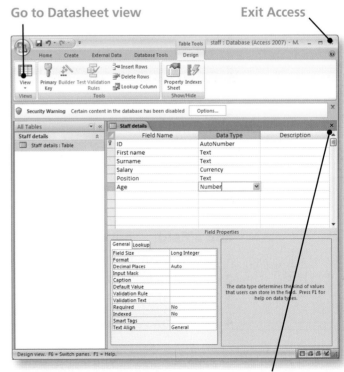

Fig. 3.7 All field names

Close the table

Adding or deleting fields

If you do not want to retain the ID field, or change your mind about other fields, you can delete them very easily. You can also add fields to your table if you want to do so after it has been created.

Fig. 3.8 Warning to save table details

delete fields

1 Open the table in **Design view**.
2 Click on the pale blue square next to the field name when the pointer shows a black arrow. The selected row will display an orange border.
3 Click on the **Delete Rows** button and confirm the deletion when a warning message appears.

Insert row   Delete row

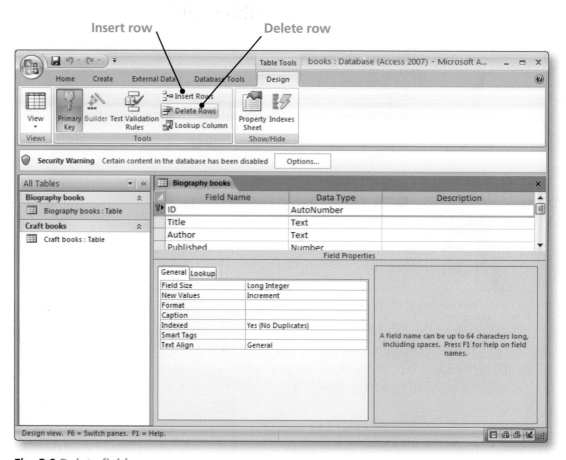

Fig. 3.9 Delete field row

add a field

1 Click in the next empty row to add a field at the end of the list.
2 To insert a field, click to select the row below the position for the new field.
3 Click on the **Insert Rows** button.
4 A new row will appear and you can now enter the field name and data type.

Renaming tables

If at some stage you decide to rename your table (or other objects you create), it is a straightforward process but the object must be closed before you can do this.

rename a table

1 Right-click on the object name in the navigation pane.
2 Select **Rename**.
3 Type a new name for the object.

Designing a table in Datasheet view

For more complex or business-orientated databases, a different way of designing a table is offered by Access 2007. This involves selecting field names from a ready-made list.

design a table using the field list

1 After creating a new file, click in the first **Add New Field** column.
2 Now click on the **New Field** button.
3 Scroll down the list of Field Templates offered and select an appropriate name.
4 Drag it up to the table or double-click so that it replaces the Add New Field name.
5 Appropriate data types such as currency or number will have been set automatically for each field name listed. If incorrect, click in the **Data Type** box and select an alternative.
6 Continue to work through the list to add further field names.
7 Click on the **Save** button to name and save the table.
8 The table is now ready for adding records.
9 Add new fields at any time by reopening the Field Templates list and selecting a new name.

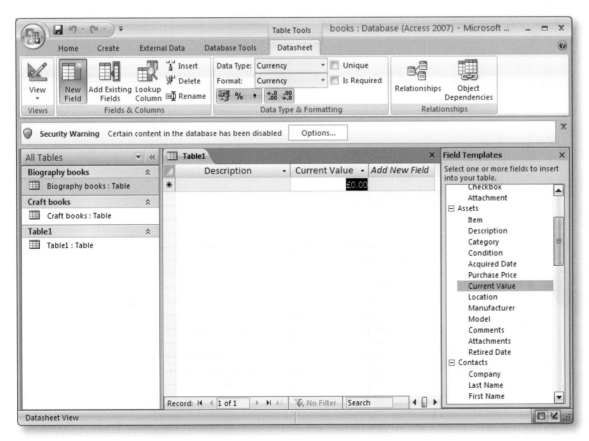

Fig. 3.10 Designing a table in Datasheet view

Closing a table

You can have a database file open with any tables that it contains closed, or with a selected table open on-screen.

close a table

1 Click on the table **Close** button showing a cross.

Or

2 Right-click on the named tab in the main window and select **Close**.

close the file but keep Access open

1 Click on the **Office** button and then click on **Close Database**.

exit Access

1 Click on the database file **Close** button.

Or

2 Click on the **Office** button and click on **Exit Access**.

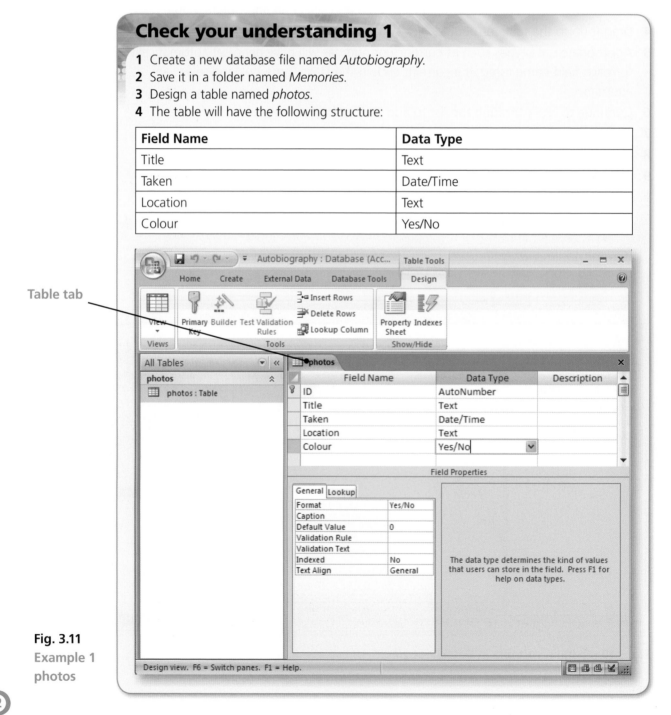

Check your understanding 1

1 Create a new database file named *Autobiography*.
2 Save it in a folder named *Memories*.
3 Design a table named *photos*.
4 The table will have the following structure:

Field Name	Data Type
Title	Text
Taken	Date/Time
Location	Text
Colour	Yes/No

Fig. 3.11

Example 1
photos

3 Maintaining a database

Opening a database file

Either navigate to a named Access file and open it directly, or open Access and then browse for the file.

open a file within Access

1 Click on the **Office** button.
2 Database files you have already created and opened recently will be listed in the **Recent Documents** window. Click on one to open.
3 Otherwise, click on the **Open** button to open the dialog box.
4 Navigate to the folder containing the database file.
5 Select its name and click on **Open**.

Fig. 3.12 Open recent database

Navigating through a table

Database tables can hold thousands of records. As well as scroll bars that will appear to allow you to scroll up and down, you can use the navigation buttons visible at the bottom of the screen.

These show which record is selected at any time, and allow you to move to the first or last record, to the next or previous record and to the first empty record if you want to add new data.

You can also click into the **Current Record** box and type in a number over the entry showing. Press **Enter** to move to that record.

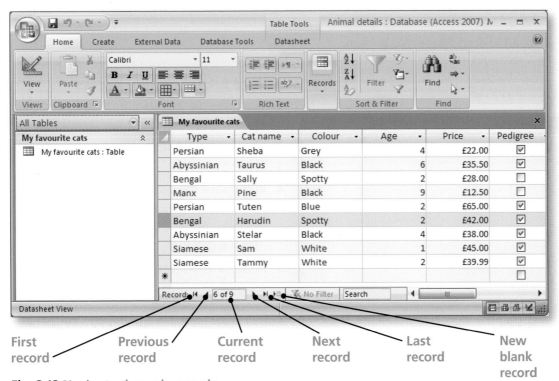

Fig. 3.13 Navigate through records

Saving

You will already have seen that database files are created (**saved**) before any data is added and that you save tables at the time they are created or amended.

To save a copy of the entire database you are working on – for example, as a backup – you can either copy it across between folders on the desktop or open the **Save As:** dialog box and save a copy with an appropriate name. To help identify it clearly, this could include the date the copy was created, a version number and even the word 'backup'.

Fig. 3.14 Select format for backup

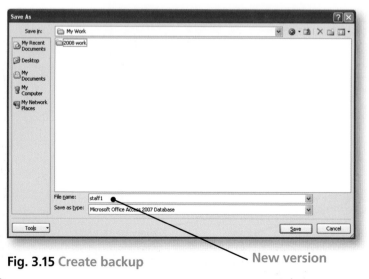

Fig. 3.15 Create backup　　　New version

make a backup within Access

1　Open the file you want to copy, but do not open any tables.

2　Click on the **Office** button.

3　Select **Save As**.

4　In the *Save the database in another format* section, select a suitable file type – for example, Access 2007 or an earlier version of the application.

5　In the Save As window, choose the location in which to store the copy and check that the name is appropriate – for example, add numbers for newer versions.

6　Click on the **Save** button to complete the save.

Entering records

Once the basic table structure has been established, you can add information. In the same way that you enter data into an Excel spreadsheet or Word table, simply click into a cell and start typing. Move across the row to the next cell by pressing the **Tab** key or clicking with the mouse. If your table still has an ID field, you will not be able to type into it as numbers are assigned automatically as you complete the rest of the row.

The structure of a database table encourages efficient design, as only one item of data can be entered into each field. Where possible, it is even more efficient to use codes, for example, H for half, F for full or Q for quarter, as this will simplify keying in and help avoid clerical errors.

Note that databases consist of records – you should not try to enter data down columns but always complete one full row at a time.

You will not be able to add records between those already present. Add a new record at the bottom of the table where an asterisk (*) is displayed.

As is always the case when working with data, accuracy is very important. Don't forget to check your work regularly.

Navigation pane   Named tab

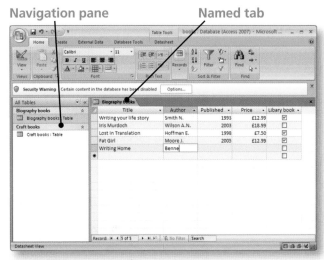

Fig. 3.16 Enter records

add records

1   Open the database file.

2   Double-click on the named table showing in the **All tables** navigation pane or the tab in the main window to open it on screen.

3   If you are entering records into a newly created table, switch to **Datasheet view**.

4   Click under the first field name and enter the details. For Number, Currency or Date data types, the default format will be applied automatically.

5   You will see a pen symbol next to the record you are completing.

6   Move across the row, entering further details. If you use the Tab key, you will be able to type over any entries such as £0.00 that may appear automatically. Otherwise, you may need to delete unwanted characters.

7   A Yes/No field may display a box. Click inside for a Yes tick, and leave empty for a No.

8   You will find that records are saved automatically, so closing the table will retain the data.

amend entries

1   Click on the entry to place the cursor inside the cell and use **Backspace** and **Delete** as normal to amend characters or figures.

2   Move to the cell with the Tab key.
    a Start typing to replace an entry
    b Press the **Delete** key to erase the entire entry.

check records

1   Proofread the data carefully by eye to check for errors that will not be picked up by the built-in spelling or grammar tools.

2   Go to **Records – Spelling** on the Home tab to use the spellchecker. In the window that opens, select alternative spellings when offered or change a misspelt word manually and then click on **Change** to update the table or **Ignore** to check the next word.

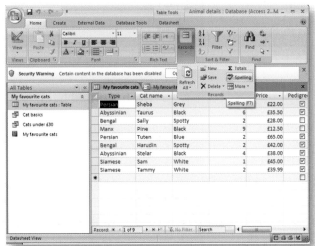

Fig. 3.17 Check spelling

delete records

1 Click on the pale blue square to the left of the record to select the entire row.

2 Press **Delete** on the keyboard.

Or

3 Click on the **Records** command on the Home tab and select **Delete**.

4 You will be warned that you cannot undo this action, so make sure you want to go ahead before clicking on **Yes**.

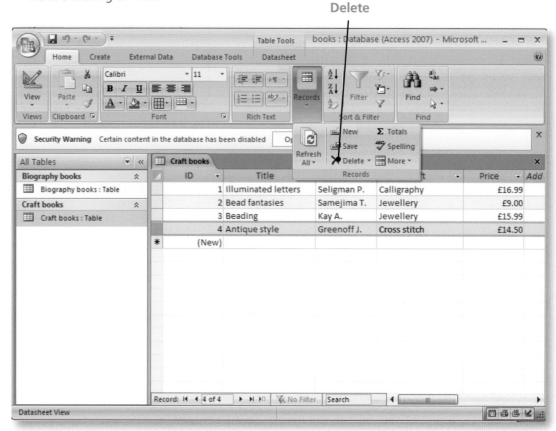

Fig. 3.18 Delete record

Check your understanding 2

1 Open the database file *Cooking* provided on the CD-ROM accompanying this book.

2 Open the *Savoury recipes* table.

3 Add the following two records:

  a **Toad in the Hole, Sausage, 60, £4.50**

  b **Hash, Corned beef, 35, £5.00**

4 Delete the entire record for **Bolognese**.

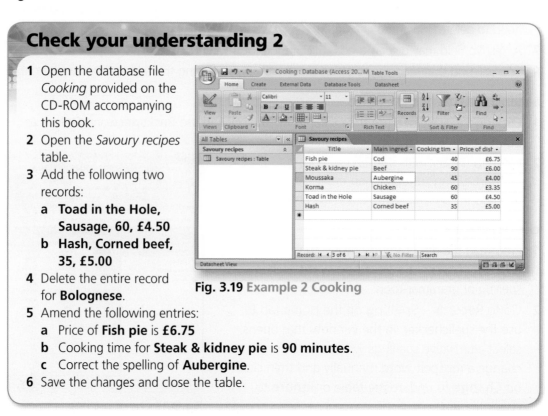

Fig. 3.19 Example 2 Cooking

5 Amend the following entries:

  a Price of **Fish pie** is **£6.75**

  b Cooking time for **Steak & kidney pie** is **90 minutes**.

  c Correct the spelling of **Aubergine**.

6 Save the changes and close the table.

Regional dates

You may notice that, when entering dates, the format is incorrect for your particular region. For example, in the UK the day always precedes the month. You can apply the correct regional settings from the Control Panel.

check regional settings

1 Go to **Start – Control Panel**.
2 Open the **Regional and Language Options** window.
3 If necessary, change the entries in the **Standards** and **Location** boxes by selecting from the drop-down menus.
4 Click on **OK** to save your settings.

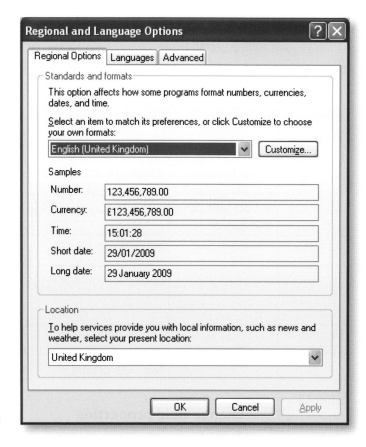

Fig. 3.20 Regional options

Widening columns

As with any table of data, it is likely that the default width of field columns is not enough to display some long entries in full. Widen them in the same way that you widen columns in Excel.

widen a column

1 Position the pointer on the line between field names to the right of the column you want to widen.
2 When the pointer shows a two-way arrow, hold down the **mouse button** and drag the column boundary to the right.
3 The new position will show as a black vertical line.
4 Let go when you reach the correct width.
5 You can also double-click the **mouse** to set the width to the longest entry (see pages 142–3).

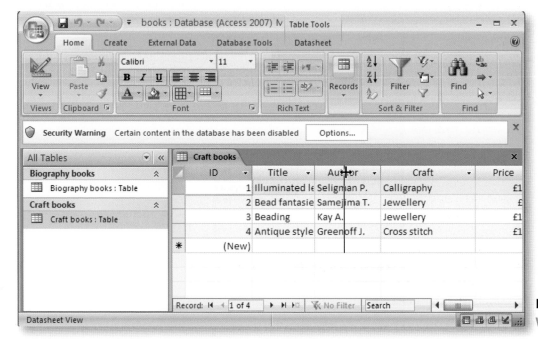

Fig. 3.21 Widen column

Field properties

So far, you will have accepted the default settings for each data type when you created your tables.

It is often necessary to change field properties and this is usually carried out in Design view. The most common properties are shown in the table below.

Data Type	Text	Number	Currency	Date/Time
Field size	Limited to 225 characters and you can reduce this amount to save space	The default is a Long integer, i.e. no decimal places displayed		
Format		You will need to set this to Double to display any decimals	It is set to display £ but you can change this to $ or none	Usually set as long time, e.g. 5:34:23 PM, or short date e.g. 12/11/2008. You can select long or medium, e.g. 12-Nov-2008
Decimal places		Usually none set so you can select the required number	Usually set at 2 but you can select none or 1	

Table 4.1

change field properties

1 Go to **Design view**.
2 In the field name column, click on the field whose properties you want to change.
3 In the Field Properties box, click in the appropriate cell to select from a drop-down list of alternative entries or type in an entry.
4 Repeat with any other fields.

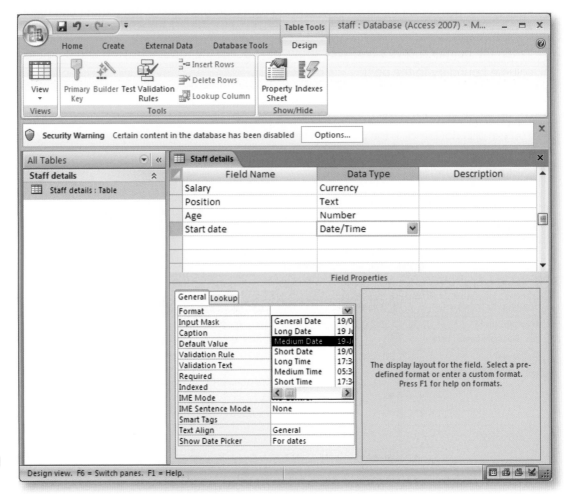

Fig. 3.22

Changing field properties

5 Save the table before returning to **Datasheet view** or closing the file.
Or
6 In Datasheet view, click on the **Format** box below the Data type box to select a different number, currency or date format. There are also shortcut buttons to increase or decrease decimal numbers, add percentage or currency symbols and include a thousand separator.

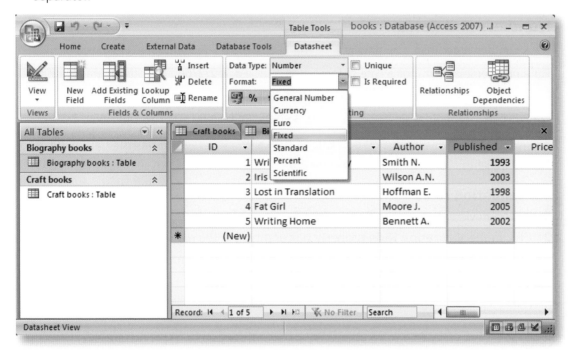

Fig. 3.23 Properties in Datasheet view

Validation rules

To make sure people working with a table only enter appropriate data, you can restrict what is entered by enforcing a **validation rule**. If this is broken, an error message – the validation text – will appear, offering guidance on how to complete the entry correctly.

For example, if your recipes must all be cooked in less than two hours, you can display an error message if anyone tries to enter a cooking time for a recipe that is over 120 minutes.

Validation rules must use acceptable expressions so that they can be interpreted by Access. These include the following:

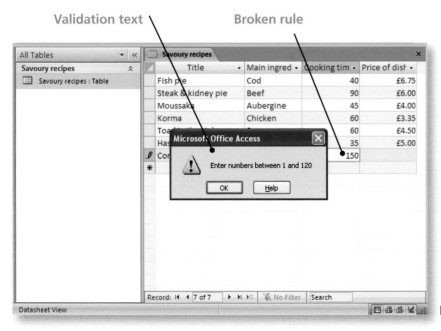

Fig. 3.24 Validation text

Text

For a single entry or range of text entries, put the allowable text between inverted commas.

For example, to allow only London, you would enter **'London'**.

To limit entries to London, Paris or Rome, you would enter **'London' Or 'Paris' Or 'Rome'**. To reject an entry, use <> – for example, **<>London** will reject the entry of London.

Numbers and dates

For a number larger than… or date after… use >   e.g. **>0**   (it cannot be a negative or zero)

For a number less than… or a date before… use <   e.g. **< 2/3/06** (before 2nd March 2006)

For equal to… or less than… use <=   e.g. **<=5**   (it cannot be more than 5)

For equal to… or more than… use >=   e.g. **>= 50**   (it must be 50 or above)

Between two numbers use > And <   e.g. **>3 And <10**   (any number between 3 and 10)

For not equal to… use <>   e.g. **<>20**   (not 20).

set validation rules

1 In Design view, click on the field you want to set the rule for.

2 Click in the **Validation Rule** property box and type in the expression.

3 Click in the **Validation Text** property box and type in the error message users will see if their entry breaks the rule.

4 Return to **Datasheet view** and test that the rule works.

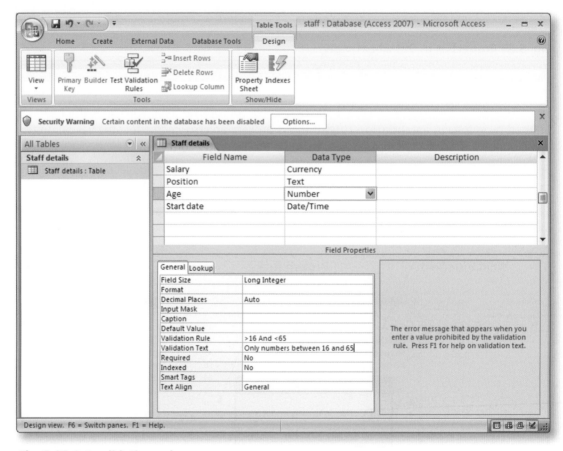

Fig. 3.25 Set validation rule

Check your understanding 3

Note: Validation rules and changing field properties are not on the New CLAiT syllabus. This exercise can be used to stretch your abilities after careful perusal of pages 138–40.

1 Open the file *Autobiography* you created for Check your understanding 1 (or use the file provided on the CD-ROM) and then open the *photos* table.

2 Enter the following records:

Title	Taken	Location	Colour
The Eye	02/10/2007	London	No
Houses of Parliament	14/02/2005	London	Yes
Seaside fun	06/07/2004	Bournemouth	Yes
Storm	11/11/1998	Falmouth	No
Celebrity	02/09/2003	Bristol	Yes
Heaven	15/08/2002	Patisserie Valerie, London	Yes

Fig. 3.26

3 Widen all columns to display the data in full.

4 Change the properties so that the date is displayed as a long date – for example, **2nd October 2007**.

5 Reduce the Field size for **Title** to 100.

6 Set a validation rule to ensure that only dates earlier than 1st January 2008 can be entered.

7 Try entering the following record to check that the rule works:

Title	Taken	Location	Colour
Chocolate	02/04/2008	London	Yes

Fig. 3.27

8 Change the year to **2006**.

9 Save and close the file.

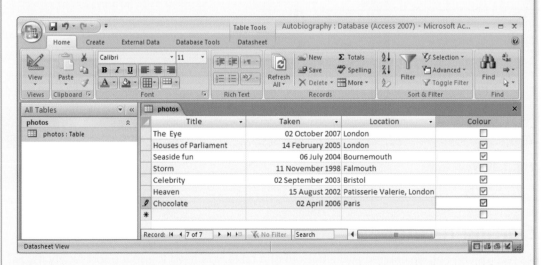

Fig. 3.28 Example 3 field properties

Forms

As well as entering data into a table, you can create an object in Access designed for data entry. This is a **form**. Instead of seeing all the records in your table, you will now only see one record at a time. Move between fields in the record by pressing the **Tab** key and use the Record navigation buttons to move to earlier or later records.

create a form

1 On the Create tab, click on **Form**.
2 A form will appear showing the first record in your table.
3 To add records, click on the **New (Blank) Record** button at the bottom of the screen and start entering the data.
4 Click on the correct tab in the main window to move between the form and the table.

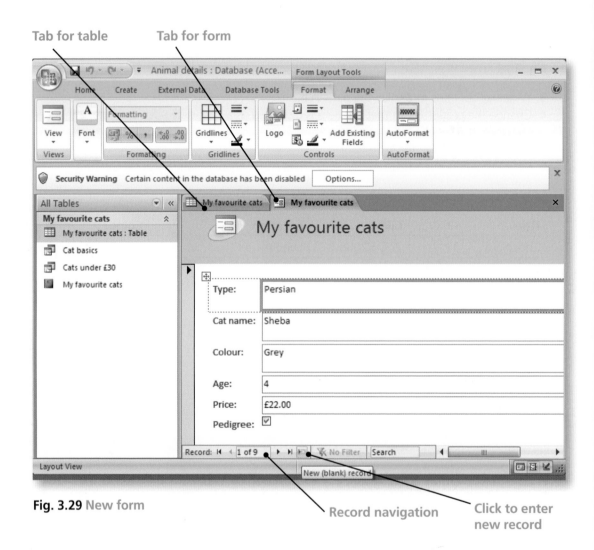

Fig. 3.29 New form

Sorting records

As records can only be entered at the bottom of a table, you need to use the sort facility if you want to rearrange them into a different order.

sort records

1 With the table open in **Datasheet view**, click on one entry in the field on which to base the sort.
2 On the Home tab, click on the **A–Z** button for an alphabetical or ascending order sort – for example, to reorder the records from the smallest to largest number or earliest to latest date.

3 Click on **Z–A** for a sort in descending order.
4 Entire rows will be reordered so that data is not split within a record.
5 If necessary, click on the **Clear All Sorts** button to return to the original order.

Sort in
alphabetical order   Clear sort

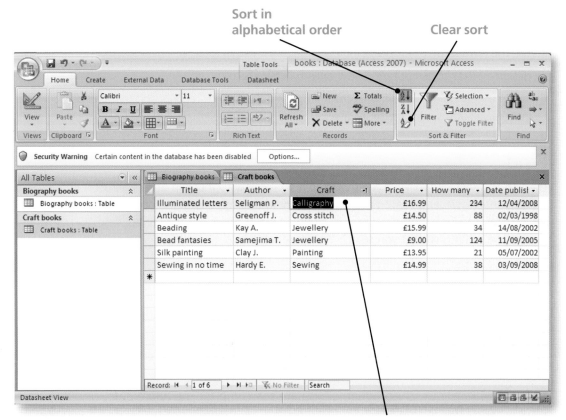

Fig. 3.30 Sort records   Field for the sort

Check your understanding 4

1 Open the database file *books*, provided on the CD-ROM accompanying this book.
2 Open the *Biography books* table.
3 Sort the records in descending order of year published.
4 Now sort the records in ascending order of price.
5 Close the file without saving these changes.

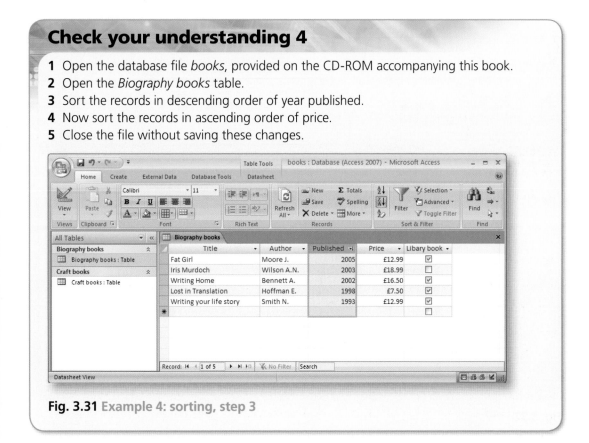

Fig. 3.31 Example 4: sorting, step 3

4 Searching for records

Once your database has been set up, you can search for records that match specific **criteria**. For example, you might want to know which items cost under £2, any places that are within 10 miles of London, or how many people in the database are named Jones.

As a database can contain thousands of records, you need to be able to search it quickly and efficiently. There are three different methods that you can use to locate specific records:

● use the **Find** facilities to locate individual records held in a table

● design a **Filter** to temporarily show only matching records

● create a new object known as a **Query** that will display the records and that can be customised and saved for future use.

Find

The find and replace tools in Access work in a similar way to those in other Microsoft Office applications. However, to save time when searching through a large number of records, they are set by default to look through entries in a single field. If this is not the correct field, you must change the settings so that you search the entire table.

find specific records

1 Click on the **Find** button on the Home tab.

2 Enter the text or numbers you are searching for into the **Find What:** box.

3 Check in the **Look In:** box. If a field is showing that is not the correct field (for example it may have picked up the field where you last left the cursor), select the table name.

4 In the **Match:** box, check whether you are searching for the entire entry or only part of an entry (for example, a figure that has a £ symbol will not be located if you are matching the Whole field).

5 Having found the first record, click on **Find next** to locate further matching records.

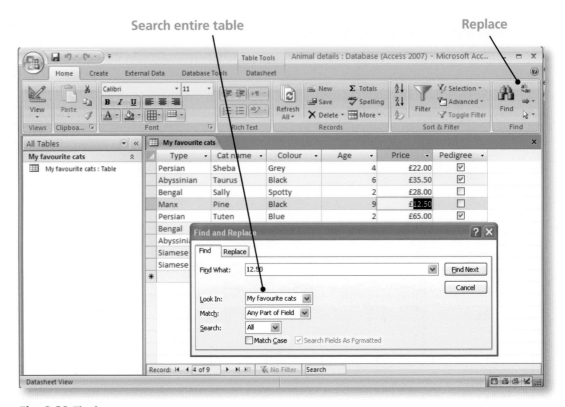

Fig. 3.32 Find

replace entries

1 Click on the **Replace** button.

Or

2 Click on the **Replace** tab if the **Find and Replace** window is open.

3 Type the original entry into the **Find What:** box.

4 Type your replacement entry in the **Replace with:** box.

5 If you are happy to do so, click on **Replace All** and all entries will be changed.

6 Otherwise, click on **Find Next**, check the entry by eye and click on **Replace** to replace the entry or **Find Next** to leave it in place and move on.

To maintain case when replacing, make sure that the box named **Match Case** – on both **Find** and **Replace** tabs – is ticked.

Check your understanding 5

1 Open the database *Jobs*, provided on the CD-ROM accompanying this book.
2 Find the first record for someone starting work in 2007.
3 Find the next record meeting this criterion.
4 Now find details of anyone working in Abingdon.
5 Use the Replace tool to replace **St Mary's** with **St Margaret's**.
6 Save and close the file.

To maintain case when replacing, make sure that the box named Match Case – on both Find and Replace tabs – is ticked.

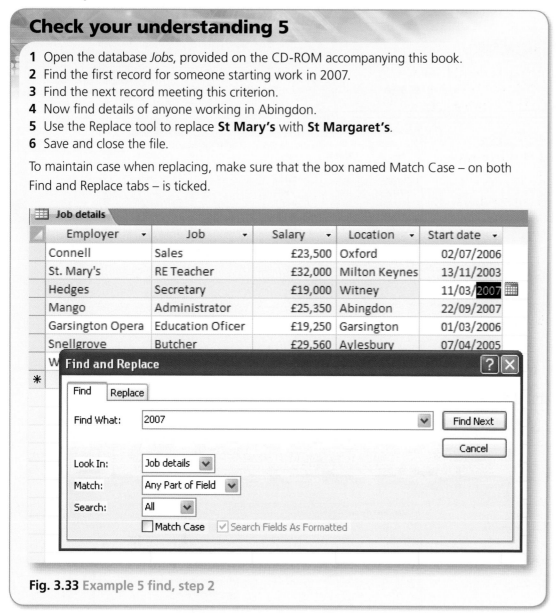

Fig. 3.33 Example 5 find, step 2

Filters

A filter can be applied that will hide any records that do *not* match your criteria, leaving only those records on-screen that match. This subset of the table can be printed and you can then take off the filter and perform a new search, or search through this limited range of records.

Where you have a Yes/No field showing a tick in a box, take care that you do not alter the setting if selecting that particular field.

If you are filtering on one criterion, you can use **Filter by Selection**. For several criteria, you need to **Filter by Form**.

apply a selection filter

1 Click on one example of an entry that matches your criterion.

2 Click on the **Selection** button in the Sort & Filter group.

3 Select from the options available: for example, you can look for records containing or not containing selected text or that equal or are more or less than a particular number.

4 For figures such as prices or dates, if you click on **Between** you will be offered a box and can type in which range to search.

5 All records matching the selected criteria will be displayed and the rest of the table will be hidden.

6 You can now print out the records.

7 To remove the filter and view the entire table, click on the **Toggle Filter** button.

8 You can also click on the **Filter** button for a range of sorting options and to clear the filter.

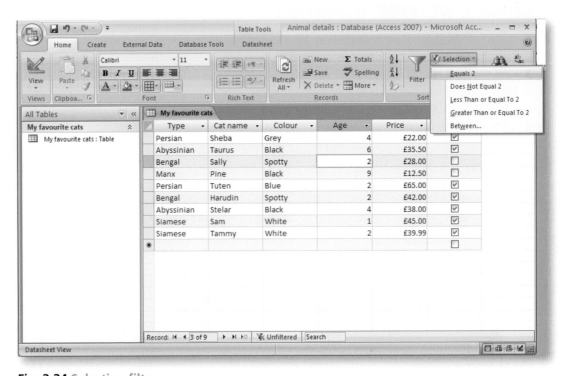

Fig. 3.34 Selection filter

Fig. 3.35 Clear filter

Check your understanding 6

1 Open the file *Sports*, provided on the CD-ROM accompanying this book.
2 Use a filter to display only those records for members joining between 1 July 2007 and 30 March 2008.
3 Remove the filter.
4 Use a new filter to find records for all female members. (You should find only three.)
5 Close the file.

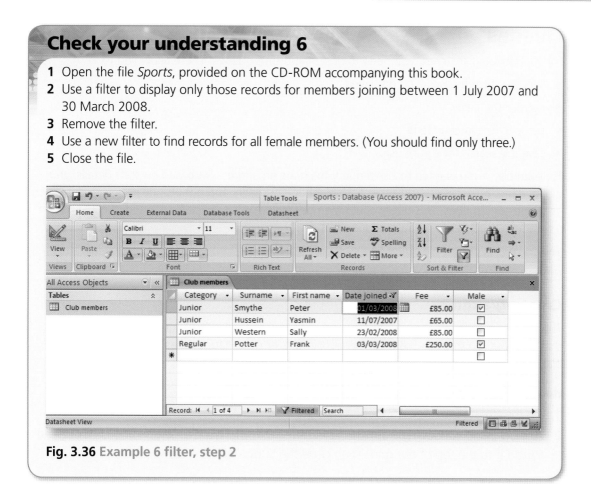

Fig. 3.36 Example 6 filter, step 2

filter by form

1 In the Sort and Filter section, click on **Advanced – Filter by Form**.
2 You will see all your field names and an empty row for your entries.
3 For each criterion, click in the relevant field box and either select an entry from the drop-down list or type in an expression such as > (greater than) or <> (not equal to). (See page 140 for a list of acceptable expressions in validation rules.)
4 Check the form carefully – for example, make sure a previous criterion has not been left as set by mistake – and then click on **Toggle Filter**.
5 Matching records should be found.
6 Take off the filter by clicking on the **Toggle** button again.

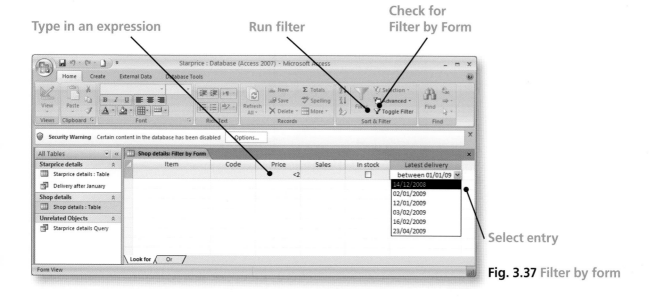

Fig. 3.37 Filter by form

Queries

For sophisticated searches, you need to design and save queries. These allow you to:

- specify which fields will be displayed
- reorder the fields
- set specific search criteria
- save the search for future use.

For example, if you wanted to use a query to create an address list based on staff details, you would select only names, addresses and telephone numbers and not include irrelevant data such as salaries or job titles. This query could then be saved so that, as staff changed, it could be run regularly to produce up-to-date address lists.

You could also design the query so that it only included staff who had joined in the last five years.

Creating a query

There are two different ways to create a simple query in Access 2007: use the **Query Wizard** that will take you through the process step by step, or go to **Query Design** and start with a blank grid.

design a query using the grid

1 On the Create tab, click on **Query Design**.
2 A Show Table window will appear. Select the table you want to search and click on **Add** to add it to the top of the grid. Then close the Show Table window.

Selected table to search

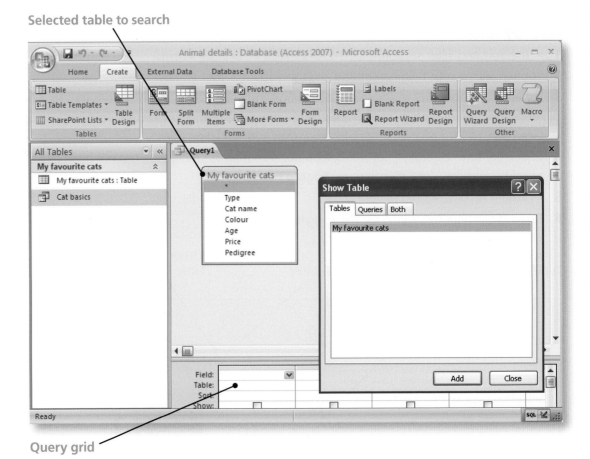

Query grid

Fig. 3.38 Show Table window

3 The table will display a list of all the fields it contains. You can now select which fields to be displayed each time you run your query. There are three ways to do this:

   a Double-click on a field name to add it to the grid.

   b Click on and drag each field name onto the Field row of the grid.

   c Click in the Field row cell and select the field name from the drop-down list.

Note that the table name will be added to the grid automatically. This is useful when searching across a number of different tables.

Running the query

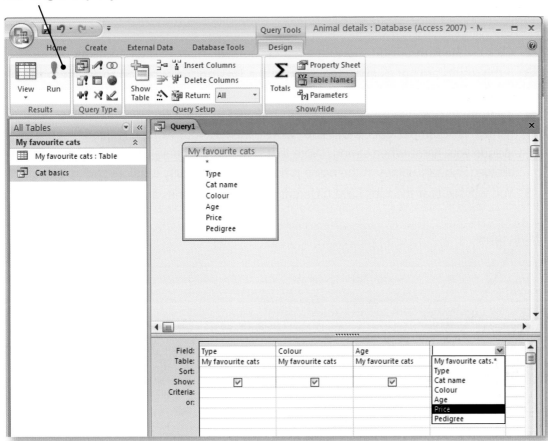

Fig. 3.39 Adding fields to query grid

4 Now set the search criteria for the relevant fields, using acceptable expressions and no formatting. For example:

   a To find only those cats costing less than £30, you would enter the expression **<30** in the Criteria row for the Price field.

   b To find only black cats, you would enter **black** in the Criteria row for the Colour field.

   c Where there is a Yes/No box displayed in the table, enter the text **Yes** or **No** in the Criteria row.

   d For dates, use **>** or **<** and enter the last day in December or first day in January to find earlier or later *years* – for example, <1/1/07 would find any dates earlier than 2007.

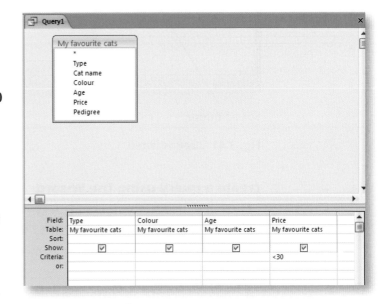

Fig. 3.40 Criteria for query

5 Access adds quote marks round text, # symbols round dates and nothing round numbers when you click on another cell in the grid.

6 At this stage, you could set a sort order for the resultant records by clicking in the **Sort** row for the appropriate field and selecting **ascending** or **descending**.

Running a query

To check that the correct records have been found, you need to run the query. This reveals all the matching records displayed in the order of the selected fields.

run a query

1 Click on the **Datasheet view** button.

Or

2 Click on the **Run** button showing a red exclamation mark in the Results group.

3 If the results are not as expected, click on the **Design view** button to return to the grid and check the criteria you have used.

4 If you try to close the query, you will be reminded to save it first with a suitable name – for example, *Cats under £30*. To help identify your work, it is good practice to include your name when saving. (Note that some punctuation, such as a full stop, is not allowed in query names. If the name is not accepted, simplify it before saving again.)

5 You will see that the tabs have different symbols for queries and tables.

Main table

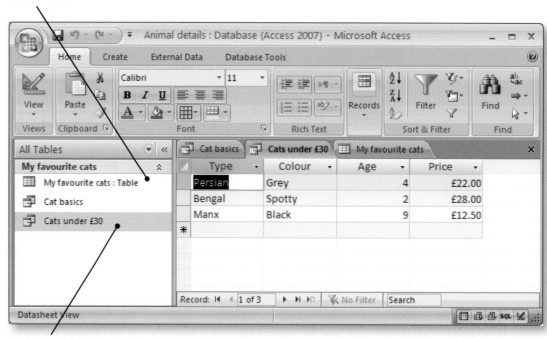

Fig. 3.41 Queries listed

create a query using the Wizard

1 On the Create tab, click on **Query Wizard**.

2 In the first window, click on **OK** to select the Simple Query Wizard.

3 In the next window, select the named table you are going to search in the Table/Query box.

4 Click on the first field you want to search or display when the query is run and click on the **Add** button to add it to the Selected Fields window.

5 Repeat with other fields in turn.
6 To add all the fields in the table, click on the double-arrow **Add** button.
7 To remove any unwanted field added by mistake, select them and click on the **Remove** button.

Table to be searched

Add field

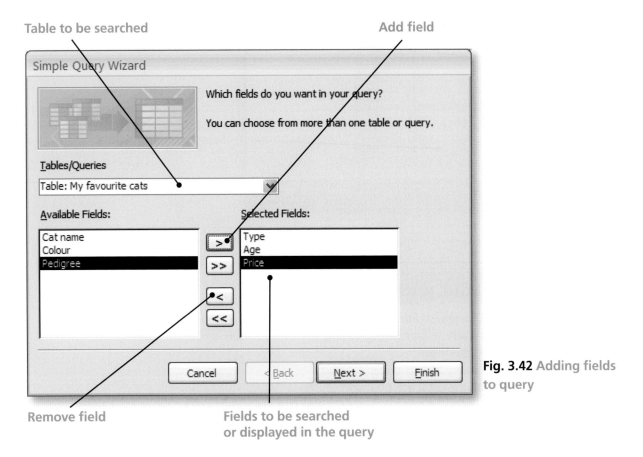

Fig. 3.42 Adding fields to query

Remove field

Fields to be searched or displayed in the query

8 Click on **Next** to move through the steps.
9 Unless you are going to perform calculations, leave the Detail option selected.
10 Name the query and click to open and view its contents.
11 If you want to add search criteria, click to modify it in Design view or go to this view later.
12 Click on **Finish**. You will see all the records that have been located and only the data held in the fields you chose to display.

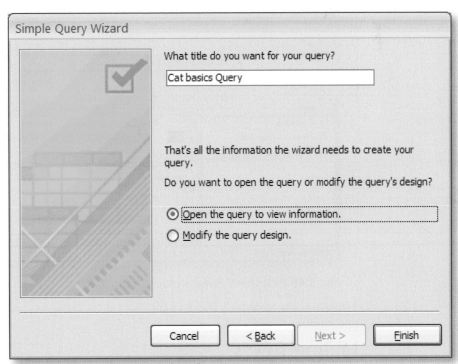

Fig. 3.43 Finished Query Wizard

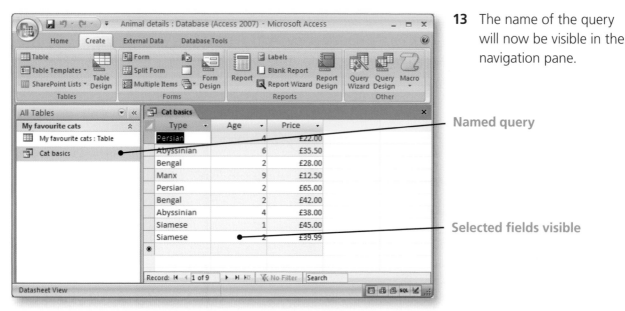

13 The name of the query will now be visible in the navigation pane.

Named query

Selected fields visible

Fig. 3.44 Query name in pane

Check your understanding 7

1 Open the database *Jobs*, provided on the CD-ROM accompanying this book.
2 Design a query to find all jobs paying less than £25000.
3 Display all the fields.
4 Save the query as *Jobs under £25000*.
5 Now open the database *Courses*.
6 Design a query to find any courses beginning in July with places for ten or more people.
7 Display *only* the Sport type, Start date and Number of places.
8 Save as *Sports places*.

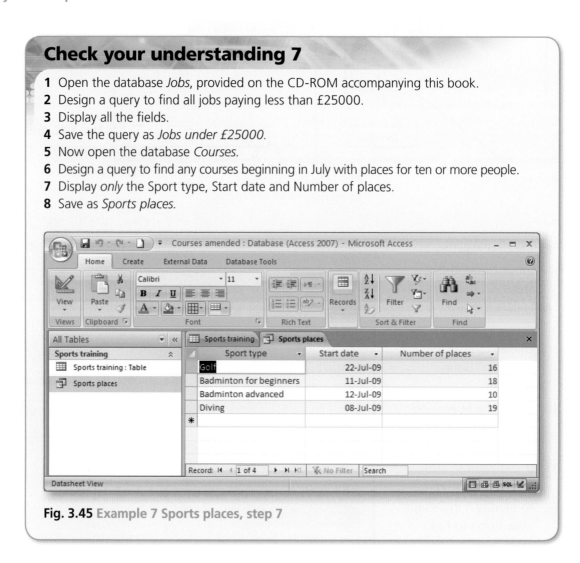

Fig. 3.45 Example 7 Sports places, step 7

Hiding fields

To carry out a search, you must include the search field in the query grid so that you can add the relevant criteria. However, if you don't want that field displayed when the query is run, you can hide the field in Design view.

hide a field

1 Design the query in the normal way, including the search field in the grid.
2 Run the query to check that the correct records have been found.
3 Return to Design view and take off the tick in the Show box.
4 Now run the query again and you will see that the same records are displayed but they no longer include the hidden field.

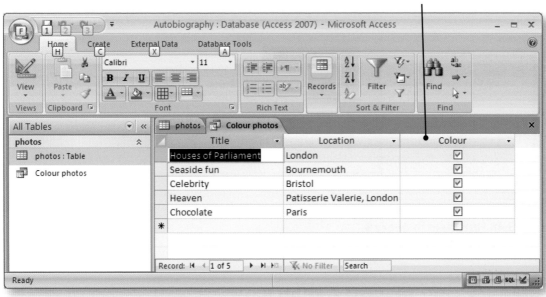

Fig. 3.46 Hide field in query 1

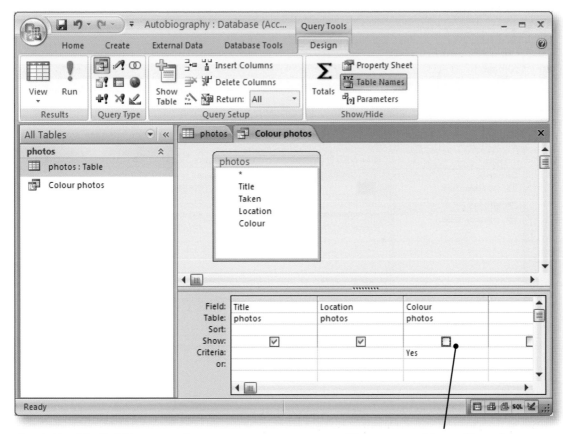

Fig. 3.47 Hide field in query 2

Colour field no
longer visible

Fig. 3.48 Hide field in query 3

Check your understanding 8

1 Open the *Jobs* database on the CD-ROM.
2 Design a query to find any jobs started after 2005. Display *only* the Job, Employer, Salary and Location fields.
3 Save as *After 2005*.

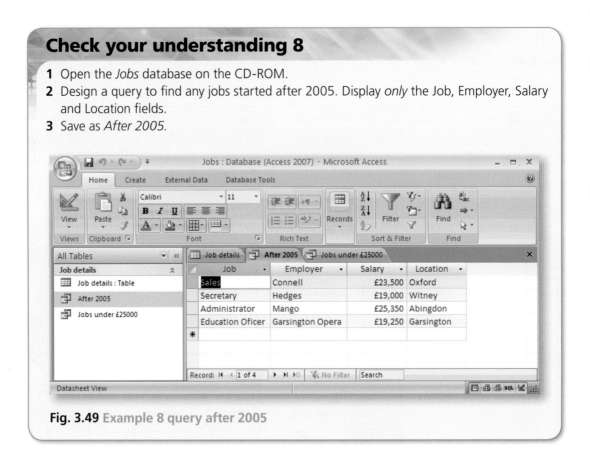

Fig. 3.49 Example 8 query after 2005

Reports

As well as printing out records in the form of a basic table or query, Access offers the option to create new objects known as reports. These can be based on either a table or a query and can display all or a selected range of fields. In Access 2007 they are created in the form of a table where you can select any column or row to format as you like.

Certain entries may appear automatically (for example, totals for columns of numerical data) but these can be deleted just like any table entry, and you can also use the database tools to carry out your own calculations such as totalling or averaging a range of figures.

You can use the wizard to create your report in steps or you can allow Access to create a basic report automatically.

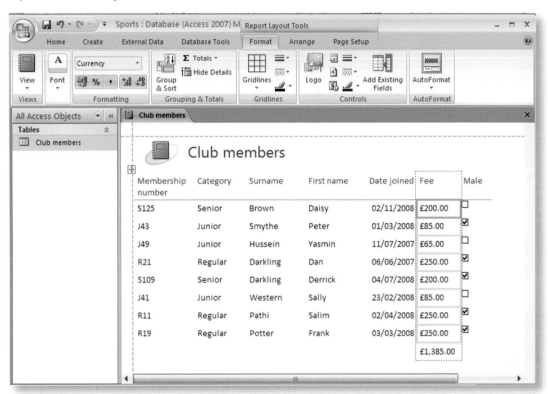

Fig. 3.50 A report

produce a quick report

1 Open the table or query or create a new query on which to base the report.

2 On the Create tab, click on **Report**. (For more control over the design, click on **Report Wizard** and follow the steps, which are very similar to the Query Wizard.)

Fig. 3.51 Create tab with Report button — Report button

3 A new report will appear and the **Report Layout Tools** commands will be available.

4 Click on any field name or title to change the entry.

5 If the report is too wide, click on any heading or column of data to drag in the column boundary. You could also apply new formatting such as realigning headings or decreasing font sizes to reduce the size of the overall report.

6 Click on any numeric fields and use options on the **AutoSum** button to remove an unwanted total (by taking off the tick next to its name) or carry out a different calculation.

7 Click on any entry and press **Delete** or right-click for the delete option to remove unwanted items such as a logo, header or footer text.

8 Select the entire table and add gridlines or borders by selecting one of the styles available.

9 Click on **Auto Format** to select from a range of ready-made report styles.

10 When you try to close, you will be asked to save the report. Type in a new name or it will have the same name as the table/query on which it is based. Its name will appear on a new tab showing the green report icon. To edit the title once it has been set and saved, you can single-click on the report in its save location, and overwrite with the new title.

Note: To return to Layout view after the report has been closed, right-click the tab in the navigation pane or select the option from the drop-down arrow below the View button.

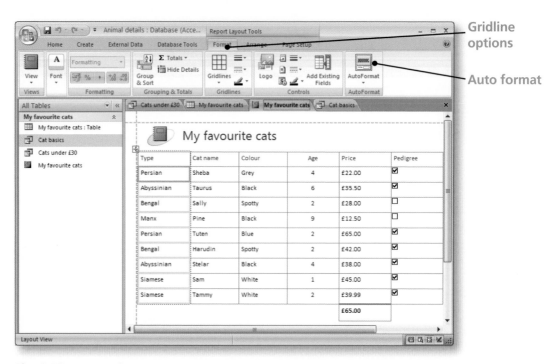

Fig. 3.52 Layout view

Fig. 3.53 Different report views

Check your understanding 9

1 Open the database *Courses*, provided on the CD-ROM accompanying this book.
2 Create a report based on all the records in the *Sports training* table.
3 Remove the total at the bottom of the Price column.
4 Make the heading title text bold.
5 Save as *Sports Training Report*.

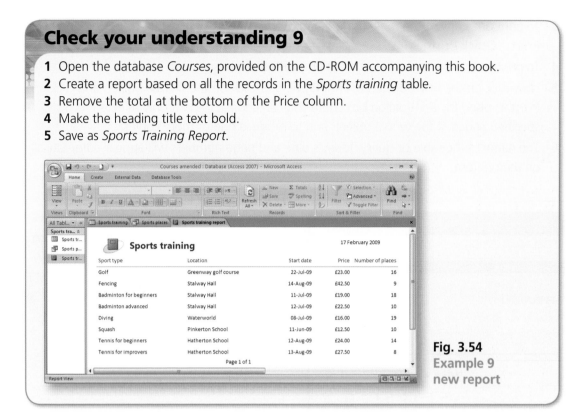

Fig. 3.54
Example 9
new report

5 Printing

You can print out the details for any object that has been created, including tables, filtered tables, queries and reports. All objects will print in portrait orientation by default.

print a table or query

1 Open the table in Datasheet view.
2 It is a good idea to check first in Print Preview that all records are displayed in full. To do this click on the **Office** button and go to **Print – Print Preview**.

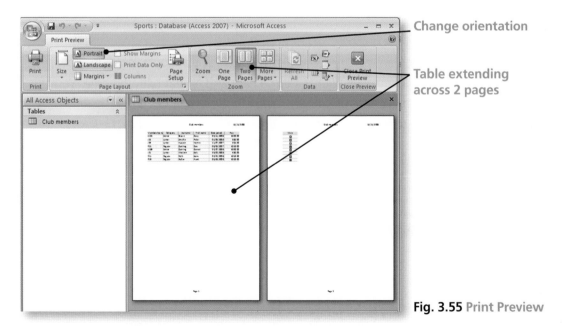

Change orientation

Table extending
across 2 pages

Fig. 3.55 Print Preview

a Zoom in to see more detail by clicking in the bottom right-hand corner to increase magnification.

b Check if you will need to widen any columns.

c Change to **Landscape** orientation if some field names are missing and the table extends across more than one page.

3 To print one copy of the table using default settings, click on the **Office** button and go to **Print – Quick Print**.

4 To print selected records, select them first with the mouse.

5 Now click on the **Print** button in Print Preview or click on the **Office** button and click on **Print** to open the Print dialog box. Here you can choose to print only selected records, specified pages or the whole object, and to produce one or more copies.

6 The name of the table or query, today's date and page numbers will appear automatically on the printout.

What to print   Number of copies

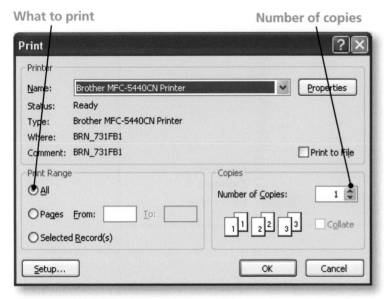

Fig. 3.56 Print dialog box

By default, Access normally adds the date and time as the Report Header and the page numbers as the Page Footer.

If you notice in Print Preview that items are missing, you can add them in Design view. They will appear in code and the header or footer area will be expanded so that they fit.

add items

1 Click on the **Design view** button.

2 On the Design tab, click on the **Date and Time** button in the Controls group.

3 In the window that opens, select your preferred date and repeat with the time. You can also take off the tick in the date or time checkbox to remove either entry.

4 Click on **OK** and you will see a small box with the code **=Date()** added to the Report header.

print a report

1 Right-click, then click on the drop-down arrow below the View button or click on the **Office** button to go to Print Preview.

2 Complete the checks as above and print in the same way.

Report headers and footers

Reports in Access can have two headers and footers:

● Report Header and Footer – added to the beginning and ending of the report in the top and bottom margins

● Page Header and Footer – entries at the top and bottom of each page.

5 For page numbers, click on the **Page Numbers** button, select your preferred style and position and click on **OK**.

6 The code for page numbers will appear in the Page Footer section. It may appear as **='Page' & [Page]** or longer for an entry showing the page plus the complete number of pages in the report.

Note that in Design view you can select any box and drag it to a different area – for example, if you want to change the position for the page numbers. You can also edit any entries such as the Report or Field Name titles by clicking in the boxes and amending the text.

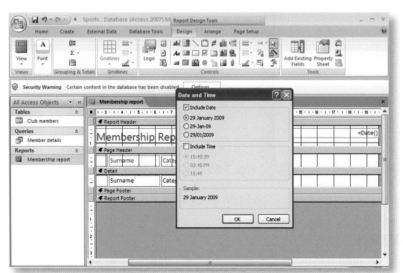

Fig. 3.57 Date and time

Check your understanding 10

1 Open the database file *Sports*, provided on the CD-ROM accompanying this book.

2 Create a query to produce a list of all members showing just their first name, surname, category and date of joining.

3 Save as *Member details*.

4 Create a report based on this query.

5 Save it as *Membership Report*.

6 Print one copy of the report in portrait orientation to fit on one page.

7 Now reopen the *Club Members* table and print only the first five records. Make sure all details are fully displayed.

8 Close the file.

Fig. 3.58 Example 10 report

Fig. 3.59 Example 10 print selected records

CLAiT Assignment

TASK 1

1 Open the database file *Shopping*, provided on the CD-ROM accompanying this book.

2 Open the table *Starprice details* and rename it *Star prices*.

3 Print a copy of all the records (Figure 3.60).

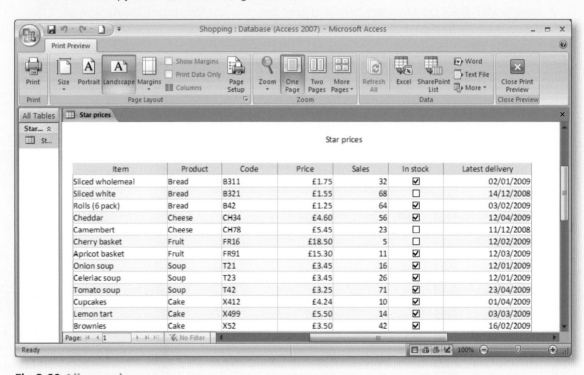

Fig 3.60 All records

4 Add the following three items:

   a Madeira, Cake, X99, £6.45, 12, In stock, 11/2/09
   b Vegetable soup, Soup, T54, £3.75, 46, Not in stock, 12/1/09
   c Pitta, Bread, B67, £9.99, 28, In stock, 14/3/09

5 Make the following amendments to the data:

   a Celeriac soup should be Celery soup.
   b The price of Sliced white is £1.85.
   c Only **9** apricot baskets were sold.
   d Delivery of Tomato soup was 28th April 2009.

6 You want to use codes for the products. **Use Replace to** change all entries as follows:

   a Bread becomes B
   b Cheese becomes Ch
   c Cake becomes Ca
   d Soup becomes T
   e Fruit becomes Fr

7 Delete the record for Onion soup as this has been discontinued.

8 Save the table.

9 Change to **landscape** orientation and print out the updated records, making sure all entries are displayed in full (Figure 3.61).

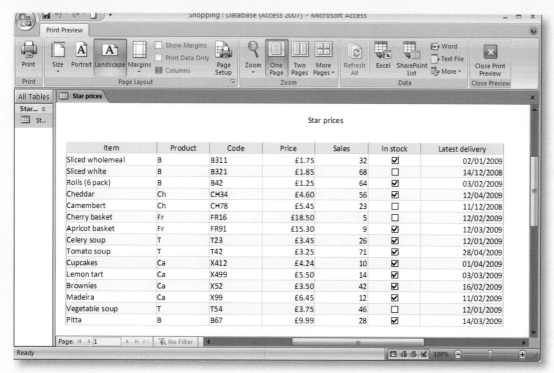

Fig 3.61 Updated

TASK 2

1 Set up a query to find all records of items selling 28 or more that are In stock. Display only the Item, Price and Sales.

2 Sort in descending order of Price and save as *Good sales in stock*. Print a copy of the records (Figure 3.62).

3 Create a report based on this query and name it *Good Sales*.

4 Make sure the date and page number are displayed on the printout and print a copy in **portrait** orientation (Figure 3.63).

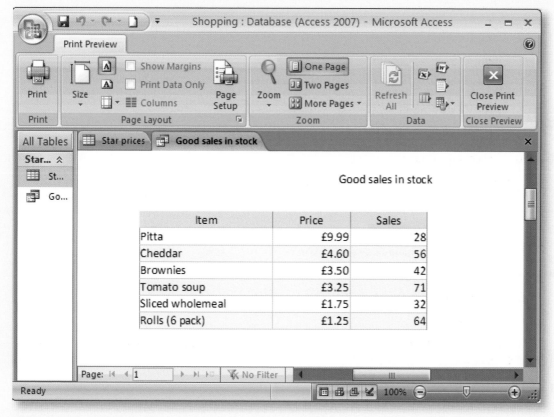

Fig 3.62 Good sales query

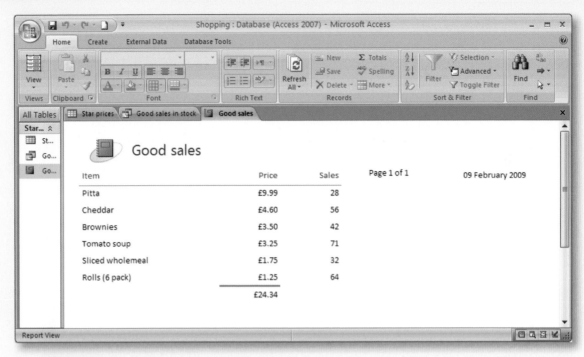

Fig 3.63 Report

TASK 3

1 Design a query to locate all items that were delivered before February 2009.

2 Display only the Item, Code, Price, Sales and Latest delivery.

3 Sort the records in ascending order of delivery date.

4 Print a copy of the records (Figure 3.64).

5 Finally, search for any items costing £5.50 or more that sold more than six.

6 Display only the Item, Product and Price and sort in alphabetical order of Item name.

7 Save the query with the name *Sales higher than 6* and print a copy of the records (Figure 3.65).

8 Close the file.

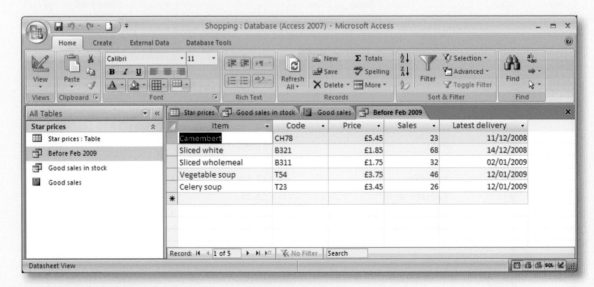

Fig 3.64 Before Feb

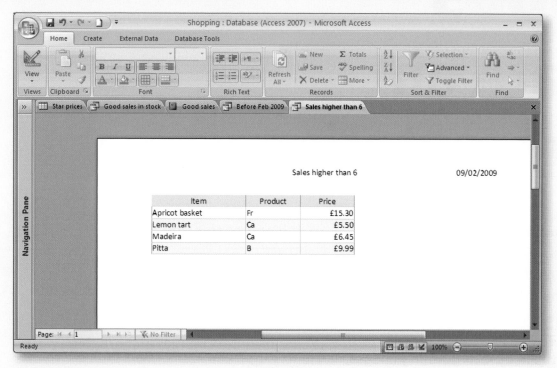

Fig 3.65 Sales higher than 6

Create an e-presentation

Applications such as PowerPoint 2007 are ideal for talks and presentations as they enable you to produce professional-looking slides to accompany your talk and even run a slide show automatically. As well as all the basic features, you can bring your presentations to life by incorporating images, sounds or movement, adding coloured or patterned backgrounds, applying whole colour schemes, animating objects or including extra information in the form of tables or charts. Slides can be printed out or you can run the slide show on a computer.

At the end of this unit you will be able to:

⊕ set up a presentation accurately

⊕ input and format data in presentation software

⊕ import/insert images and graphics correctly

⊕ save and print the presentation.

1 PowerPoint basic features

Opening PowerPoint

launch the application

1 Click on an icon if it is available on the desktop or **Start** menu.

Or

2 Go to **Start – All Programs** and click on **Microsoft PowerPoint**.

Opening a previously saved presentation

You use the same process to open presentations as any other Microsoft Office files.

Fig. 5.1 Launch PowerPoint

open a presentation

1 Click on the **Office** button.
2 If a recently opened file is listed in the Recent Documents area, click on its name to open.
3 Otherwise click on **Open** or press **Ctrl + O**.
4 Navigate to the folder location where the file has been stored.
5 Click on the filename in the main window.
6 Click on **Open**.

Working with slides

When the program opens, you will be in **Normal view**. In this view, you are presented with a single slide in the main part of the screen that is ready for text entry, together with two smaller panes – a **Slide pane** on the left that shows a thumbnail version of each slide, and a **Notes pane** where you can add speaker's notes.

The Slide pane alternates with a different pane, the **Outline pane**. This shows just the textual content of a slide.

The slide has areas set out ready for text entry that you can type into or ignore/delete. These are basically text boxes but are known as **placeholders**. In PowerPoint you will also find slides offering placeholders ready for columns of text or for inserting other content such as images, charts, diagrams or media clips.

Go to Open dialog box

Click to open listed file

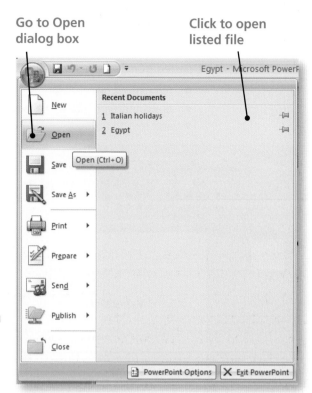

Fig. 5.2 Open a file

edit a placeholder

1 Click on any text to reveal a hidden placeholder border.
2 Click on the border to select the box.
3 Drag it to a different position on the slide if you want your text in a different place.
4 Press the **Delete** key to remove an unwanted placeholder.

Outline pane

Thumbnail of current slide on Slide pane

Text placeholder

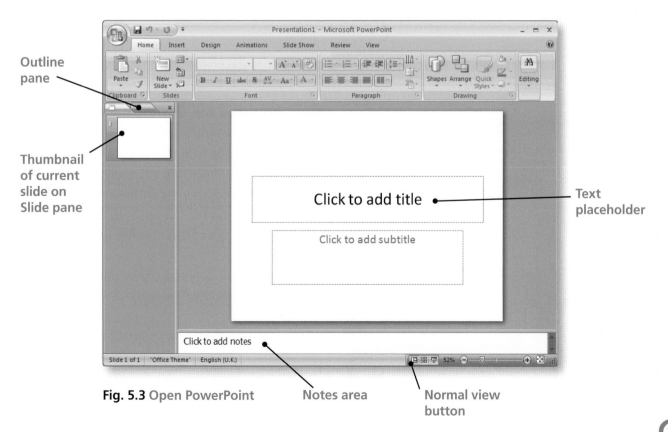

Fig. 5.3 Open PowerPoint   Notes area   Normal view button

Adding text

There are three ways you can add text to a slide, which can be typed in directly or copied and pasted from elsewhere:

- type into a placeholder
- draw and type into a text box
- add text to a shape.

Fig. 5.4 Enter text

When using a text box, use the **Shape Outline** and **Fill colour** options if you want to add or remove a visible border or add a coloured background to the words. Full details of how to do this can be found in 'Working with shapes' on page 173.

add text to a placeholder

1   Click on the placeholder to place the cursor inside the marked area.
2   Start typing in the normal way.
3   Press **Enter** to type more text on a new line.
4   Click outside the placeholder to confirm the entry.
5   The font type and size will have been set for that particular entry, but you can override the default settings using normal formatting tools.
6   As you type, the text will also appear on the thumbnail showing in the Slide pane.

Using the outline pane

As well as entering text directly onto a slide, you can also type it in as outline text.

PowerPoint makes use of *levels* of text. The top level of text on a slide is the **Title level** text, and then it moves down to **Subtitle level** text and so on. You would usually have between two and five levels of text on any slide.

Having typed text at one level, you need to *demote* the text to move down a level and *promote* it to move back up again

To demote text, press the **Tab** key on the keyboard or click on the **Increase List** (Indent) button on the Home tab. To promote up a level, hold **Shift** as you press the **Tab** key or click on the **Decrease List** (Indent) button.

Outline pane

Fig. 5.5 Increase List

enter text using the Outline pane

1   Click on the **Outline** tab.
2   Click next to Slide 1 on the pane.
3   Start typing your text. This will form the top level text. You will see it appear on the main slide at the same time.
4   Press **Enter** to start typing the top level text for the next slide.
5   To type the next level text on the *same* slide, press **Tab** or **Increase List**. This demotes the line of text down a level.
6   Press **Enter** to add a new entry at the same level, or demote or promote it to change levels.
7   When creating slides that have been set up to offer bulleted lists, each lower level of text will be indented and have a different bullet style.

add text using text boxes

1 Click on the **Text Box** button on the Insert tab.
2 Click on-screen or draw out a box of preferred dimensions.
3 Let go of the mouse and start typing inside the box where the cursor is flashing.
4 The text you type into a text box will *not* be visible on the Outline pane as it is interpreted as an object and not as normal text.

format text

1 Select individual words with the mouse, or click on any text to view the placeholder border.
2 Select the entire contents of a placeholder to format by clicking on the border.
3 Apply an alternative font type or add emphasis such as

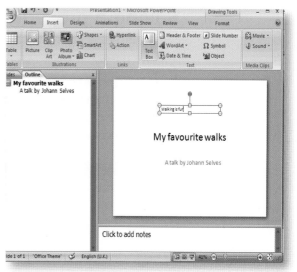

Fig. 5.6 Text Box text entry

bold, italic or underline, or colour the text from options on the Home tab. See Unit 1 for more information on formatting text.
4 Note that to apply a font size not offered from the drop-down list, type in the size and press the **Enter** key to confirm the choice.
5 You can also click on the **Increase** or **Decrease Font size** button to step through font sizes. Alignment is covered in detail on page 44.

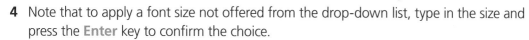

Fig. 5.7 Format text   Emphasis   Increase or Decrease font size in steps

edit text

1 Select any text and use **Delete** and **Backspace** to erase unwanted characters.
2 Click on-screen and start typing to add extra text.

For more information on editing text, see page 62.
Find and replace are explained in detail on p68–9.

Checking entries

As with any work, it is important to proofread and check for meaning as well as correct any spelling or grammatical errors.

spellcheck

1 For a single error, right-click on any red underlined word and select from alternative spellings that may be offered.
2 To check the whole presentation, click on the **Spelling** button on the Review tab.
3 In the Spelling window, click on **Ignore/Ignore All** to retain a spelling that is correct.
4 Click on a suggested alternative or manually change a misspelt word in the **Change to:** box and click on **Change/Change All** to update the slides.
5 Click on **Close** to return to your presentation.

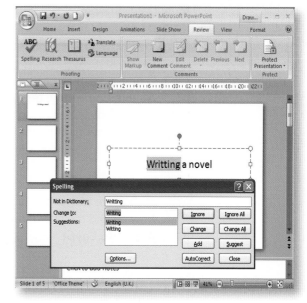

Fig. 5.8 Spell check

Saving a presentation

Presentations can include slides, handout material, notes pages or an outline of your talk. When you save the file, all these objects are saved together at the same time.

If you have created a particular style of presentation involving a number of changes and additions that you will want to use in the future, you can save time by creating a PowerPoint template. Select this option when you select the type of file to save. It will be saved with other templates and so you must look for template file types when you want to open it again.

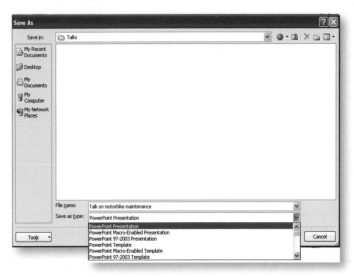

Fig. 5.9 Saving

save a presentation

1 Click on the **Save** button or go to **Office button – Save**. Or

2 Hold **Ctrl** and press **S**.

3 Select a suitable location in which to save the file.

4 If necessary, change the file type.

5 Give the presentation a filename.

6 Click on the **Save** button.

Closing

close a presentation

1 Click on the **Close** button in the top right-hand corner.

2 Click on the **Office** button and select **Close**.

exit PowerPoint

1 Close the only presentation open.

2 Click on the **Office** button and select **Exit PowerPoint**.

Check your understanding 1

1 Launch PowerPoint.

2 On the slide that appears, enter the following title text: **Visiting Egypt**.

3 Enter the following as a subtitle: **An evening of mystery**.

4 Apply a bold emphasis to the title and change the font to Arial Black or a similar solid font.

5 Underline the subtitle and change the text colour to red.

6 Now amend the title to read: **A Visit to Egypt**.

7 Check for and correct any errors.

8 Save as *Egypt* and close the file.

Fig. 5.10 Example 1 Egypt

Slide layout

Each slide that you add to a presentation, or the initial slide provided when you start a new file, will be set out in a standard way. The first slide will be a **Title** slide and will have two placeholders for title and subtitle. All other slides will be different forms of Title and **Content** slides displaying a title placeholder at the top and large placeholder for the main text and/or added objects.

To display your slide contents in different ways, you can apply a different layout selected from the range of styles available within PowerPoint.

change slide layout

1 Display the slide you want to change.

2 On the Home tab, click on the **Layout** button.

Or

3 Right-click on the slide in the Slide pane and select **Layout**.

4 Select a different layout by clicking on the sample.

5 Your slide will now display the new layout.

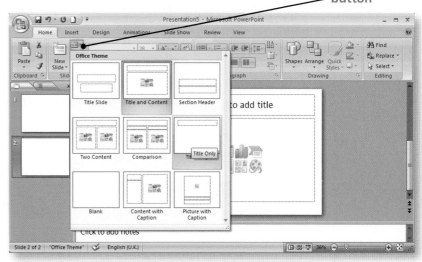

Slide layout button

Fig. 5.11 Change slide layout

Bullet points

As you type into some placeholders, bullets will be added automatically. You can remove unwanted bullets or add them where needed. Each level of text has its own bullet style applied automatically. Numbering works in exactly the same way as bullets so you can number list items instead.

work with bullets

1 Select one line, or all list items.

2 Click on the **Bullets** button on the Home tab to add bullets.

3 Click on the highlighted **Bullets** button to remove bullets.

4 Click on the drop-down arrow next to the button to select alternative styles of bullet.

5 If you change text level within a list, each level will have a different style of bullet applied by default. It will also be indented.

   a To go down a level, press the **Tab** key.

   b To go up, hold **Shift** as you press **Tab**.

Bullets button   Numbering

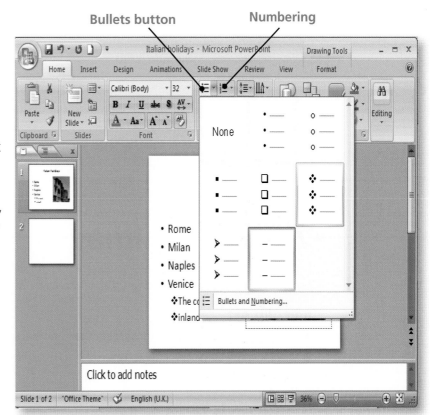

Fig. 5.12 Add bullets

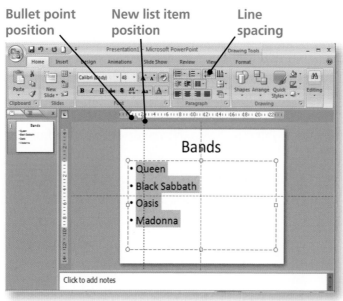

Bullet point position **New list item position** **Line spacing**

Fig. 5.13 Change list indent

6 Sometimes the bullet points or list items will be in the wrong place on the slide – for example, the text may be too close to the bullet. Change the position by dragging the bullet point or text insertion point along the ruler with the mouse. A dotted line will show the new position.

7 To increase spaces between entries in a list, apply different line spacing.

Check your understanding 2

1 Open the file *Italian Holidays* provided provided on the CD-ROM accompanying this book.

2 Click on Slide 2 on the Slide tab to open the slide on-screen.

3 On this slide, change the top-level bullet points to a different style.

4 Remove bullet points for the two items under **Venice**.

5 Add a new entry, Pisa, after Inland at the same level as the other cities. Make sure it has an appropriate bullet.

6 Click on Slide 1.

7 Change the layout for this slide to a Title slide.

8 Add the title: **Holidays Abroad**.

9 Add the subtitle: **A talk by (add your name)**.

10 Format the title text to font size 54.

11 Format the subtitle text to italic.

12 Save as *Italian Holidays amended* and close the file.

Fig. 5.14 Example 2 Italian holidays

2 Inserting images

If you want to add images to any slides, you can make use of Microsoft's Clip Art gallery or you can insert an image from file or a source such as a CD.

add Clip Art

1 Apply a slide layout that includes a Content placeholder.

2 Click on the **Clip Art** icon to open the Clip Art search pane.

Or

3 Click on the **Insert** tab and click on **Clip Art**.

4 In the search pane, enter keywords to identify the type of image you are looking for and then click on **Go**.

5 Scroll through the images that appear and click on any one to add it to your slide.

Add picture from file   Add Clip Art

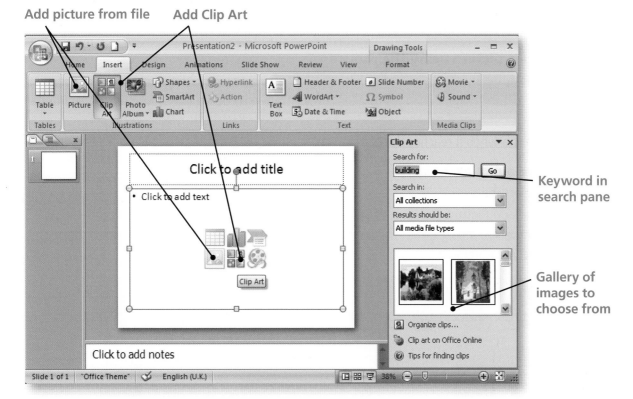

Fig. 5.15 Add Clip Art

Keyword in search pane

Gallery of images to choose from

insert a picture from file

1 Click on the **Insert Pictures from File** icon in the Content placeholder.
Or
2 Click on the **Picture** icon on the **Insert** tab.
3 When the dialog box opens, navigate to the picture file you want to insert.
4 Click on its name in the main window.
5 Click on the **Insert** button.

Selected file

Fig. 5.16 Insert picture from file   Insert button

171

Editing pictures

When the picture appears on the slide, it can be moved to a new position, reduced or increased in size and even copied to other slides or different open presentations.

resize a picture using the mouse

1 Move the pointer over a corner. It will display a white sizing handle.
2 When the pointer changes to a two-way arrow, hold down the mouse button and drag the boundary in or out.
3 Let go when it reaches the correct size.

resize a picture exactly

1 Select the picture.
2 Click on **Picture Tools – Format**.
3 In the Size area, click on the arrows in the **Width** or **Height** box to increase or decrease the measurement.

Sizing handle

Click arrow to change measure

Fig. 5.17 Resize picture

Increase or decrease measure

Maintain proportions

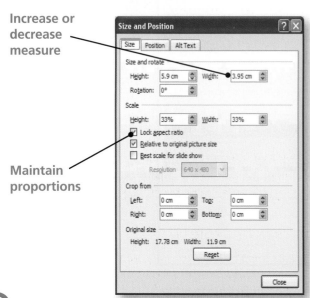

Or

4 Right-click on the picture and select **Size and Position**.

5 In the dialog box that opens, change measurements in the Width or Height boxes.

6 To keep the picture in proportion, the measurements in *both* boxes will change at the same time.

7 To alter both height and width, take off the tick in the **Lock aspect ratio** checkbox.

Fig. 5.18 Size and Position dialog box

move a picture

1 Hover the pointer over the picture until it shows a four-way arrow.
2 Hold down the **mouse** button and drag the picture to a new position.
3 To move it to a new slide, use **Cut and Paste** (see 'copy a picture' below).

copy a picture

1 Click on the picture to select it.
2 Select **Copy** from the Home tab or on the menu that will appear after right-clicking. (To move a picture, you would select **Cut**.)
3 Go to the slide where you want a copy of the picture to appear. If necessary, first open a different presentation. You may need to move other objects on the slide, such as text or page numbers, once your picture is in place.
4 Click on **Paste**.

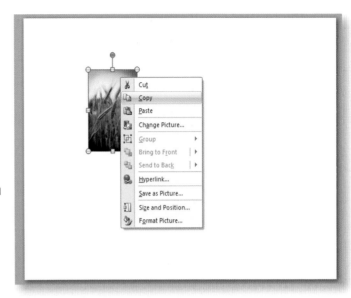

Fig. 5.19 Copy a picture

delete a picture

1 Select it and press the **Delete** key.

Check your understanding 3

1 Open the presentation *Libraries*, provided on the CD-ROM accompanying this book.
2 Apply a new slide layout to Slide 1 that has a placeholder for content.
3 Use the placeholder to open the Clip Art gallery.
4 Find any picture of a book.
5 Add it to the slide.
6 Reduce it so that it is a quarter of the original size.
7 Move it so that it is to the right of the title. Make sure it does not obscure any text.
8 Now add the image *library book* supplied.
9 Reduce it to about half its original size.
10 Position it in the centre of the slide.
11 Save the file as *Book pictures* and then close.

Fig. 5.20 Example 3 book pictures

Working with shapes

There are a number of different ready-made lines, double- or single-headed arrows and shapes that you can add to a slide. These can be resized, moved or deleted in the same way as pictures, but you can also modify them by changing the outline style, adding text or filling the shape with colour.

For lines or arrows, hold down the **Shift** key as you draw to make sure they are straight.

If you create a complex design made up of a number of different lines and shapes, you may want to resize them all or move them to a different slide. Rather than work separately with each shape at a time, you can group them all together and they can then be treated as a single shape.

add shapes

1 On the Insert tab, click on the **Shapes** arrow to reveal a gallery of different shapes and lines.
2 Click on the **shape** or **line** you want to add.
3 Click on the **slide** to add a shape of standard dimensions.
   Or
4 Hold down the **mouse** button and drag out the shape to the desired size.
5 The shape will appear in a selected state already filled with the default colour.

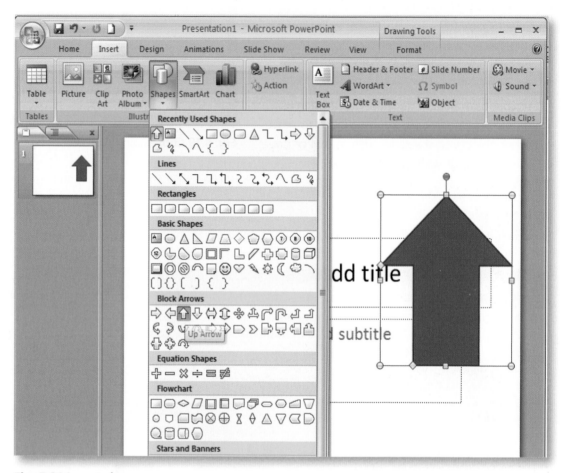

Fig. 5.21 Insert shape

Editing shapes

Once lines or shapes appear on your slide, you can resize them, move or delete them or change their formatting. Make sure the target shape is selected – showing a border and sizing handles round the edge – before choosing different options.

format a shape

1 On the Drawing Tools tab, click on **Format**.
2 To add, remove or change a fill colour, click on the drop-down arrow next to the Shape Fill button and select a different colour.
3 For a top shape to show any text or objects underneath, select **No Fill**. Otherwise, what appears as an empty shape will have a white fill colour.
4 To change the border or a line colour, click on the drop-down arrow next to the Shape Outline button and select a different colour. Select **No Outline** to remove a border completely.
5 On this menu, you can select **Weight** to change the line width or **Dash** to outline with dashed lines. There are also different styles of arrow.

6 Click on **More Lines** (or right-click and select the **Format** option) to open the dialog box. You can now make more specific changes to the shape, including changing the style of any arrow heads.

Don't forget to use **Print Preview** to check the appearance of your slides if they will be printed, as handouts for example. Before bulk printing handouts, it's best to print an assessment copy for yourself first. You may find that black and white printing demands you use fewer colours, for example, or that the number of images on each slide reduces their impact.

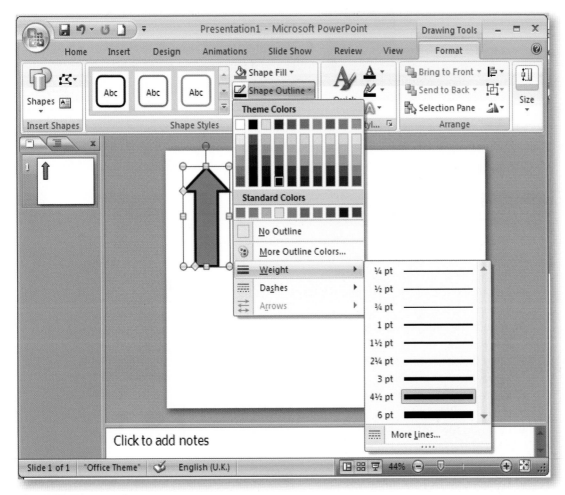

Fig. 5.22 Format shapes

add text to a shape

1 Click on the shape and start typing. Use the normal font and alignment tools to change the look or position of the text.

2 For vertical text within a shape, select an option from the **Text Direction** button on the Home tab.

3 To move between editing the text and the shape, right-click and select **Exit** or **Edit Text**.

Grouping shapes

When you want to format or copy several shapes together, you must select and then group them.

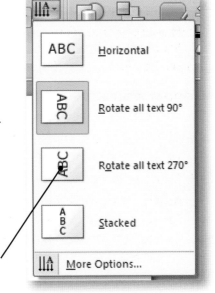

Set text direction

Fig. 5.23 Text direction

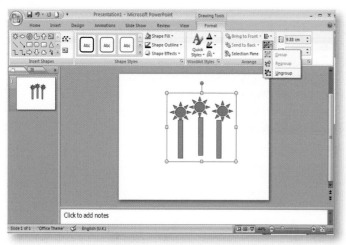

Fig. 5.24 Group shapes

group shapes

1 Click on the first shape with the mouse.
2 Hold down **Shift** and click on the other shapes in turn. They will all remain selected.
  Or
3 Use your pointer to draw a box round all the shapes to select them.
4 On the Format tab under Arrange, click on the **Group** button.
5 Your shapes will now all respond as a single shape if you copy or resize them.
6 To work on a single shape within the group at any time, click on it or first select the **Ungroup** option.
7 If you don't make too many changes, you may be able to group shapes together again by clicking on the **Regroup** option.

Check your understanding 4

1 Start a new presentation and select a **Blank slide** layout.
2 Draw a tree using two shapes from the gallery, such as stars and rectangles.
3 Resize any shapes so they are all in proportion.
4 Colour the top of the tree green and the trunk brown.
5 Group the shapes.
6 Reduce the grouped tree to half its original size.
7 Copy the shape and place the copy somewhere on the slide.
8 Resize the copy so that it is back to the original size.
9 Ungroup the larger tree and place a copy of the shape making up the top of the tree in the centre of the slide.
10 Position the two complete trees on each side of this shape.
11 Save the presentation as *Trees*.

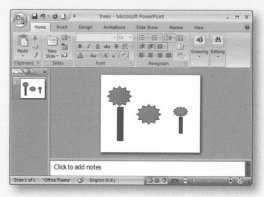

Fig. 5.25 Example 4 trees

Rotate button

Rotating shapes

You may find that the shape you add to your slide needs to be flipped over vertically or horizontally (to form a mirror image), or rotated to a different angle. You can carry out these tasks using the mouse or the menu.

rotate manually

1 Select the shape you want to manipulate.
2 Move the pointer over the green circle that will appear at the end of the rotate arm.
3 Hold down the mouse button and drag the shape left or right.

Drag to flip horizontally

Fig. 5.26 Rotate with mouse

New position for pointer

4 The pointer showing curved black arrows will be displayed as you drag and you will see a faint image of the shape in its rotated position.

5 Let go of the mouse when the shape is in the correct place.

7 To create a mirror image, drag a central white sizing handle across the shape and the image will be 'folded over' horizontally.

use the menu

1 Click on the drop-down arrow next to the Rotate button.

2 Select an option such as **Flip Horizontal** or **Rotate Left**.

3 For more exact angles of rotation, click on **More Rotation Options** to open the dialog box.

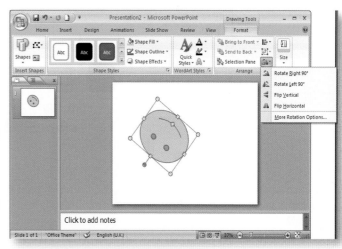

Fig. 5.27 Menu rotate options

Layering shapes

As you add shapes to the same place on a slide, they will appear on top of one another in layers. If the top shape is larger than any underneath, these will be hidden.

To make use of this layering to create complex images, you may need to remove the fill colour for a top shape or reorder shapes by bringing those underneath forward or sending those on the top back one or more layers.

layer objects

1 Add the first object to the slide.

2 Add another one and place it on top.

3 To view the underneath shape, click on the **Format** tab and choose one of the following.

  a Remove the Fill from the top shape by selecting **No Fill** from the Shape Fill menu.

  b Select the top shape and click on **Send to Back** in the Arrange section of the ribbon.

  c Select the underneath shape and click on **Bring to Front**.

Fig. 5.28 No fill

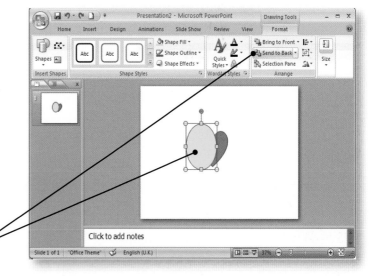

Top shape before clicking Send to Back

Fig. 5.29 Layer shapes

  d If there are more than two layers and you want to position a shape between other shapes, click on the arrow next to the correct Arrange option and choose **backward** or **forward**.

Fig. 5.30 Bring to front

177

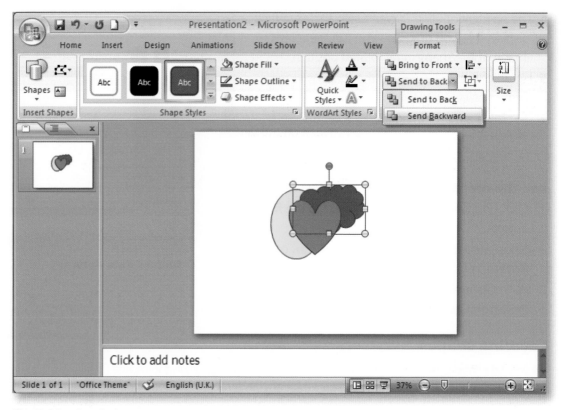

Fig. 5.31 Bring in between

Check your understanding 5

1 Start a new presentation.
2 Add four shapes to the slide to represent a cloud, heart, sun and bent arrow.
3 Fill each shape with a different colour: blue (cloud), yellow (heart), black (sun) and red (arrow).
4 Position the shapes on top of one another with the cloud at the bottom, then the heart, then the sun and finally the arrow on top. Make sure you can see a small part of each shape.
5 Reorder the shapes so that the sun is on top and the bent arrow is underneath all the shapes.
6 Flip the bent arrow so it is pointing in the opposite direction.
7 Rotate the heart so it is pointing upwards.
8 Remove the fill colour from the sun.
9 Close the file without saving.

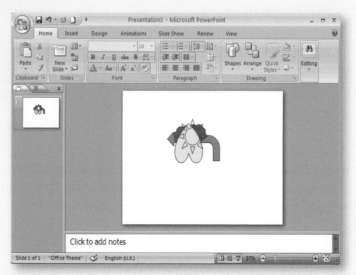

Fig. 5.32 Example 5 layer shapes

3 Working with text and graphics

There are different ways you can position text, pictures, shapes and any other objects on your slides. The simplest is to apply different slide layouts. You can choose one, for example, that offers a text placeholder on the left and placeholder for content such as a picture or chart on the right. You can also add objects to any slide and then:

- align them centrally or to the left or right on the slide
- align the top, bottom or sides of one object with another
- align them with different parts of the slide itself such as the top or bottom edges
- view gridlines or guides and position objects by eye using these markings
- view and use the vertical and horizontal rulers
- distribute objects equally on the slide.

align objects

1 Select the object. To select more than one, hold down the **Ctrl** key as you click on subsequent objects.

2 For pictures, click on the **Format** tab under Picture Tools. For other objects such as text boxes and shapes, the Format option will be under Drawing Tools.

3 Click on the drop-down arrow next to the Align button and, if necessary, select the correct option – to align objects to the Slide or to Selected Objects.

4 Select an align option such as **Centre** or **Top**.

5 When aligning to the slide you will have the option to distribute the images equally across the slide, either horizontally or vertically.

Gridlines

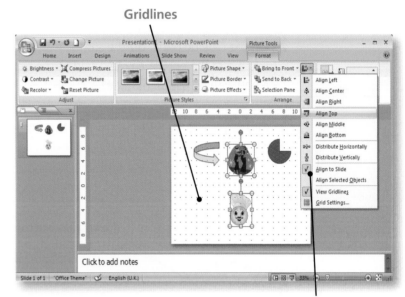

Fig. 5.33 Align pictures

Align to Slide option chosen

use guides, gridlines and rulers

1 Add dotted gridlines and add or remove drawing guides by clicking on **Grid Settings**, or choose this option on the View tab.

2 If using the gridlines or guides, drag each shape to your preferred position with the mouse, matching the position by eye to the dots or lines.

3 Always use the guides if you want to divide the slide into quarters and work in one particular quarter.

4 To use the ruler, display it from the View tab. You will then see a dotted line mark the ruler position as you drag an object vertically or horizontally along the slide.

Ruler   Guide line

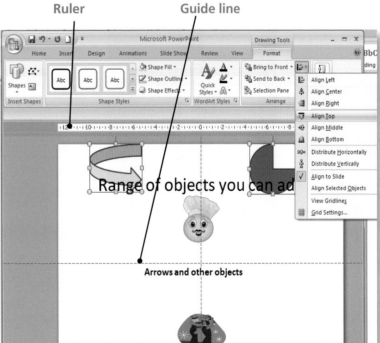

Fig. 5.34 Guides

4 Presentations

When you first open PowerPoint, one slide is always ready to work on. To create a full presentation, you need to be able to add extra slides. You also need to know how to make amendments such as copying or deleting slides, how to navigate your way through the slides as you build up the presentation, and how to run your slide show on a computer.

Adding new slides

There are two different methods for adding new slides – using thumbnails on the Slide or Outline pane or using the ribbon.

add new slides

1   In the Slide pane, click on a thumbnail of any slide and press **Enter**. A new slide will appear below it.

Or

2   On the Outline pane, do the same. If you have already added text to the slide, make sure you are at the end of any text and at the right level to create a new slide, or you will start a new line on the same slide.

Or

3   Click on the **New Slide** button on the Home tab and a new slide will appear on-screen.

4   It will be obvious which is the current slide, as it will be highlighted in the Slide pane and its number will appear in the bottom left-hand corner of the screen.

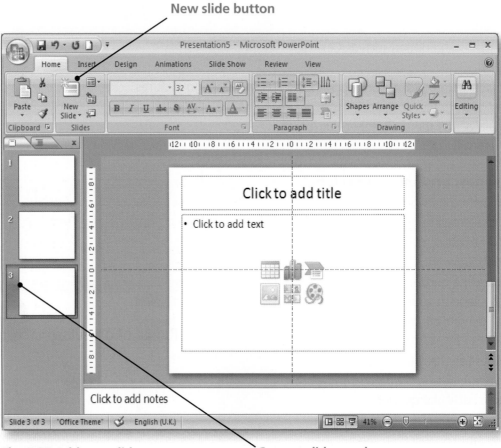

Fig. 5.35 Add new slide

move between slides

1 Click on the **Previous** or **Next Slide** navigation button showing double arrows to the right of the main slide.
  Or
2 Click on a numbered slide in the Slide pane.
  Or
3 Press the **Page Up** or **Page Down** keys on the keyboard.

delete an unwanted slide

1 Select the slide.
2 Press the **Delete** key.
  Or
3 Press the **Delete Slide** button on the Home tab. It displays a red cross.
  Or
4 Right-click on the slide and select **Cut**.

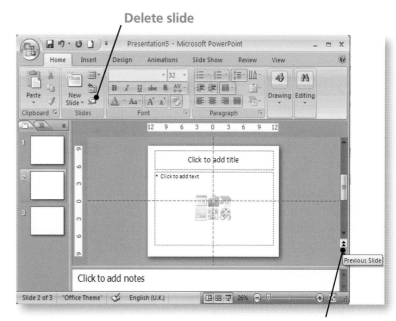

Fig. 5.36 Navigation

Delete slide

Navigation buttons

Check your understanding 6

1 Start a new presentation.
2 Add four new slides.
3 On each slide, enter the text **Slide number** (put in the correct number).
4 Navigate through the presentation from Slide 1 to Slide 5 and then display Slide 1.
5 Delete Slide 3.
6 Close the file without saving.

Reordering slides

If you find you prefer your slides in a different order, there are two ways to change their position. Either drag slide thumbnails on the Slide tab, or first go to the Slide Sorter view that displays all the slides in the presentation. You can then drag slides into different positions in this view.

move slides

1 On the Slide tab, click on the target slide.
2 Use the pointer to drag it to its new position. Its progress will be marked by a horizontal grey line.
3 When you let go of the mouse, the slide will drop into place.
  Or
4 Click on the **Slide Sorter** view button (or go to this view from the View tab).
5 Drag the target slide to a different position. This time, its progress is marked by a red vertical line.

Slide 3 being moved between 1 and 2

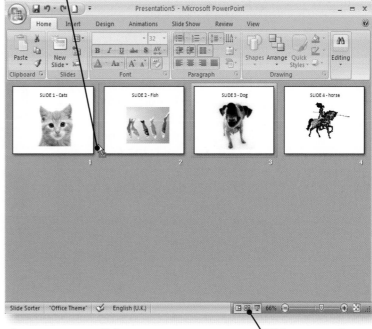

Fig. 5.37 Move slides

Slide sorter view

181

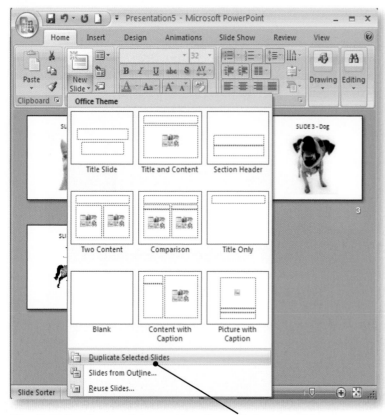

Fig. 5.38 Duplicate slide   Duplicate Selected Slides

Duplicating slides

If you want to create a number of very similar slides, it is quicker to duplicate them and then edit their contents rather than key in everything from scratch each time.

duplicate slides

1 Click on the slide(s) you want to copy.
2 Click on the **Copy** icon on the Home tab.
3 Click on **Paste**. A copy of the original slide(s) will appear and you can move it to a new position or edit its contents.
   Or
4 Click on the drop-down arrow next to the New Slide button in the Slides group on the Home tab.
5 In the layout gallery, click on **Duplicate Selected Slides**.

Check your understanding 7

1 Open the presentation *all the animals*, provided on the CD-ROM accompanying this book.
2 Create a new slide and give it the title: **SLIDE 5 – Birds**.
3 Insert an appropriate Clip Art image on the slide. Resize it if necessary so that it does not obscure any text.
4 Now reorder all the slides so that they run from Slide 5 (first slide) to Slide 1 (last slide).
5 Duplicate the first slide (showing the bird image) and move this copy so that it becomes the very last slide in the presentation.
6 Change the title of the last slide to **SLIDE 6 – Birds**.
7 Finally, delete **SLIDE 3 – Dog**.
8 Save the file as *Animals reordered*.

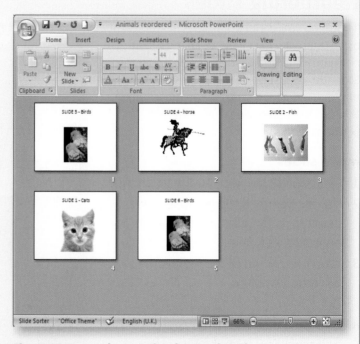

Fig. 5.39 Example 8, Animals reordered

Watching presentations

At this stage it is worth remembering that watching slide shows can be quite tiring! It is therefore important to keep the audience in mind when creating a presentation and apply certain basic rules:

- only use a small amount of text per slide
- use pictures in place of text where possible
- limit the number of points you want to make on each slide
- keep colours coordinated and from a sensible palette
- don't overuse bullet points.

Using the Slide Master

When you are working with a long presentation and want to improve its appearance, maintain a consistent look or add extra items, it can be time-consuming to make the same changes to a number of individual slides. Instead PowerPoint provides a quick way to amend all the slides in the presentation, by using the **Slide Master**.

This slide stores information about the layout and formatting of all the slides. If you make a change to the Slide Master, it is translated throughout the presentation.

It can be particularly useful if you create a complex presentation. You can concentrate on the textual content and then use the Slide Master to apply the most appropriate fonts and font sizes throughout the presentation.

view the Slide Master

1 Click on the **View** tab.

2 Click on **Slide Master**.

3 In the Slide pane, click on the slide type you want to amend. Title slides are slightly different in appearance so you must select **Slide 1** in the Slide pane to amend the Title slide of a presentation as well as the rest of the slides.

edit the Slide Master

1 When the slide appears in the main window, you will be able to see the default font type for different levels of text, font sizes and list formatting that has been applied.

2 Click on any element to make changes and use the normal font options available, for example, on the Home or Slide Master tab. If you have not already defined these elements in your presentation, the default settings will be overridden and your new choices will be applied to every slide.

3 You can add images or objects to the Slide Master and they will then be visible on every slide. (Note that to remove items from your presentation that have been added in this way, you will always have to return to the Slide Master view as you will not be able to access them in Normal view.)

4 You can also amend the style of bullets applied to the different levels of text.

5 To return to your presentation, click on another view such as the **Normal view** button at the bottom of the screen or the **Close** button on the Slide Master tab.

Amendments will also apply to the title slide

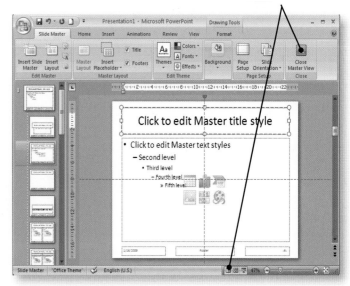

Fig. 5.40 Slide Master

Return to normal view

Fig. 5.41 Edit Slide Master

Check your understanding 8

1   Start a new presentation and save it as *Cooking*.
2   Create a three-slide presentation by adding two new slides.
3   Give Slide 1 the title **Cooking** and add the following text: **Cooking is a favourite hobby for many people**.
4   Give Slide 2 the title **Making Bread**.
5   Add the following text: **It is easy to make the following types of bread:** Remove any bullets if one appears.
6   Add the following four items as a bulleted list: **White loaf, Wholemeal loaf, Rolls, Speciality breads**.
7   Give Slide 3 the title **Jam Making**.
8   Go to Slide Master view and make the following changes.
    a   Change the title font to Algerian size 40.
    b   Change the main text font to Arial Black size 32.
9   Add a suitable picture from the Clip Art gallery and position it on the slide. Make sure it will not interfere with the text on any of the slides.
10   Change to a different top-level bullet style.
11   Return to Normal view and check that new formatting has been applied and the image is on all the slides.
12   Save and close the file.

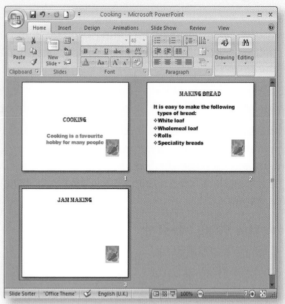

Fig. 5.42 Example 9 Cooking

No background   Options   Find other colours

Fig. 5.43 Background

Backgrounds

You can add a coloured background to one or more slides in your presentation by applying a background design. These can be solid colours, gradients or even pictures. In PowerPoint 2007 backgrounds are grouped into themes. These associate each background with a range of colours and styles of text and border that coordinate well and that are all applied together automatically.

add a background

1   Select a slide and then click on the **Design** tab.
2   In the background group, click on **Background Styles** to open the gallery.
3   A range of related themes is displayed alongside.
4   Right-click on a background style.
5   In the menu that appears, select the correct option to apply the new colour to all your slides or just the selected slide.

6   If you want to change the basic colour of the background, select the **Format Background** option.

7   Select a solid rather than gradient fill if preferred and choose from a palette of colours.

8   Click on the **Apply to All** button to apply the new colour throughout the presentation.

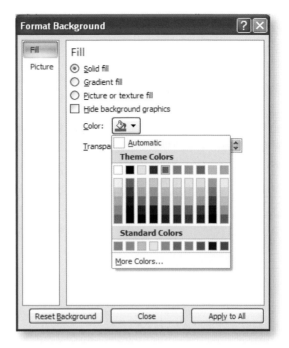

Fig. 5.44 Format Background

Check your understanding 9

Open any presentation and apply a coloured background to all the slides.

Running a slide show

To make use of your computer's sound, image and video facilities, you need to run a PowerPoint presentation as a slide show. This means that the menus will disappear and each slide will be displayed in full on the screen. Depending on the audience, you may want to run slide shows on a single computer monitor or projected onto a large screen.

Slides will appear one after the other when you click on the mouse button or press the **Page Down** key, although there are facilities to run a show automatically and to add special effects when you introduce whole slides (transitions) or different objects on a slide (animations).

run a slide show

1   Click on the first slide you want to view.

2   Click on the **Slide Show** button at the bottom of the screen.

    Or

3   Click on the **Slide Show** tab and click on **From the Beginning** in the Start Slide Show group.

4   You can also press function key **F5** to start the slide show.

5   Keep clicking the mouse to move through the slides.

6   To leave a slide show before you reach the last slide, press the **Esc** key on the keyboard.

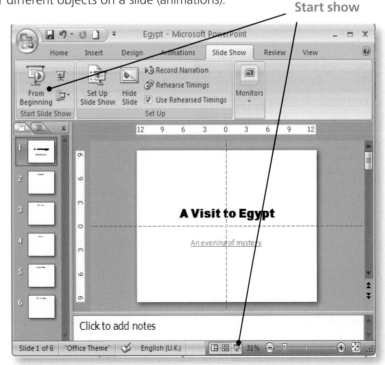

Fig. 5.45 Run slide show

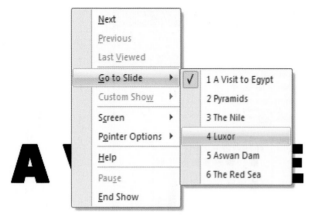

Fig. 5.46 Pointer device

Navigating within a slide show

It is common when running a slide show for different audiences to want to display slides out of order or to skip some slides altogether. You can do this by using the pointer to jump to a different slide during the show.

go to a different slide

1 Right-click on the current slide during a slide show.
2 Click on Go to Slide.
3 Click on the name of the next slide you want to display.
4 It will now appear as the next slide.

Check your understanding 10

1 Open any presentation you have created that is made up of more than two slides, or create a new one. Make sure each slide has a title so that you know when it is being displayed.
2 Run the presentation as a slide show.
3 Now run it again but, this time, use the pointer to jump from Slide 1 to Slide 3 or 4.
4 Jump back to Slide 2.
5 Close the file.

Resolution

If your presentation will be viewed on a projector, it is important that any images you use to illustrate your slides are set to the correct resolution (the number of pixels on the horizontal and vertical axes that set the sharpness of the image). This should be equal to the device resolution –for example, 1024 x 768 pixels, together with a safety margin. This will allow for the increase in physical size and ensure that images remain sharp and vibrant. So a full-sized image would be 1024 x 768 pixels or a little over, and one filling half the slide would be 512 (1024/2) x 384 (768/2).

The reason for setting the image resolution first is that if you increase the size of an image once it has been added to a slide, you are not changing the number of pixels, which is the true measure of resolution, but just the image's physical size.

Printing

As well as printing out each slide as if it was a document page, you can output PowerPoint presentations to the web and also print different aspects of the file that relate to the slide's use as an aid for talks. You can print:

● the text outline of a presentation
● a single slide, selected slides or all the slides
● black and white or coloured slides
● handouts for an audience that contain a thumbnail image of each slide
● notes pages for the speaker that contain word-processed notes alongside a thumbnail image of the slide.

You can also print onto different media such as 35 mm slides or overhead transparencies as well as paper.

This means that you have to take care to select the correct options before printing. You must also check that the slide or page will print out with the correct orientation. The default setting is for slides to print out in Landscape and handouts or notes pages to print out in Portrait orientation.

check a presentation before printing

1 Click on the **Office** button and select **Print – Print Preview**.

2 Check the **Print What:** box to see what has been selected and change if necessary.

3 Retain or change the orientation.

4 Close the preview or print directly from this view.

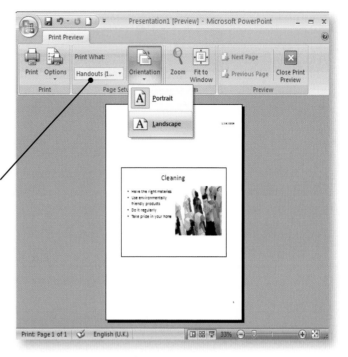

Item being printed

print a PowerPoint presentation

1 For a single set of all the slides in the presentation applying default settings, click on the **Office** button and select **Print – Quick Print**.

2 For other options, select **Print** to open the Print box.

Fig. 5.47 Preview before print

3 Click on the drop-down arrow in the Print what: box to select the output you want.

4 Select an option such as **Current Slide** or enter slide numbers if you want to restrict what you print. If you only want to print slides 2, 5, and 7, for example, you should enter 2, 5, 7 in the Slides field, under Print Range.

5 If printing handouts, select the number of thumbnails to print on each page.

6 Change from colour to black and white if required, by selecting this option in the Colour-grayscale box found below the Print what: box.

7 Change the number of copies if necessary.

8 Click on **OK** or first check your printout by clicking on the **Preview** button.

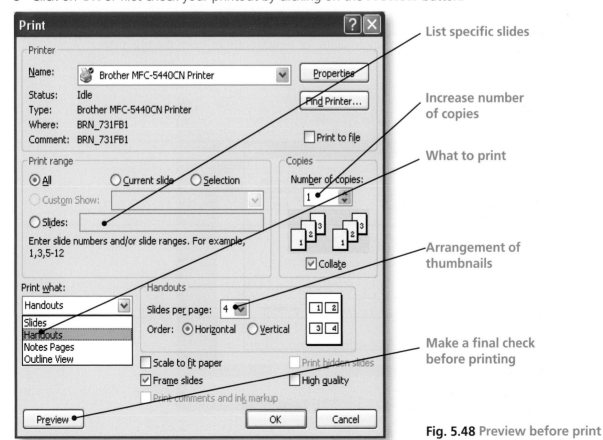

List specific slides

Increase number of copies

What to print

Arrangement of thumbnails

Make a final check before printing

Fig. 5.48 Preview before print

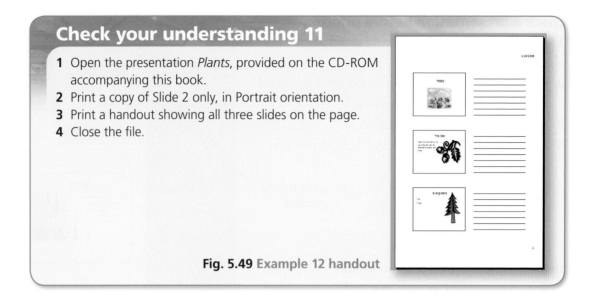

Check your understanding 11

1 Open the presentation *Plants*, provided on the CD-ROM accompanying this book.
2 Print a copy of Slide 2 only, in Portrait orientation.
3 Print a handout showing all three slides on the page.
4 Close the file.

Fig. 5.49 Example 12 handout

Headers and footers

You can add details to your slides or printouts as headers and footers that will be positioned in the top or bottom margins. These can include the automatic date or time, slide or page numbers and other details. Many entries will be positioned automatically in set areas of the slide but they can be dragged to different places if preferred.

create headers and footers

1 On the Insert tab, click on **Header and Footer**.
2 In the window that opens, you can make the following choices:

   a Click on the correct tab to add entries to slides, handouts or notes pages.

   b Click on **Date and Time** and either select an automatic entry from the drop-down list of styles or enter your own fixed date that will not be updated.

   c Click for slide/page numbers.

   d Click in the Footer box to add your own entry in the box. There is also a Header box for notes and handouts.

   e Apply entries to all or single slides, or remove entries from the title slide.

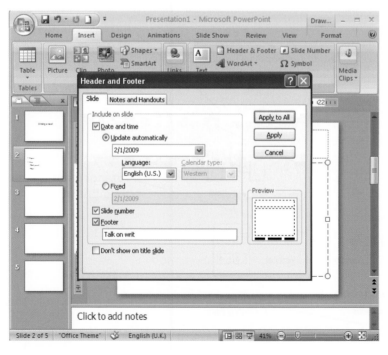

Fig. 5.50 Header and footer

Check your understanding 12

1 Reopen *Plants.*
2 Add today's date and slide numbers to all the slides.
3 Add a note in the footer that reads **Save our environment**.
4 Print out one slide that shows these details.

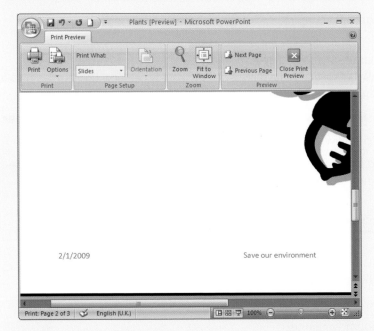

Fig. 5.51 Example 13 plant header, showing date and footer text

CLAiT Assignment

TASK 1

1 Set up a master slide as follows. This master slide layout must be used for all slides:

   a Slide orientation to **portrait**

   b Text styles as follows:
   Title – bold, centred, large sans serif font (e.g. Arial)
   Main text/1st level – italic, left aligned, medium serif font (e.g. Times New Roman), no bullets
   2nd level – italic and underlined, indented, smaller serif font and any style of bullet

   c At the bottom of the slide display **your name,** an **automatic date** and a **slide number**.

2 Format the background to yellow.

3 Insert the image *plant.jpg* in the top right corner so that it appears on all slides. This image may be resized but must not touch or obscure any text. Make sure the image is kept in its original proportions.

4 Save the presentation using the filename *garden1* and use it for the rest of the assessment.

TASK 2

1 Create Slide 1 and enter the title *Garden Centre Unlimited.*

2 Enter the following text in the main placeholder (frame):

   a *Makes your garden bloom* – main text
   b *Presentation by (your name and today's date)* – 2nd level

3 Create Slide 2 and enter the title *The Garden Centre's Philosophy.*

4 Add the following text:

   To promote a friendly and helpful environment
   To provide the best service possible
   To increase plant sails and advice gardener

5 Create Slide 3 and enter the title *Our Aims.*

6 Add the following as a list, set at the levels shown:

   We aim to create a welcoming place to buy or browse (level 1)
   We aim to increase sales staff by the end of this year (level 1)
   Staff are fully trained to help customers and care for the plants (level 2)
   We aim to increase our uptake of landscape materials (level 2)
   We aim to surpass local provision of gardening services (level 1)

7 Proofread and use the spellcheck facility to check the accuracy of text on all slides.

8 Save the presentation keeping the filename *garden1*.

9 Print the presentation as a **handout** with three slides to a page (Figure 5.52).

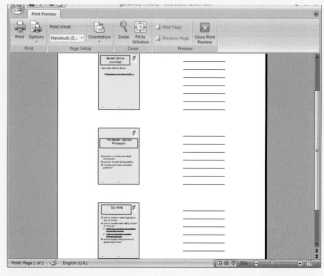

Fig. 5.52 Handout

TASK 3

1 Make some amendments to the presentation:

  a Create Slide 4 and enter the title *Where we are.*

  b Create a plant shape (see example below) on this slide using auto shapes. Position this between the title and the footer area. The flower head should be red and the pot brown.

  c Make sure the shape does not touch or overlap any text.

  d Between the shape and the title, insert the image file *map.jpg* from the CD-ROM and resize it if necessary to fit neatly without overlapping any text or images.

  e Replace the word *Garden* with the word *Planting* wherever it appears in the presentation (four times). Make sure you match case.

2 On Slide 3 promote the line *We aim to increase our uptake of landscape materials* to become a 1st level line of text.

3 Save the presentation using the new filename *garden2*.

4 Print Slides 3 and 4 as individual slides, one per page (Figure 5.53).

Task 3

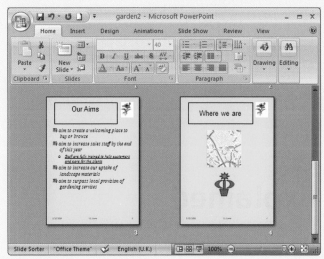

Fig. 5.53 Slides 3 and 4

TASK 4

1 On Slide 3 titled *Our Aims* delete the line 'We aim to surpass local provision of gardening services'.

2 Change the order of the slides so that Slide **4** titled *Where we are* becomes Slide **3**.

3 Add the following two items at 2nd level text to Slide 4 after *materials: Rockeries, Patios*. Make sure they display bullets.

4 Save the amended presentation using the new filename *garden3*.

5 An outline view printout is required. Enter your **name** as a header or footer for this print and print the presentation in **outline view** to display the text on **all four slides** (Figure 5.54).

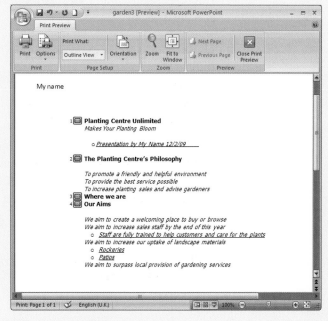

Fig. 5.54 Outline

Online communication

A basic grasp of Internet technology and an understanding of its power in providing access to vast amounts of information as well as the means to communicate electronically (using electronic mail or email) are vital in today's world. This unit introduces you to Internet technology and shows you the best ways to communicate and browse effectively.

(Although there are now methods for accessing the Internet via mobile phones or games consoles, this chapter concentrates on computers that use fixed telephone lines.)

At the end of this unit you will be able to:

➔ identify and use email and browsing software

➔ navigate the World Wide Web and use search techniques to locate data

➔ transmit and receive email messages and attachments.

1 The Internet explained

The Internet is the name given to networks of computers that are linked together and that enable computer users to send and receive information electronically.

One of the most important roles of the Internet is to allow you to view multimedia pages of text, images, sounds and video. These pages are known as web pages, and the millions of pages currently available make up the World Wide Web (also known as WWW or 'the web'). The collection of interlinked pages published by a single organisation is referred to as a website.

Basic requirements

To use the Internet, you need the following:

- computer
- telephone connection
- **modem** or **router** – a modem is hardware that converts the digital computer signals to analogue so that they can be sent via the telephone system. Most modern computers come already fitted with an internal modem. A router is also needed if you have networked computers, as information can then be directed or 'routed' to specific machines
- **Internet Service Provider (ISP)** – organisations that provide access to the Internet when you set up an account with them
- **Browser** – the software required to view web pages. Common browsers include Internet Explorer, Firefox and Opera.

Accessing the Internet

Each page on the web has a unique address, its URL (Universal Resource Locator). When you want to view web pages, you connect to the Internet by starting up the browser (usually by clicking on a link provided by your ISP) and a web page will appear in the main window. The same page will open each time you make a connection and is known as your home page.

Internet speed

Internet speed is a measure of the number of kilobits or megabits of data transferred per second (kbps or mbps) and affects how fast each web page loads. There are two types of Internet connection that you can have: dial-up and broadband. More and more people are switching to broadband as it is much faster and therefore allows you to watch videos, listen to music or view large images more quickly.

Dial-up can transfer 56 kbps whereas broadband speeds can range from 512 kbps to 8 mbps per second.

A slow Internet speed can be caused by a variety of factors, including:

- the number of applications accessing the Internet at the same time
- the quality of the line
- how many people are sharing the same connection
- your computer settings, which may not be configured efficiently
- the time of day (more people are online in the evenings)
- the capacity of a particular website to handle the traffic it receives
- your distance from the telephone exchange.

Why use the Internet?

There are so many possibilities when you have access to the Internet that it is hard to imagine life without it. Here are just a few things you can do with Internet access:

- send messages electronically to people across the world
- watch or read the news and get instant updates
- listen to music
- watch films
- check the weather or what's on TV
- publish your own videos
- buy second-hand goods on auction sites such as www.ebay.co.uk
- see people you are communicating with via webcams
- make friends through social networks
- instant messaging with anyone online at the same time
- check definitions and spellings and use translation services
- go shopping, banking, buy tickets…
- read books, newspapers and magazines
- get expert help from forums or discussion boards
- download free programs
- join a newsgroup community made up of people with similar interests
- publish your digital camera photos to share with friends and family
- take an online course.

Advantages and disadvantages of using the Internet

The services listed above indicate the value of using the Internet. Some of the main advantages include:

- speed – web pages of information download onto your computer in seconds
- low costs – emails can be sent around the world for little or no cost, and you can carry out price comparisons across a range of suppliers to find the cheapest
- convenience – you can find information, order goods, book last-minute holidays or tickets, transfer money or send messages all from your computer

- global audience for your own web pages
- no time constraints – you can pay bills, watch films or go shopping in the middle of the night.

Of course there are also disadvantages. These might be:

- receiving unwanted malicious programs (viruses) that can cause havoc to your machine or files
- suffering identity theft or fraud if your credit card or other personal information is intercepted
- spam – your mailbox can become clogged with unwanted advertisements or messages
- excessive use – the web can be addictive and can affect your health as well as social life.

Web page addresses

A typical web page address is

http://www.bbc.co.uk/doctorwho/index.shtml

The unique address of any web page is made up of various elements. These help to identify the organisation that publishes it, its contents and any folder pathway where the individual file is stored:

> **http://** shows that the page is published using a particular set of rules known as **h**yper**t**ext **t**ransfer **p**rotocol
>
> **www.** means it is on the World Wide Web
>
> **bbc.** is the name of the organisation
>
> **co.uk**. shows it is a British company
>
> **/doctorwho/** – forward slashes show the pathway where the file is stored
>
> **index.shtml** is the actual page title, with the extension *shtml* showing that the page was written using HTML (**h**yper**t**ext **m**ark-up **l**anguage)

The main part of the address – bbc.co.uk – is known as the **domain name**. This identifies the site where the file is stored. Every computer accessing the Internet is given a unique number or **IP** (Internet Protocol) address, but these can be hard for people to remember. Domain names are used as a substitute.

Depending on the type of organisation publishing the web pages, the extension after the dot will vary. For example:

- co.uk – British company
- com – international company
- gov.uk – local or national government
- org.uk – public body or charity
- ac.uk – British educational establishment
- net – network, commonly used by ISPs.

File transfer

As well as addresses beginning http://www., you will find http://ftp. This denotes a file transfer site using **File Transfer Protocol** which is the system used to exchange files over the Internet. Commonly you might want to do this when downloading software such as virus checkers (see below) or image editing programs, or publishing (uploading) pages to your own website.

Viruses

There is one group of programs that you won't want to download. These are viruses, designed to interfere with the workings of your computer. Viruses are distributed across the Internet maliciously and may be downloaded automatically when you visit particular sites, or you can be infected from emails or even by using portable media such as CDs.

The only way to protect your machine is to install virus-checking software and make sure that it is updated and run on a regular basis.

Behaviour on the Internet

When communicating with others on a network, users are expected to behave in a socially acceptable manner. This behaviour has been given the term **netiquette**. Groups normally establish their own rules but it often means that, for example, when using email or discussion forums and newsgroups:

- messages should not be in the form of spam (sending multiple messages such as advertisements)
- message content should not be inflammatory or cause offence
- you should avoid using capital letters in the main body of the text – this is known as SHOUTING
- you should not invade other people's privacy.

Check your understanding 1

1 Why do you need a modem to use the Internet?
   a To establish rules for downloading files
   b To convert digital to analogue signals
   c It increases Internet speed

2 How do you normally connect a computer to the Internet?
   a By using the telephone line
   b Via email
   c By satellite

3 How is Internet speed measured?
   a Kilograms
   b Miles per inch
   c Kilobits per second
   d Gigabytes

4 What do the initials ISP stand for?
   a Internet standard protocol
   b International service provider
   c Internet service provider
   d Internet service protocol

5 What is a browser needed for?
   a Sending emails
   b Viewing web pages
   c Connecting to the Internet

6 Which part of the URL http://www.pearson.com/education/timetable.html is known as the domain name?
   a http://
   b pearson.com
   c www.
   d timetable.html

7 Name two advantages of using the Internet.

8 Which of the following is a browser?
   a ISP   b HTTP   c Opera   d Broadband?

9 Which extension would normally be part of the URL of a charity?
   a gov.uk   b org.uk   c ac.uk

10 Which of the following breaks a common rule of netiquette?
   a Using an incorrect URL
   b Viewing too many web pages
   c Sending advertising material by email
   d Spending a long time browsing the Internet

2 Connecting to the Internet

Selecting an ISP

When setting up your own Internet access, you will need to choose an appropriate service provider. As there are so many companies offering this service, the choice is very wide. The best choice for you personally will depend on a number of factors:

1 **How much will you be using the Internet?** If you only plan to send the odd email message and check a few web pages each day, then the cheapest option might be a Pay As You Go dial-up service. There is no subscription, but each time you connect, the length of time you spend on the Internet will be charged in the same way as making a local phone call. For more use per month, it may be cheaper to pay a monthly subscription that will cover all your Internet activity. (To save money, dial-up users are advised to compose and read all their email messages offline and only connect for the few seconds it takes to send and receive messages.)

For anyone hoping to browse for a number of hours each day, or view videos and download large files, it is better to select a broadband service. These are all on subscription and the cost depends on the connection speed and number of web pages you think you will access each month.

2 **Do you want a combined package?** Many broadband providers also offer telephone and TV programmes as well, and so these can work out cheaper than buying each service separately.

3 **How much downloading will you carry out?** Some packages limit the number of pages you can visit or files you can download, so the heavy user may require a more expensive package that has no download limits.

4 **Do you want help if you have problems?** Many ISPs have free helplines where you can get technical support, but others charge for these services or do not offer them.

5 **What speed do you require?** Dial-up will always be far slower and will limit what you can do on the Internet, but some slower (and therefore cheaper) broadband services may be good enough for your purposes. You usually only need to decide if you will be a light, medium or heavy user of the Internet before signing up for an account.

Signing-up

To make life easier, there are now many websites that will help you compare ISP services and work out the best deal to suit your personal needs. You can then visit the organisation and get set up online. New computer users will normally sign up with an ISP when they purchase their machine, so they are ready to access the Internet straight away. Use the comparison websites – perhaps at college, work or in a library – so that you choose an appropriate provider. Once you have an ISP, switching to a cheaper or better package is very easy.

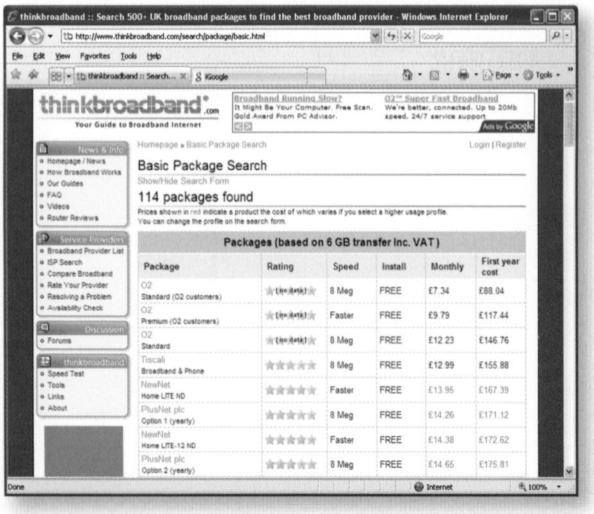

Take care to check the small print – many services require you to stay with them for a minimum of 12 or 18 months and they may also have a low introductory offer price that rises after a few months.

When you are ready to switch, just inform your current service provider that you want to do so, ask them for the MAC (Migratory Access Code) key that is required and make sure you have been with them the required minimum length of time so there are no penalty charges for early withdrawal.

At the present time, many broadband packages suitable for normal home use, which may also provide a router free of charge, cost about £8 to £15 per month.

Fig. 8.1 ISPs compared

3 Locating information

Selecting a browser

For many years, the browser used by the majority of Internet users was Microsoft's Internet Explorer. (The examples in this book are based on Internet Explorer 7.) Now other programs have become popular, such as Firefox, Safari and Opera, and, at the time of writing, the search engine Google has just brought out Chrome. You can have more than one system on your computer at the same time, so you might like to try a new one for a change. Fortunately, they all work in very similar ways.

use a browser

1 Find the icon for the browser on your desktop or Start program.

2 Click on it.

3 The browser will open up to display your home page.

The browser window

When the browser application opens, you will see a typical window with menus, buttons and a web page filling the main part of the screen. The various parts of the window that you need to work with are:

- **Control buttons** – to maximise, minimise or close the window

- **Address box** – this displays the URL of the page you can see or wish to open

- **Go** – visit the URL typed into the Address box

- **Refresh** – reload a page that hasn't loaded properly

- **Stop** – cancel loading a page, perhaps if it is taking too long

- **Search box** – type in keywords to help locate relevant information

- **Back button** – click to return to a previous page

- **Forward button** – click to move forward through opened pages

- **Favourites** – this stores the selected addresses of pages you may want to revisit and also lets you track pages visited in the past

- **Page** – offers options such as saving or editing web pages

- **Print** – click to print out the page

- **Home** – this returns you to your opening home page (Note: A website has its own Home page that usually introduces the organisation and is often known as the welcome page)

- **Index** – usually provided on web pages as a navigational aid

- **Menus** – links to more options.

2 separate browser icons

Fig. 8.2 Browser icon

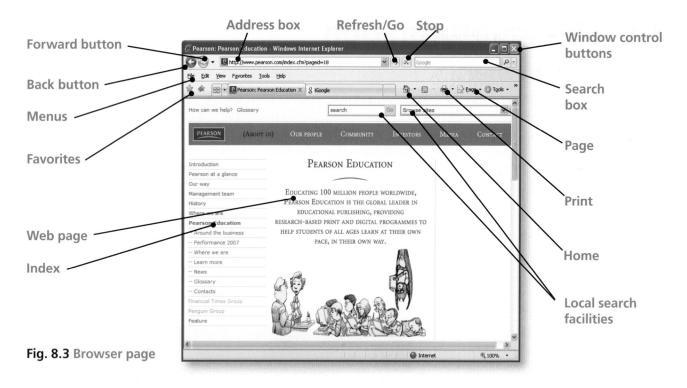

Fig. 8.3 Browser page

Navigating the web

To find information, you have to open a relevant web page. This can be carried out in two different ways:

- use the full URL
- click on one of the links placed on an open page. These are known as **hyperlinks** and will open a related page. They are usually identified by coloured text (although images do not appear any different) and the pointer changes to a hand when over any hyperlink image or text.

Using URLs

It is often perfectly clear where information will be found. For example, train timetables will be available from www.nationalrail.co.uk; background details of many BBC TV programmes will be set out at www.bbc.co.uk; and information on driving licences will be available from www.direct.gov.uk.

To visit the website of a known organisation, all you need is its Internet name and likely extension – for example, if it is a company (co.uk), academic institution (ac.uk) or government site (gov.uk).

Fig. 8.4 Hyperlink pointer   Click hand pointer to open new page

open a page using the URL

1. Type the full URL into the Address box. You do not need to start http:// but must include the domain name and all punctuation (such as forward slash or full stops).

2. Press **Enter** or click on the **Go** button (a green arrow that alternates with the **Refresh** button) and wait a few seconds for the page to load.

Check your understanding 2

1 Go to www.wikipedia.org – an encyclopaedia site.
2 Click on the **English hyperlink**.
3 Click on any picture to view it in an enlarged view.
4 Use your **Back** button to return to the previous page.
5 Move forward a few times by clicking on any hyperlink text of interest.
6 Use the **Back** button to return to the opening page.
7 Now go to your own home page.
8 Close the browser and, if necessary, disconnect.

Using search engines

In many cases, it won't be clear which website contains the information you are looking for. You will then need to visit a site known as a **search engine** that has been created specifically to help you search the web for relevant information.

The words you type – known as **keywords** – will be used to locate web pages that contain the same words. Although many sites listed will not be relevant, a good search engine should identify at least a few websites worth following up.

Some browsers already offer a limited search facility, but it is usual to visit a search engine site as you can then customise your search.

use a search engine

1 Use a keyword box if displayed in your browser window.
   Or
2 Type the full URL of a search engine into the Address box and press **Enter**. Popular search engines include www.google.co.uk., www.yahoo.co.uk and www.ask.com. Some, such as www.webcrawler.com, carry out 'meta searches', which means they search the search engines.

Fig. 8.5 Search engine list

3   When the search engine main page opens, enter your keywords or phrase into the search box provided and then press **Enter** or click on the **Go** or **Search** button.

4   The result will be lists of websites – usually 10 or 20 per page. Scroll down the list and click on the main title of any page listed that appears to provide relevant information. The new page will open.

5   To help you decide which websites to visit, read the first part of the entry under the link and check the name of the website you will be visiting.

6   Use your **Back** button to return to the list to follow up other pages.

7   Note that some of the links on the page are sponsored.

Effective search techniques

With so much information available, it is a good idea to try to reduce the length of a search list so that you only have a short but relevant group of websites to visit. Here are a few ways to do this:

● Click on a link on the page or add 'UK' as a keyword to limit the search to UK websites only, if this is important.

● Click on an **Images**, **Maps** or other special link if you want to search for these rather than carry out a general website search.

● Type several words between quotation marks to limit the results to pages that contain those words next to each other.

● Enter a whole sentence if you are not sure which keywords to select – search engines ignore *and, the* etc.

● You can add a **plus** (+) sign in front of words that must be included, or a **minus** (–) sign to omit pages containing specific words

When searching, you should always take care to select information that is appropriate for your needs. While this can be obvious – football results from 1987, for example, when you're searching for last season's results – often you will need to use your judgement to determine whether or not you have found the information you are looking for. Try using different keywords as your search terms, and don't forget that sometimes you will need to click through a few links before you get a successful result.

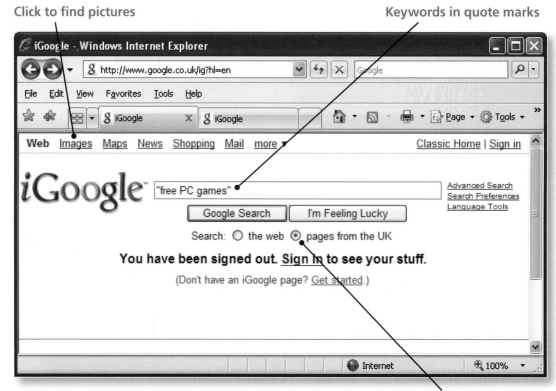

Fig. 8.6 Search techniques

Check your understanding 3

1 Go to any search engine site.
2 Search for more detailed information about *netiquette*.
3 Now start a new search. You want to find a job as an IT technician anywhere in the world. Enter appropriate keywords into the search box and produce a list of relevant websites.
4 Note down how many sites are listed altogether.
5 Follow up one or two of these and then return to the list page.
6 Now amend your keywords to find out if there are jobs in the UK.
7 Carry out another search for jobs in your nearest large town.
8 Note down the number of sites resulting from this search. (It should be far fewer!)
9 Finally, change your keywords and use quotation marks or + or - symbols to limit the search to job descriptions, with no pages offering vacancies being displayed.

Fig. 8.7 Example 3 search for jobs

Using directories

In the early days of the Internet, many search engines organised databases of websites they had reviewed and catalogued into a hierarchy. These search websites were known as directories. A directory search involves working down through this hierarchical structure to reach the bottom level containing a small group of related websites. Some search engines still work on this basis, although it can mean missing a large number of more relevant sites.

carry out a directory search

1 Visit a website such as www.ukdirectory.co.uk.
2 Click on a top-level link such as **Entertainment**.
3 Use the index on each page to work down through the levels.

Lower level   Route taken

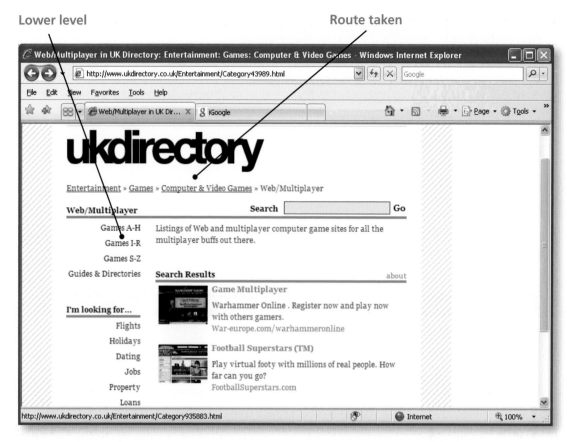

Fig. 8.8 Using directories

Check your understanding 4

1 Go to a directory site such as www.ukdirectory.co.uk.
2 Work through their categories to find out about any motorcycle training courses in your area.
3 Now carry out a similar search using a search engine.
4 Which search was the most helpful?

Add favorites button   Amend page name   Create a new folder to store the URL

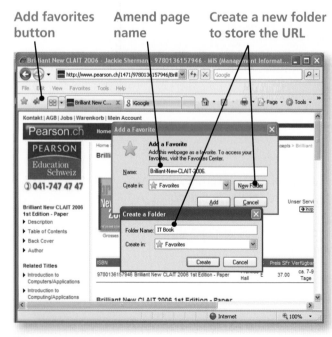

Fig. 8.9 Add favorite

Bookmarking pages

No one can retain in their heads the full URL of all pages visited, so browsers offer users a folder where they can store a link to any page they come across when browsing that they might want to revisit. This is known as **bookmarking** the page. In Internet Explorer the folder is known as the **Favorites** folder.

bookmark a page

1 With the page open in the browser window, hold **Ctrl** and press **D**.

Or

2 Click on the **Add to Favorites** button showing a yellow star and green cross.

Or

3 Open the Favorites menu and click on **Add to Favorites**.

4 Retype the page name if it is too long, and click on the **Add** button. This will store the URL at the bottom of the list of favourite websites.

5 If you prefer, you can first select an appropriate subfolder in which to store the URL from the **Create in:** box. You could also create a new folder at this stage by clicking on **New Folder** and entering a suitable name.

6 Click on **Add** to place the URL inside the folder and close the box.

visit a bookmarked page

1 Click on the **Favorites** button.

2 Click on the folder containing the bookmark and then click on the URL.

3 The page will now open.

Favorites list   Click to open the page

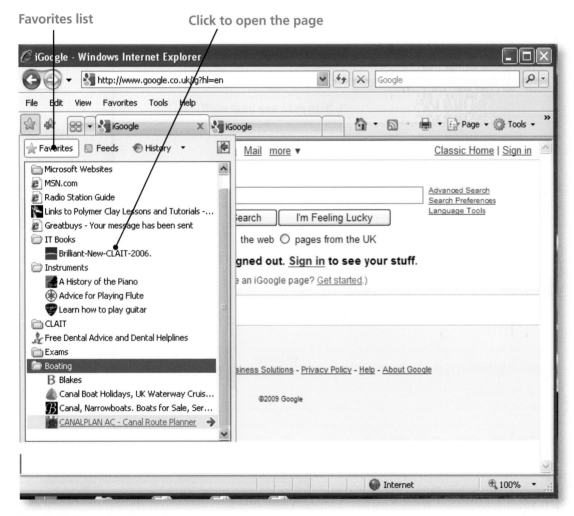

Fig. 8.10 Open bookmark

Revisiting pages visited some time ago

During a computer session, it is easy to retrace your steps by clicking on the **Forward** or **Back** toolbar buttons. But what if you want to revisit a website visited earlier in the week? Fortunately, a record of all pages accessed is kept for some time in the **History** folder and you can work through this to locate the page.

use History

1 Click on the **Favorites Centre** button.

2 Click on the circular **History** button.

3 Click on the heading to view pages visited – for example, on one day this week or a few weeks ago.

4 If there is a long list of web pages and you want to find particular URLs, click on the down arrow next to the History button to reorder the list by website name alphabetically or in the order in which they were visited, rather than by date.

Click to view pages visited last week

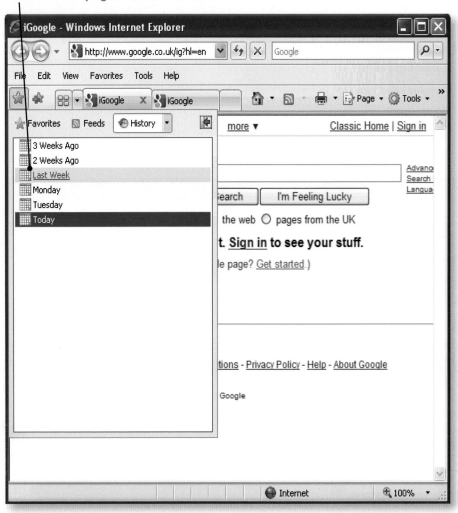

Fig. 8.11 History

Check your understanding 5

1 Use a search engine to find a page displaying information about a wind instrument such as the flute.

2 Bookmark it and save it in a new folder named *Instruments*.

3 Carry out a new search for websites containing information on a different instrument such as the piano.

4 Add the URL of this page to the Favorites *Instruments* folder.

5 Repeat this search to add the URL of a page on guitars. (Make sure you bookmark pages from different websites each time.)

6 Use your Favourites list to reopen the page about flutes.

7 Finally, check which pages were visited on your computer last week.

Fig. 8.12 Example 5 using bookmarks

Saving information

Each time you access a new page, this is 'downloaded' temporarily from the Internet and you view, watch or listen to it on your screen. You can also save Internet files as documents, audio, image or sound files, or download whole programs that you can then install on your computer.

Web pages are multimedia files that can comprise a mix of file types. When saving a web 'page', you need to decide if you want all the elements saved together or you want a simplified version. You can also save pictures showing on a page separately as image files.

save a web page

1 Click on the **Page** button or **File** menu.
2 Select **Save As**.
3 Check the name and change it if necessary to make the file easy to locate on your computer.
4 Choose how to save the page from the options in the **Save as type:** box:
   a **The complete page**, including all images, sound or video files etc.
   b **Archived**, where the various components are consolidated as a single file.
   c **In HTML** (the code in which the page was written).
   d Only the **textual content** of the file.
5 Select a location for the file in the **Save in:** box.

Folder location   Page name   Page button

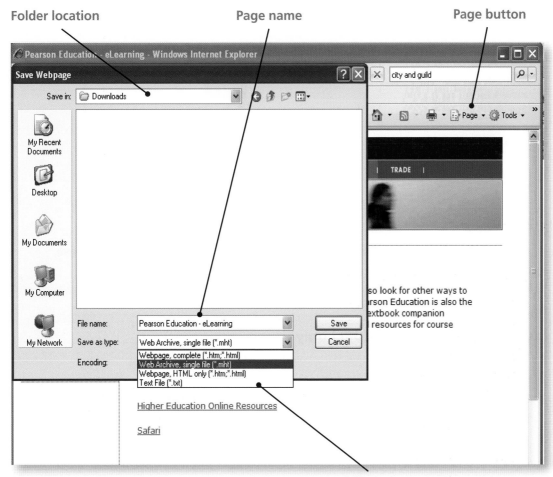

Fig. 8.13 Save web page   Type of file being saved

6 Press the **Enter** key or click on **Save**.
7 To open the page at a future time, perhaps to print it, go to **File – Open** or use the Search facility from the desktop and search the folder in which the page is stored.
8 A page saved as a whole web page will open into the browser. A text-only file may open into a text-editing program such as Notepad.

save web page images

1 Right-click on the image and select **Save Picture As**.

2 When the Save As window opens, check the type of file being saved in the **Save as type:** window. Normally, images on web pages are **JPEG** or **GIF** files and so should be saved in these formats.

3 Continue saving in the normal way.

4 To open the image, perhaps to print it, go to **File – Open** or use the desktop search facility and search the folder in which the picture was stored. Depending on how it is accessed, it may open into the default image-editing program on your computer.

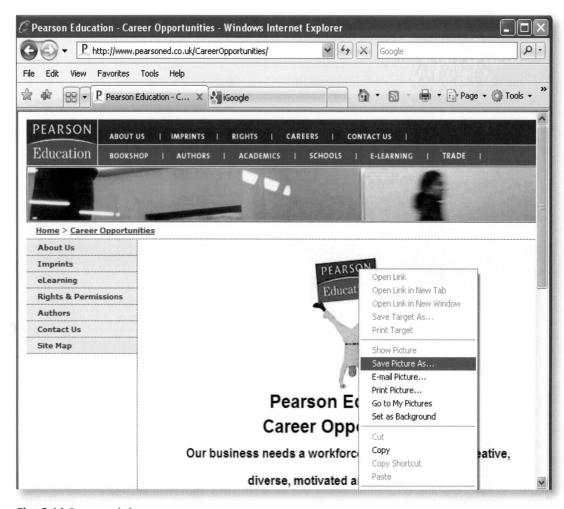

Fig. 8.14 Save web image

save a web page address (URL) only

1 Navigate to the right page.

2 Click in the **Address** box to select it.

3 (If this does not select the whole address but just places the cursor inside the box, right-click and click on **Select All** first.)

4 Right-click on the address and select **Copy**.

5 Paste this address into a word document or email, for example, to pass it on or retain it for the future.

Previewing web pages

Printing web pages is straightforward, except that a web page is not the same as a document page. There may be a great deal of content below the part visible on-screen and this may extend over a large number of printed pages. It is a good idea to check your printout in Print Preview first of all, so that you can limit the printout to fewer pages or change the orientation if not all the information is fully visible.

preview web pages

1 Click on the drop-down arrow next to the Print button and select this option.
   Or
2 Go to File – Print Preview.
3 Check the number of pages – these will show at the bottom of the screen and will also
   be printed in the top corner of each page.
4 View other pages by clicking on the Next or Previous page arrow.
5 Click a different orientation button to change from Portrait to Landscape.
6 Click on the Setup button to make more detailed changes such as to the margins or
   paper sizes.
7 Click on the Print button to open the Print box.
8 Click on the Close button to return to normal web page view.

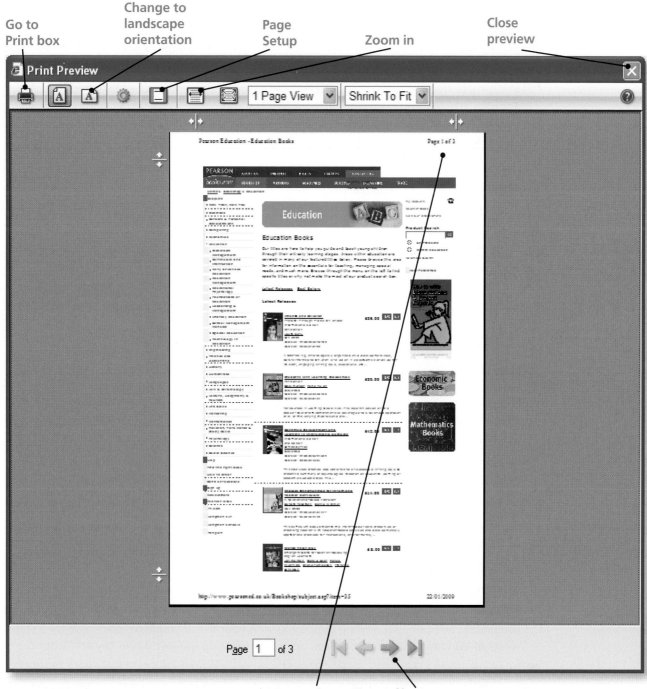

Fig. 8.15 Print Preview

Printing web pages

Once you have sorted out what and how your page will print, you can print it out.

print web pages

1 Click on the **Print** button to print out all the pages using the default settings.
2 To change any settings, open the **Print** box from the Preview page or go to **File – Print**.
3 If necessary, limit the printout by choosing an option such as printing the current page or only page 1 or 2.
4 Set the number of extra copies you want to print.
5 Click on the **Preferences** button to change printer settings – for example, to print in colour or black and white.
6 Click on **Print**.

Check your understanding 6

1 Go to any website.
2 Print a copy of the first part of the web page only, onto a single piece of paper.
3 Save and print just the textual content of the page.
4 Save any image from the page onto your computer.
5 Print a copy of the image.

Closing the browser

At the end of an Internet session, click on the **Close** button on your browser window. For dial-up, you will need to click on a **Disconnect** button, but for broadband the connection stays open all the time.

4 Internet security

Despite its many advantages, the Internet can be an unsafe place and measures need to be taken to keep data secure.

Methods for maintaining security include the following.

- **Installing, using and updating virus checkers on a regular basis.** New viruses are written every day and protecting your computer from infection must be undertaken rigorously. Many virus checkers are available to download free from the Internet, such as Avast or AVG, and others can be purchased from companies such as Sophos, MacAfee and Norton.

- **Keeping your passwords secure.** Every time you are asked to create passwords, you need to think about how to stop them being discovered by others. Methods include:

  o using a mix of upper- and lower-case letters, numbers and symbols rather than easy-to-identify words

  o never writing them down or passing them on to others

  o changing them regularly

  o not using the same one for all your Internet activities.

- **Locking your computer when in a shared office or room.** Without having to sign out completely, this can stop anyone tampering with your files if you leave your desk for a short while. In Windows machines, you can do this by pressing the **windows** key and letter **L**.

- **In appropriate situations, using digital signatures with emails.** These are a form of electronic signature that authenticates the identity of the message sender. They can be useful, for example, when sending legal documents by email. Other similar security systems involve encryption, whereby the message content is 'scrambled' and only those with the key to the code used can decipher them.

Computer legislation

There are many laws related to computer use that are there to protect your personal information or work. There are two laws that concern most people: Data Protection and Copyright.

The Data Protection Act

This has eight principles governing the use of data that concerns identifiable individuals. It states that personal data will:

1 be processed fairly and lawfully

2 be obtained only for specified and lawful purposes, and not further processed in any manner incompatible

3 be adequate, relevant and not excessive

4 be accurate and where necessary kept up to date

5 not be kept for longer than is necessary

6 be processed in accordance with the data subject's rights

7 be secure; appropriate measures shall be taken against unauthorised or unlawful processing, accidental loss, destruction or damage to personal data

8 not be transferred to a country or territory outside the European Economic Area (EEA) unless there is adequate protection in place.

Copyright law

You may think that just because someone has published a painting, photo, computer program, video or song on the Internet it means it is free to use. But this is not the case. Copyright law means that programs and files cannot be used without the express permission of the originator unless they are clearly 'free of copyright'. Some infringements of copyright have become known as 'piracy'.

5 Working with email

Why use email?

There are a number of advantages to using email rather than conventional means of communication such as post, telephone and fax:

* It is very cheap. To send one hundred email messages to people in other countries takes a few seconds at local telephone costs, rather than the expense of stamps or long-distance phone calls.
* No one has to be at home to receive messages, as you can download your emails when it is convenient.
* You can send messages instantly, day or night.
* Copies are always created.
* Emails are sent instantaneously, whereas letters can take several days.
* When replying, the content of previous messages can be included to remind everyone what has been discussed earlier.
* Messages can be retrieved wherever you are in the world.

There are also disadvantages, such as:

* You cannot send emails to people who do not have computer access.
* They are never completely secure.
* You can be inundated with unwanted bulk mail (spam).
* Email addresses change often and can be difficult to locate.

Sadly, there is no telephone directory equivalent for email addresses and, as people change their ISPs and hence their email addresses quite often, it can be hard to track down someone's details. Some websites trawl the web looking for names, but this is very hit-and-miss.

6 Email

There are two ways you can send and receive electronic messages:

- using software installed on your computer (see page XXX for more details)
- accessing your messages online from any computer connected to the web.

It is very useful to be able to use email without having to own your own computer and you can do this by using **webmail** (web-based email services). Many websites offer free mail services to users and these include www.google.co.uk, www.yahoo.co.uk, www.hotmail.com, www.gmx.com and www.postmaster.co.uk.

Email addresses

Whatever system you use, you will need to create two entities: an email address and an associated password. For webmail systems, when you enter both entities correctly into the log-in box, you will be able to access your messages.

The email address is made up of three parts:

- your name, nickname or combination of name and numbers – for example, *Jackie_sherman* or *jsherman5*
- the @ symbol
- the domain name of the email server where your messages are stored – for example, *hotmail. com* or *postmaster.co.uk* for webmail or your ISP's server – for example, *aol.com* or *virgin.net.*

Your address will therefore look something like this:

jsherman5@postmaster.co.uk

As with all forms of address, accuracy is important if you want your message to arrive at the right destination. When entering an email address, double-check it for errors before sending the email.

The structure of an email message

Every message you send or receive is made up of a number of parts. When sending a message, the boxes must always be completed accurately.

- **To:** this is where you type the full email address of the person you are writing to.
- **Cc:** this will contain the full email address of anyone you want to receive a copy of the message. For more than one person, each address should be separated by a semi-colon.
- **Bcc:** sometimes you will want to send a copy of an email to someone without the other recipients knowing you are doing so. You add their email address in this box to send a 'blind copy'.
- **Subject:** here is where you enter a short description of the content so that it is clear what the message is about.
- **Main window:** this is where your message goes. Usually it is similar to a letter but less formal in style. Between friends (but not for work messages) you can even include **emoticons** where punctuation symbols represent emotions such as smiley faces :-).

Attachment: An attachment is a file that is added to an email. They can be pictures, documents, or even sound or video clips. The larger the attachment, the longer an email will take to send. Many institutions have limits governing the size of attachments that can be sent or received.

Note that you do not need to add your own email details – these will be included automatically. One of the risks of an email account is messages from unknown users. While these can be messages you'd like to see – an old friend getting back in touch, for example, or the HR officer from a company you've just applied to – often they aren't.

When you receive an email from an unknown address and you are suspicious that it is spam (or otherwise malicious) you should delete it immediately. Make sure that you don't open attachments from unknown senders – these are often viruses designed to attack your computer.

Opening Outlook 2007

Most Windows computers already have a basic email system, Outlook Express, pre-loaded. A more sophisticated version can be installed that also offers a calendar, task management and other facilities. The email application that forms part of the Microsoft Office 2007 suite is Outlook 2007.

The advantage of a computer-based system is that if you have a dial-up connection you can work offline composing, reading or gathering information with no charges being incurred.

launch Outlook

1 Click on the icon visible on the desktop.

Or

2 Find it on the Start menu or from the All Programs list.

Fig. 8.16 Launch Outlook

The Outlook system

The mail part of Outlook provides a number of folders in which to store messages. There is also an address book labelled Contacts where you can store email addresses for easy reference.

The mail folders are as follows:

Deleted items – labelled **Trash** in some other systems

Drafts – for unfinished messages

Inbox – storage for all incoming mail

Junk email – for unwanted messages identified as spam

Outbox – a folder that will hold completed messages temporarily until you are ready to connect to the Internet and send them

RSS feeds – this will automatically store regular programs related to news, blogs or entertainment that you have chosen to receive

Sent items – copies of all messages you write

Search folders – these are virtual folders that will display the results of any searches you carry out.

You can change the way you view your messages by selecting a different option from the **View – Current View** menu. For example, you can add a small preview pane in which to read the first part of any message or list all the messages received during the last seven days.

close Outlook

1 Click on the **Close** button in the top right-hand corner.

2 If you still have messages to send, you will be reminded to save or send them.

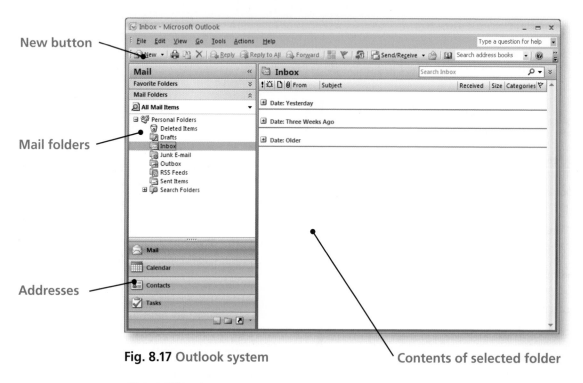

Fig. 8.17 Outlook system

Contents of selected folder

Sending messages

When you create a new message, you will see text and paragraph formatting tools above the main window and can use these to add bullet points, change fonts, add emphasis or realign text, but bear in mind that some email systems will not show these details when your message is received. (See Unit 001 for more details on formatting, bullet points and text alignment.)

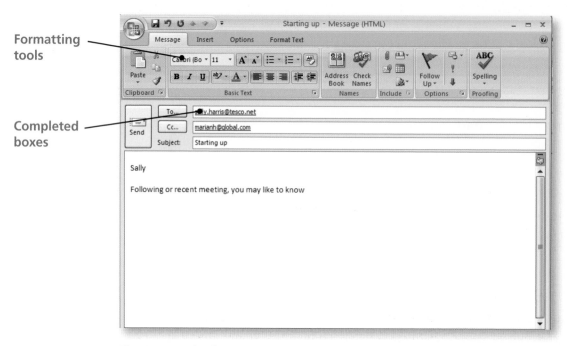

Fig. 8.18 Outlook compose

send a message

1 Click on the button labelled **New** in the main window. (If a mail folder has not previously been selected, you will need to click on the down-facing arrow next to the New button and select **Mail message**.)

2 Complete all the boxes as set out earlier.

3 Make sure when entering your message that you observe Internet 'netiquette' (see page 195).

4 Click on the **Send** button to send the message straight away.

5 Where you are connected to the Internet all the time, the message will be sent immediately. For dial-up users working offline, messages will be stored in the Outbox until you connect and send them.

6 To keep a draft of a message to continue working on later, click on the down arrow next to the Save Sent Item button on the Options tab and select the **Drafts** folder.

Or

7 Simply close the message and it should be saved.

8 Copies of all sent messages should be saved automatically in the Sent Items folder. If they are not appearing there, go to **Tools – Options**. On the Preferences tab, click on **Email – Options** and check the box labelled **Save copies of messages in Sent Items folder**.

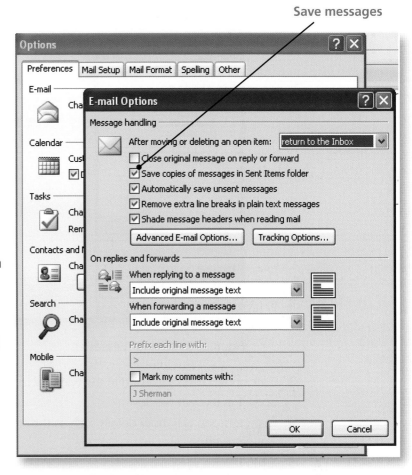

Save messages

Fig. 8.19 Outlook options

You will need to find a friend or colleague willing to reply to your messages in order to carry out the exercises.

Check your understanding 7

1 Open Outlook 2007.

2 You are going to send a message to your friend with a copy to yourself.

3 Complete the **To:** box with their full email address.

4 Complete the **Cc:** box with your own email address.

5 Add the subject **Testing**.

6 Enter the message **This is a test message. Hope it arrives**.

7 Sign your name and send the message.

Reading messages

Each time you open your email system, or if you click on the **Send/Receive** button, any new messages waiting for you will be delivered to your Inbox. Unread messages will appear in bold and the number of unread messages will appear in brackets next to the Inbox.

read messages

1 Check for new messages.
2 Click on the **Inbox** folder name on the left to display its contents in the main window.

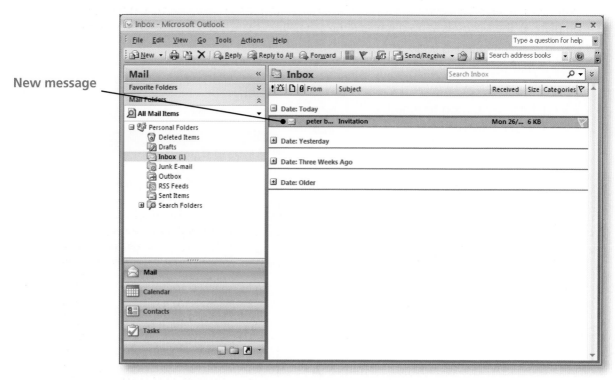

Fig. 8.20 Receiving messages

3 Click on any message listed in the window to view it in a preview pane, or double-click to open it in its own window.
4 Each message will show details such as the sender, subject matter, size and the date it was received.
5 If you receive several messages at the same time, move through them by clicking on a **Next** or **Previous** button or return to the Inbox and click on the details of each message in turn.

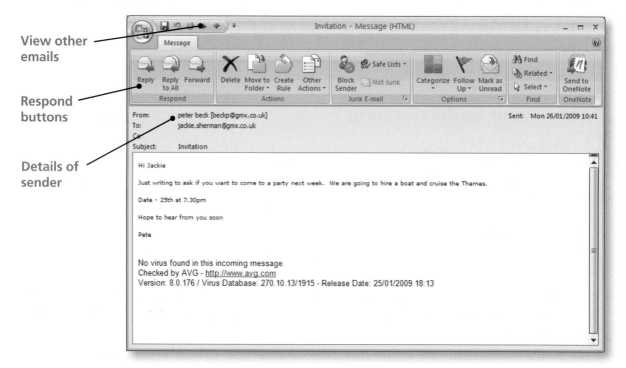

Fig. 8.21 Opened message

Blocked messages

Some messages will be moved automatically to the Junk E-mail folder as Outlook 2007 is set up to recognise certain phrases or types of message as spam. You must check this folder regularly, in case a normal message has been moved there by mistake. You can also add unwanted senders to a list of blocked email addresses so that future messages from them will be moved automatically.

block a message

1 Right-click on the message you want to block.

2 Select **Junk E-mail**.

3 Click on the option to **Add Sender to Blocked Senders List**.

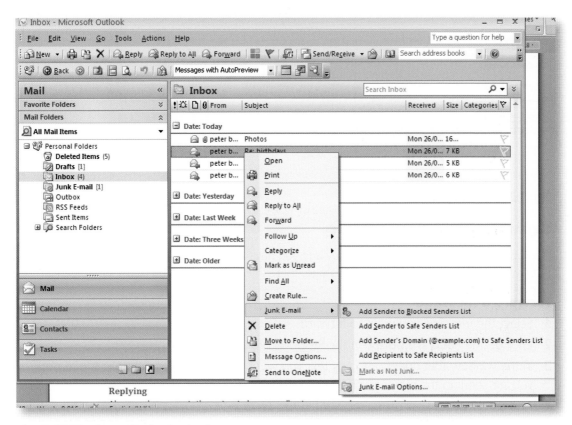

Fig. 8.22 Block sender in Outlook

Replying

Above each message in the main window, as well as in an opened message window, there are two different reply buttons:

● **Reply** will send a reply to the author of the message only.

● **Reply to All** will send the reply to anyone else who received a copy of the original message, as well as its author.

reply to a message

1 Select the message in the Inbox, or open it on-screen and click on the appropriate **Reply** button.

2 In the window that appears, add your reply text in the main window above the original text that is normally left in place as a reminder. (You can delete or edit all or some of this text if it is not helpful to retain it.)

3 The recipient's email address and the subject of the message (preceded by *Re.*) will have been added to the message automatically.

4 Click on the **Send** button to send the message straight away.

5 After sending, a copy of your reply will be saved in the Sent Items folder and the original message you received will remain in the Inbox.

Recipient's details added automatically

Send message

Your reply typed here

Original message

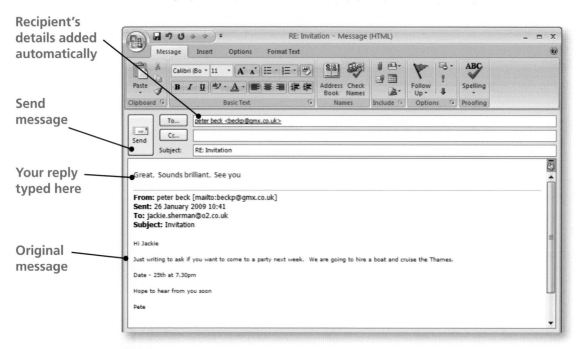

Fig. 8.23 Replying in Outlook

Forwarding a message

If you want someone else to see the message you have received, you can forward them a copy. If there were any files attached to the message, these will be sent on at the same time.

forward a message

1 Select the message you want to forward.

2 Click on the **Forward** button in the Respond group.

3 In the window that opens, add any text you want to include – for example, the reason you are sending the message on.

4 Add the email address of the recipient in the **To:** box.

5 The subject will have been added automatically, preceded by *Fw:*.

6 Send the message.

Check your understanding 8

1 Send your friend a new message. Give it the subject **Birthdays**.

2 Add the message **Did you know my birthday is on...** (add the date). **Please let me know yours**.

3 Sign and send the message.

4 Read the answer you receive from your friend.

5 Reply to them with the text **Good, I will make a note of it**.

6 Open your **Sent Items** folder and check that a copy of your original message and reply are visible.

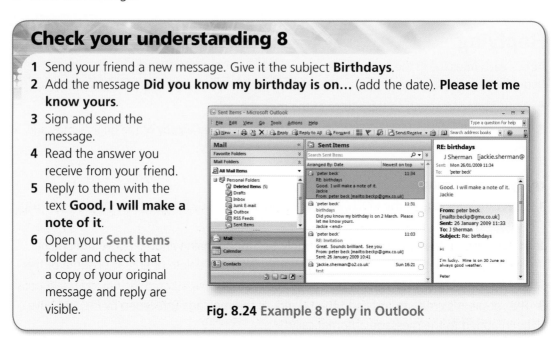

Fig. 8.24 Example 8 reply in Outlook

Checking messages

Before sending a message, particularly when it is formal or important, you need to check for accuracy. As well as reading through, use the built-in spellchecker to help you.

spellcheck a message

1 Correct any words underlined in red manually, or right-click and select the correctly spelt alternative offered.
2 To check the whole message, click on the **Spelling and Proofing** button.
3 Work through the message, selecting alternatives from the Suggestions box or changing words manually.
4 Click on **Change** or **Change All** to correct one or all entries of this word in the message or **Ignore Once/Ignore All** to leave them as they are typed.
5 Click on **Cancel** to close the spelling window.

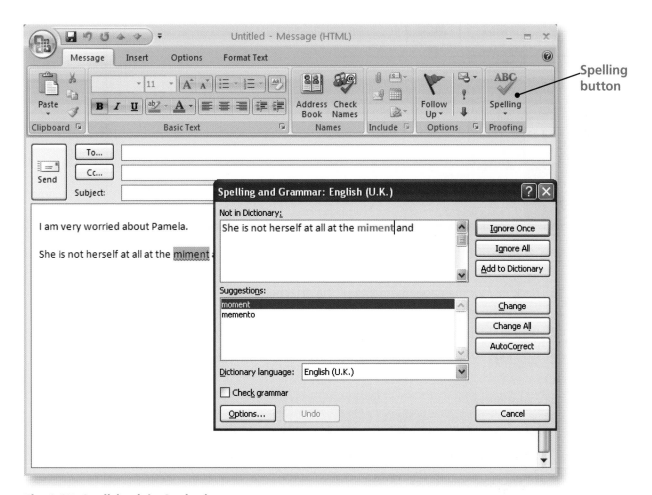

Fig. 8.25 Spellcheck in Outlook

Working with attachments

One of the advantages of using email is to be able to send and receive files such as photos, videos and shared word-processed documents, and these are all known as **attachments**. If you receive an attachment, you can save it outside your email system and read, print or work on it in the normal way.

Some files can be very large and difficult for recipients to download onto their machines. For this reason, image files sent electronically are normally in **JPEG** or **GIF** formats, and all types of file can be reduced in size by using compression (zipping) programs.

attach a file

1 Start composing your message.

2 Click on the **Attach File** button on the **Message** tab showing a paperclip symbol.

3 In the **Insert File** window that opens, navigate to the folder containing your target file.

4 Click on its name.

5 Click on **Insert**.

Attach button

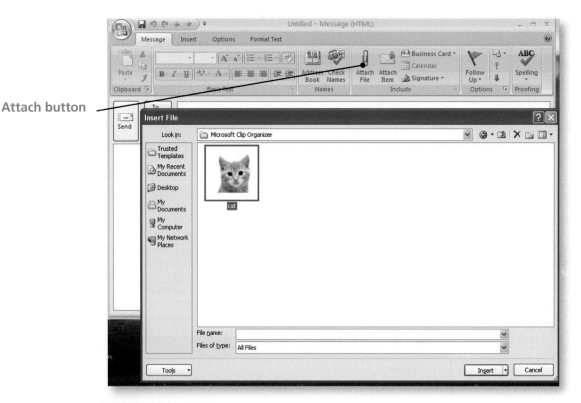

Fig. 8.26 Attach files in Outlook

6 Back in your message, the name of the attached file will be displayed in a new box at the top of the message.

7 Repeat the process if you want to send more than one attachment.

8 Continue to write and then send the message as normal.

Attached file

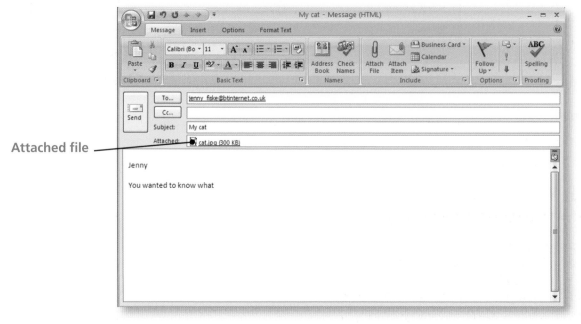

Fig. 8.27 Attached file with Outlook message

Receiving an attachment

When a message arrives in your Inbox, you can tell if it has a file attached.

- There may be a paperclip symbol next to the message details.
- When you open the message, you will see the details of any attachments at the top of the message.

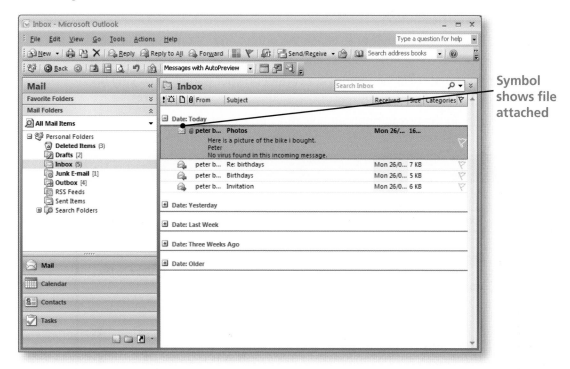

Symbol shows file attached

Fig. 8.28 Receive attachment in Outlook

work with attachments

1   Open the message.

2   Double-click on the attachment file name to open the file fully. You will be shown a warning message and need to click on **Open**. The file will open into a suitable program such as an image-editing program.

3   Once open, you can save it using the normal procedure for that program.

4   If you are worried about the origin of the attachment, click on the **Save** button in the warning message so that you can virus-scan it later.

Fig. 8.29 Warning for attached files in Outlook

5   You can also save an attached file without opening by right-clicking or clicking on the **Office** button and selecting **Save As – Save Attachments**.

6   Save the file as normal into your computer filing system.

Check your understanding 9

1   Start a new message.
2   Attach any file saved onto your computer.
3   Send it to your friend.
4   Ask them to send you a message with a file attached.
5   Save the attachment you receive into your filing system.

Printing messages

Sometimes you may want to keep a hard copy of a message you receive – for example, a code is often required at the box office or station if you have bought tickets online and been sent confirmation by email.

print an email message

1 Click on the **Office** button.
2 Click on **Print – Print Preview** to check the output. You should see that all message headings such as the sender, subject and date have been added automatically.
3 Click on **Print** and check all settings are correct on your printer by clicking on **Preferences**. Then print as normal.
4 You can click in the box to print out any attached files at the same time.

Print layout

Print attachments

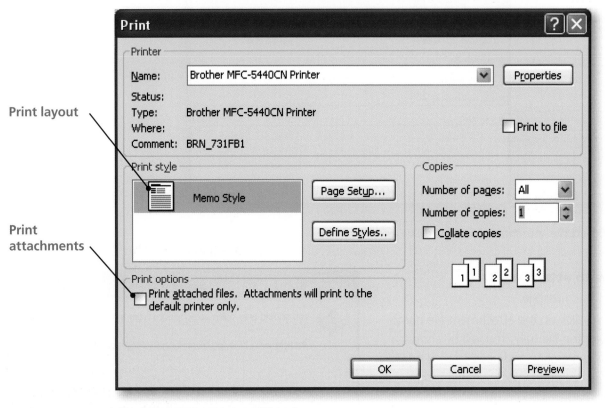

Fig. 8.30 Print email in Outlook

Deleting messages

You can delete open messages or those that arrive in your Inbox that you don't want to open.

delete a message

1 For open messages, click on the **Delete** button showing a black cross.
   Or
2 Select an unopened message in the main window.
3 Click on the **Delete** button showing a red cross.
   Or
4 Right-click and select **Delete**.
   Or
5 Press the **Delete** key.
6 The message will be moved to the Deleted Items folder.
7 If you make a mistake, move the message out again using one of the move options (see pages 221–2).

Check your understanding 10

1 Locate and print a copy of the attachment you saved earlier.
2 Delete the original message your friend sent that had the file attached.
3 Check that this deleted message has appeared in the Deleted Items folder.
4 Print any email message you have received and check that the subject, date and name of the sender are all visible on the printout.

Managing messages

After a time, your Inbox will fill up with incoming mail and it will be hard to locate past messages easily. In the same way that you set up a hierarchy of folders for computer files, it is a good idea to set up folders and subfolders within the Inbox or Sent folder to store related messages.

Once these have been created, you can quickly move current messages into the correct folders. All new emails should also be filed as soon as they arrive. (You can also copy messages into different folders by using the Copy rather than Move options.)

To view all the messages in a subfolder, click on the name of the subfolder and its contents will appear in the main window.

One important issue with email messages is that they take up space. It is vital that unwanted messages are deleted so that the system has space for more. If emails have important attachments, these should be stored outside the email system so that the message can then be removed.

Where past messages have to be stored for a certain length of time, Outlook also has an **archive** facility where a sweep is made of the system on a regular basis and messages past a certain date are moved there automatically.

While emails can be filed into folders within Outlook – or a webmail system – they can only be accessed when the relevant program is open. If you save or back up your emails on your hard drive (see page 222 for instructions), you can view them offline as well. Emails saved in this way can be filed with other documents on your hard drive or network.

create folders

1 Right-click on the **Inbox**.
2 Select **New Folder**.
3 In the window that appears, give the new folder a suitable name.
4 Click on **OK**.
5 The folder will appear underneath the inbox.
6 Continue to make as many folders as you need, and subdivide them further if necessary.

move messages using the menu

1 Open the Inbox to reveal all the messages.
2 Click on one or select several messages at once.
3 Right-click and select **Move to Folder**.
4 Select the correct folder in the Move Items window. To see all the new folders, you may have to click on a + symbol next to the Inbox to reveal all the subfolders.
5 Click on **OK** to close the window.

New Inbox folder

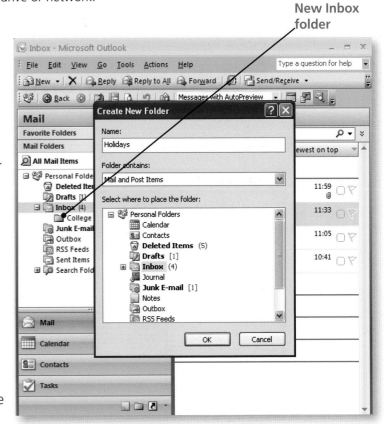

Fig. 8.31 New folder in Outlook

Fig. 8.32 Move messages in Outlook

move messages using the mouse

1 Open the Inbox to reveal all the messages.
2 Click on one or select several messages at once.
3 Click and drag a message from the right-hand pane across the divide towards the target folder.
4 Let go of the mouse and the message will drop inside.
5 If you drag with the right mouse button, a menu will appear and you can select Move or Copy.

You can also save emails outside of Outlook – on a flash drive, for example, or on your hard drive. To do this, select the email you would like to save. Go to File then Save As. Enter your chosen file name, and then in the drop-down menu for Save As Type choose Outlook Message Format. Choose where you would like to save the email, and click Save.

Check your understanding 11

1 Create two new Inbox folders labelled *Birthdays* and *Time Off*.
2 Move a message you have received related to birthdays into the *Birthdays* folder.
3 Move any other messages into the *Time Off* folder.
4 Delete one message in the *Time Off* folder.
5 Finally, restore the deleted message back to the Inbox.

2 Addresses and contacts

So that you can send email messages, you need to have at hand the email address of anyone you wish to write to. If they have ever sent you an email, their address will be held on your system. If they have not previously sent you an email, you need to add it to your Contacts address book.

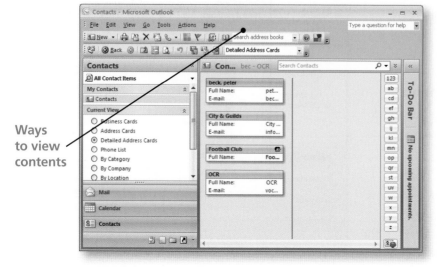

Ways to view contents

Fig. 8.33 Open contacts

Opening contacts

Contacts is available from the main Outlook window.

open Contacts

1 Click on the folder name in the main window.
2 Depending on the selection, you will see the names arranged as a list or as small cards, with alphabetical tabs down the side to help you move through the addresses.

add a new contact

1 Click on the **Contacts** folder name.
2 If organised as a phone list, click into the top empty row and type the details here. To add further information, double-click the row and a new Contacts window will open.
  Or
3 Click on the **New** button.
4 In the window that opens, add as much information as required. You must always add the name, full email address and display name.
  Or
5 Select an incoming email message.
6 Right-click on the address in the **From:** box.
7 Click on **Add to Outlook contacts**.
8 A New Contact window will open with some of the details already completed.
9 If you want to, add extra details such as their postal address and telephone number.
10 Click on the **Save & Close** button to save the details.

Retain details

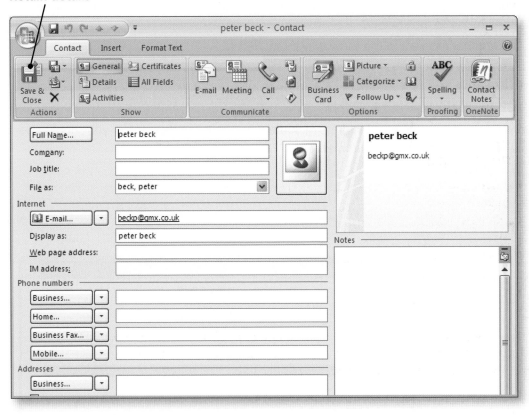

Fig. 8.34 Add to contacts

edit a contact

1 Open Contacts.
2 Double-click on the target name.
3 Change any entries as required.
4 Click on **Save & Close** to update the details.

delete a contact

1 Open Contacts.
2 Select the details.
3 Right-click and select **Delete**.
  Or
4 Press the **Delete** key.

Check your understanding 12

1 Add the following two addresses to your Contacts folder:
   a Name: John Gray
   b Email address: j.gray@swapshop.co.uk
   c Name: Mary Hopkins
   d Email address: maryhopk@sanderson.net
2 Add the address of your friend taken from one of their messages.
3 Now amend John Gray's address to read: j.gray5@swapshop.co.uk
4 Finally, delete Mary Hopkins's details from your Contacts folder.

Using contacts when composing

When creating a message, you can add the email addresses of anyone in Contacts very easily.

add Contacts to a message

1 Start the new message.
2 Click on the **To:** button. This opens up a list of your Contacts in a Select Names window.
3 Select the recipient in the top window and double-click on their details. These will be added to the To: box below.
4 Add another recipient in the same way if required.
5 Click on **OK** to return to the message.
6 If sending copies, click on the **Cc:** box in the message and double-click on names to add their email addresses in the Cc: box.
7 If you start typing the email address of someone in your Contacts folder you should also be offered their full details automatically.

Grouped addresses

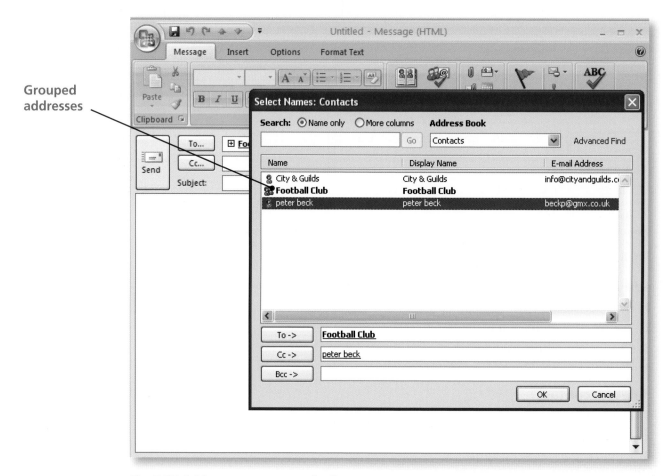

Fig. 8.35 Add contacts automatically to message

Group addresses and distribution lists

If you regularly send the same emails to a number of people, you can group their details together into a distribution list. This will be displayed as a single address in Contacts so that you can click on it to add all the addresses to your message in one go.

create a distribution list

1   Click on the drop-down arrow next to the **New** button and select **Distribution List**.
2   When the window opens, type a name for the group – for example, *Football Club*.
3   To add addresses already held in Contacts, click on **Select Members**.
4   Double-click on the name of anyone you want to add to the group to place their name in the Members box.

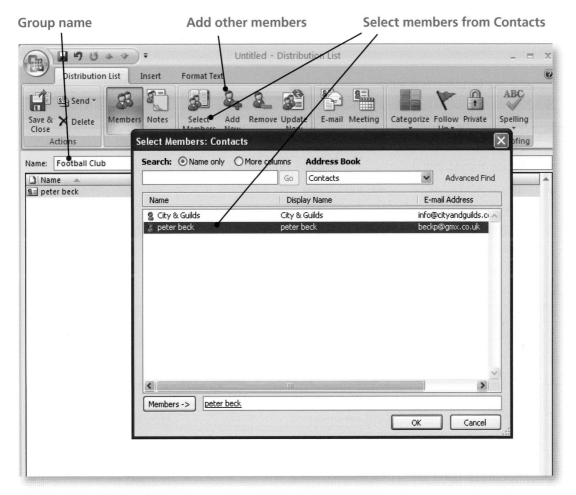

Fig. 8.36 Distribution list

5   Continue until everyone has been added and then click on **OK** to close the window.
6   To add further members, click on **Add Members**.
7   Enter their details in the boxes and click on **OK**. Click on the checkbox if you also want to add their details to the Contacts folder.
8   Click on **Save & Close** to update the details.
9   The group title will be visible in Contacts in bold with several faces next to it. Click on its name to add all the addresses to your messages.

Printing contacts

You can follow normal printing procedures to print out the details of any contact in your Contacts folder.

print a contact

1   Select the **Contact**.

2 Click on the **Office** button.

3 Go to **Print – Print Preview** to check how the details will appear.

4 To change any settings such as paper size or orientation, click on the **Page Setup** link.

5 Click on **Print** to produce a copy.

6 Note that an open Contact will only print in memo style, but a closed Contact can be printed in various styles, depending on what style you are using to view the contents of the folder.

7 Note that if printing a distribution list, the group name will appear on page 1 and the members' details on further pages.

Searching

Once you have built up a large Inbox or Sent folder full of messages, you need to be able to locate an important message quickly. You may also want to find an address in order to edit a Contact.

locate an email message

1 Click on the **Mail** folder.

2 For a quick search, click in the **Inbox Search** box and type in key words such as the sender's name or subject matter.

3 Click on the double down arrows to open up a larger window to enter further details.

4 Click on **Add Criteria** to fine tune the search, e.g. to search by date or locate only messages with attachments.

5 Matching messages will be listed below the Search box and the first may also be displayed if you are using a reading pane.

Search box

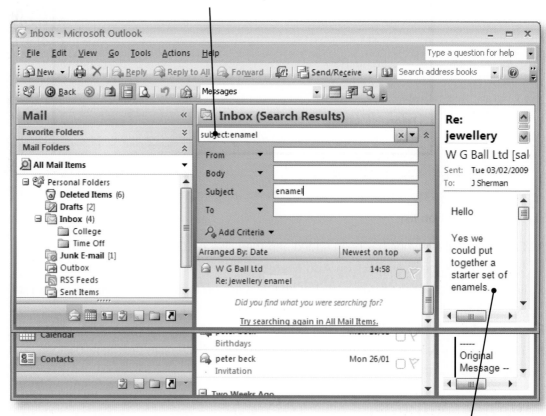

Fig. 8.37 Outlook find message   Reading pane

search for a contact

1 Click on the Contacts folder name.
2 Click on the drop-down arrow in the Search box and make a selection – for example, to Search All Contacts.
3 Enter all or part of the email address or other details.
4 The related contacts should be listed.
   Or
5 Enter the details for your search in the Search address books box. If you have more than one address book, select Contacts.
6 When you press Enter you will be taken to the Contacts entry for that person.

Search address books

Search box

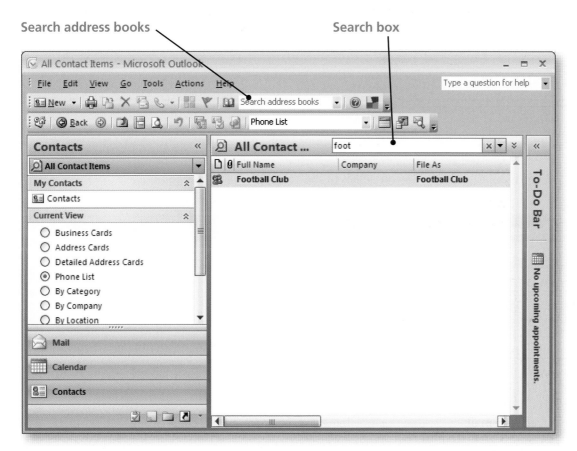

Fig. 8.38 Search contacts

Check your understanding 13

1 Use the search facilities to locate all messages from your friend.
2 Now search for John Gray's email address.
3 Create a distribution list with the name Work Group. Add the following members:
   a John Gray
   b Your friend
   c Samantha Foley (sam.fol@virgin.net). Do not add her details to your Contacts folder.
4 Print out a copy of John Gray's email address entry.

CLAiT Assignment

(Ask a friend to send you an email with the subject *Camera pictures* and containing the text *We can all benefit from advice about using a camera.* It should have the file *camera* from the CD-ROM as an attachment.)

TASK 1

1 Log-in to your email system and open your Inbox.

2 Read the message from your friend titled *Camera pictures*.

3 Save the image file *camera* outside your email system.

4 Use the reply facility to send your friend a reply, adding the following text: *I do agree. I find taking pictures with my new digital camera quite tricky.*

5 Add your name.

6 Check your message for errors.

7 Make sure a copy of your message is saved.

8 Send your message.

9 Add the following contact to your address book:

10 Tom Stills, tomstills4@camera-weekly.co.uk

11 Produce a printout showing details of this contact in full (Figure 8.39).

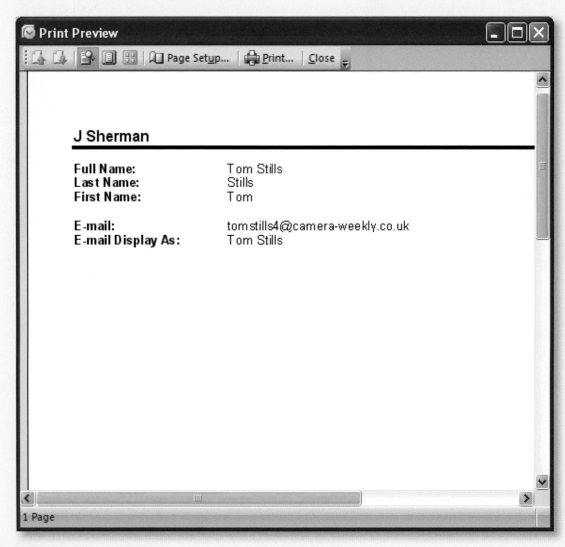

Fig 8.39 Print of contact

TASK 2

1 You are going to forward the original message. Either forward it to a second friend or colleague or to yourself.

2 Add the text *This photograph may interest you.*

3 Sign your name.

4 Send the message, making sure the attachment is still attached.

5 Check that the sent message has been saved in your email system.

6 Delete the original message titled *Camera pictures* from your Inbox.

7 Take a screen print of your Inbox showing that the message has been deleted.

8 Take a screen print of your work area showing the saved *camera* image file.

TASK 3

1 Create a new email message to be sent to Tom Stills using the address from your Contacts folder.

2 Attach the file *Sunset* provided on the CD-ROM accompanying this book.

3 Add the subject *Taking Sunsets.*

4 Enter the following text: *What do you think of my recent photo?*

5 Check the message for errors.

6 Save it as a draft.

7 Print a copy of the draft message. Make sure all header details and the attachment are visible. (If necessary, include a screen print as well.) (Figure 8.40)

8 Print a copy of all sent messages.

9 Log-off from your email system.

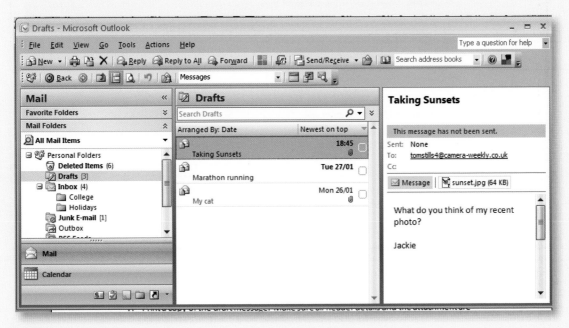

Fig 8.40

TASK 4

1 Use a search engine to locate information on downloading digital photographs from a mobile phone.

2 Open a web page that offers appropriate information.

3 Bookmark the page.

4 Print out the first page of information (Figure 8.41).

5 Now go to the Natural History Museum website at www.nhm.ac.uk.

6 Follow the links to find out when the Wildlife Photographic Competition first started.

7 Bookmark the page.

8 Print out one page of information showing the date. Circle the date on the page (Figure 8.42).

9 Save any image from the page as *wildlife image* into your work area.

10 Take a screen print of your work area showing the image file.

11 Close your browser.

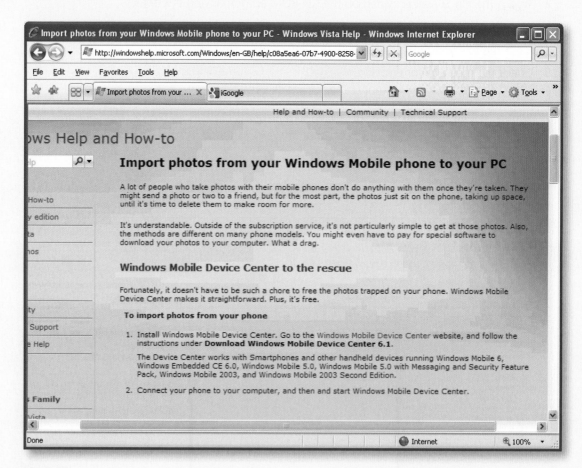

Fig 8.41

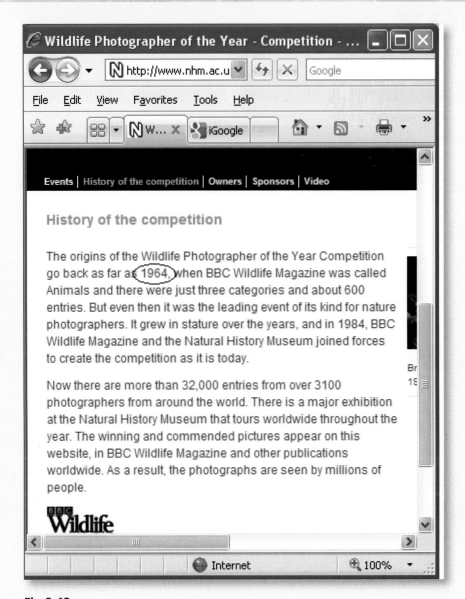

Fig 8.42

Index

Rachel 12
CLAIT (CLEIT)